'Yon's no herrin' scales, yon,' Flora stated flatly. 'No, nor mackerel either.'

'Indeed they are so,' argued Erchy but with dwindling defiance as he realised he was confronted by an expert. He glanced again at Morag but she had turned away, elaborately disinterested.

'Yon's salmon, yon!' accused Flora.

'Be quiet!' returned Erchy with a challenging gleam in his eye, but seeing Flora's conspiratorial smile he went on: 'What if they are salmon, anyway? It's pleased enough you'd be if you found one waitin' for you in the mornin', I doubt.'

'I would too,' agreed Flora with unusual lucidity. 'There's nay harm in yon.'

'The Lord puts the salmon in the rivers like he puts the berries on the trees,' said Morag piously. 'They're there for all of us, no' just the laird.'

Also in Arrow Books by Lillian Beckwith:

The Hills is Lonely
The Sea for Breakfast
The Loud Halo
A Rope - In Case
Green Hand (A novel)
About My Father's Business

Lillian Beckwith

LIGHTLY POACHED

Decorations by Douglas Hall

ARROW BOOKS

ARROW BOOKS LTD
3 Fitzroy Square, London W1

An imprint of the Hutchinson Publishing Group

London Melbourne Sydney Auckland
Wellington Johannesburg Cape Town
and agencies throughout the world

First published by Hutchinson & Co (Publishers) Ltd 1973
Arrow edition 1976
© Text and illustrations Hutchinson & Co (Publishers) Ltd 1973

Made and printed in Great Britain
by The Anchor Press Ltd
Tiptree, Essex

ISBN 0 09 911600 6

For Philip, Katy,
Tina, Neil and Anita

Contents

Vocabulary

		Approximate pronunciation
Cailleach	Old woman	Kyle-yak
Mo ghaoil	My dear	Mo gale
Ceilidh	An impromptu meeting for gossip and song	Cayley
Strupach	A cup of tea and a bite to eat	Stroopak
Oidhche mhath!	Good night	Oi she-va
Bodach	Old man	Bodak
Biolaire	Watercress	Byul-ar
Thig a 's Tigh	Come inside	Hic-a-Stoya
Thalla	Go away!	Halla
Seanachaidh	A teller of tales	Shenna-ka
Sao	Here, take it	Sho
Potach	Oatmeal mixed with water and pressed into a round cake	Pot-ak
Gogaid	A light-headed, foolish girl	Go-gad
Orra Chomais	'An amulet to deprive a man of his v.r.l.ty particularly on his wedding night, by way of vengeance (A fine thing to cure blackguards!)' *Ad literam* MacAlpine's Gaelic dictionary	Orra-shoma
Each Uisge	Waterhorse	Ek-ooska
Tha e breagh	It is fine (Good day!)	He Breeah
Crack	A gossipy chat	
Sooyan	A young coalfish	

Lightly Poached

THE sun-stained showers had put a sheen on everything. On the summer grass; on the craggy hills; on the gulls' wings; on the sibilant water and on the rocks of the shore. Even the clouds looked as if they had been polished up with a soft duster.

Between the showers I had been engaged on the urgent

task of cleaning my weed-smothered potato patch, using a hoe until my aching shoulders entreated rest when I would crouch down and pull out the weeds by hand until my knees reminded me it was time to stand up and use the hoe again. I loathed weeding potatoes. As each spring came round and I, helped by neighbouring crofters, set the seed on nests of manure along the new-dug furrows I vowed that this year I would really cherish my potatoes; that I would attend to the weeding as soon as the green rosettes appeared above the soil and would continue regularly doing a little every fine day so that, come summer, I should have a trim forest of healthy green shaws rising from the ridged black earth with a definable space, weed free and wide enough for a booted foot to tread, between each row. Thus, I promised myself, I would ensure that when the time came for harvesting I should, like my neighbours, fill pail after pail, sack after sack, with potatoes of a size that could reasonably be termed 'ware', that is, fist-sized or larger. So far, however, even the most encouraging critics would never have described my potato crop as anything but 'seed', which means of a size equivalent to a bantam's egg, or worse, as 'chats', which were hardly bigger than marbles or, as Morag, my ex-land-lady, described them, as 'bein' no bigger than a hen would swallow in one gulp'. Too small for cooking in their jackets, they had to be peeled raw and anyone who has had to endure winter after winter of coping with such puny runts will know there is no more dispiriting an occupation. I usually ended up by boiling a panful every day, mashing them with a bottle and mixing them with oatmeal and then feeding them to my cow and hens while, swallowing my pride, I would buy a sack of potatoes from someone who had worked much more dedicatedly than I and who therefore had some to spare. Alas this year again despite all my resolutions and the tactful comments of well-meaning Bruachites I had failed to get to grips with the task of weeding in time and now in midsummer except for two short rows which I had cleaned the previous morning my potato patch resembled a jungle more than an orderly forest and with the plants scarcely a hand's height the leaves had already begun to pale as a result of their contest with lusty persicary, binding buttercups and tenacious dockens. I knew they must be rescued now or never, so, ignoring my body's unwillingness and the clouds of midges which assailed me every time the breeze died and a shower threatened to obscure the sun, I continued resolutely, hoping that I could clean enough rows to yield sufficient ware potatoes for my own use. Another hour's work, I told myself, and then I could finish for the day. As I made the resolution I sighed forgetfully which resulted in my having to spit out a queue of midges which had been hovering around my mouth waiting the opportunity to explore my larynx. Kneeling down I resumed pulling at the strangle of corn spurrey which, though relatively easy to uproot, leaves a sticky deposit on the hands which proves even more attractive to predatory insects than clean flesh. I wished often that potatoes were not so essential a part of my food supplies, but to face a Bruach winter without a good store of potatoes in the barn would have been foolhardy. The crofters would have considered it suicidal.

It had been some time now since the last shower; some time since I had had an excuse to nip back for a 'fly cuppie' in the coolth and comfort of the cottage. Through my thin blouse the sun was toasting my back; the exposed parts of my body itched with midge bites; my open-toed sandals—open-toed due not to design but to wear—were full of earth and sharp grit. I was sticky, dirty, itchy and achy and I

longed for a respite. Straightening up I rested on the hoe.
The breeze had died away completely with the last shower,
leaving shreds of mist in the corries of the hills. The sea was
like a stretch of blue cambric variegated with darker
patches which, suddenly erupting into arrow-shaped shock-
waves of spray, told of shoals of mackerel pursuing their
food around the bay.

'So you're busy!' It was Morag's voice and I turned to
greet her as she tacked across the croft towards me.
Accompanying Morag was Flora, a remote kinswoman of
hers who occasionally visited Bruach on holiday from the
East Coast fishing port where she lived. Flora was famous in
Bruach as being one of a band of 'kipper lassies', the girls
who travelled from port to port throughout the herring
season and in all weathers sat out on the piers deftly gutting
and cleaning mountains of herring newly unloaded from the
fishing boats; bandying ribald pleasantries with the crews
and, reputedly, screaming imprecations with complete im-
partiality at sluggard fish porters, scouting gulls or indeed
anyone who threatened to impede their work. Flora took
great pride in being a 'kipper lassie' and always carried
around with her a photograph cut from a newspaper which
showed her along with half a dozen other lassies smilingly
busy at their gutting and seemingly oblivious of the hail and
sleet that flew around them. There was an inked ring round
Flora on the photograph because the girls were so bundled
up in clothes that identification might otherwise have been
impossible. She was middle-aged, 'all beam and bust' as
Erchy described her, and her eyes and hair were ap-
propriately kipper coloured. Her voice was as strident as a
ship's siren; her laughter piercing and when irritated her
vocabulary would, according to an admiring Hector, 'take
the feathers off a hoody-crow'. She was a good-natured,

good-humoured soul and whilst she was in Bruach the summer ceilidhs were enlivened by lurid accounts of her adventures, quarrels, flirtations and spending sprees, accounts which I no doubt would have found more entertaining had I been able to decode more than one word in six of her broad East Coast speech and that one word usually 'yon'. In her absence the Bruachites referred to her as to all 'kipper lassies' as 'Skin-a-herrin' Lizzie', though they would never have been either discourteous or rash enough to have used the nickname in her hearing. Only once did I hear it used in her presence and that was by Davy, a Glasgow-bred child without a vestige of Gaelic courtesy or reticence who with his mother was visiting a relative in the village. One Friday evening when there had been the usual batch of customers, adults and children, waiting at the weekly grocery van for their turn to be served Davy was there insolently superintending his doting mother's purchases to ensure she bought for him an ample supply of sweeties and biscuits. When Flora appeared he had left his mother abruptly, sidled round to the front of the van and begun chanting:

> 'Skin-a-herrin',
> Skin-a-herrin',
> Skin-a-herrin',
> *Lizzie.*'

In the unthinkable event of a Bruach child behaving in such a fashion the nearest adult male would have grabbed him, boxed his ears and been thanked by the embarrassed parents for administering punishment so promptly. But Davy was a foreigner and though we were all made to feel exceedingly uncomfortable by the boy's rudeness only old Murdoch admonished him with a snapped 'Whist, boy!'

and the gesture of an upraised hand. Davy ignored the old man and continued his taunting. Flora darted a glance at the mother as if giving her a chance to take action before she herself did, but the mother had retreated into an air of intense preoccupation with the small print on a packet of cream crackers and would not look up. We saw Flora's bosom swell; we saw her eyes glint and we prepared to flinch at the linguistic dexterity we expected to hear. But our ears were assailed by no fish-pier malediction. Instead Flora merely raised her voice to its most penetrating pitch and screamed: 'Aye, lad, I can skin a herrin' as quick and clean as your own mother skins the lodgers that stay in your house!'

The delighted smiles on the faces of the Bruachites were swiftly erased as Davy's mother turned first on Flora and then on the rest of us a look of concentrated venom that changed even as we watched to confusion as she realised that, isolated as Bruach was, it was not too isolated for us to be unaware of the poor reputation of the boarding house she kept in the city and that lodgers who had once endured her hard beds, scanty food and high prices never stayed long. Calling her son with an asperity that startled him into obedience she hurried him away.

'He's a wee monster, that one,' Anna Vic had said severely.

'An' his father before him,' observed someone else.

Old Murdoch took his pipe out of his mouth. 'As the old cock crows, so the young one learns,' he had declared fatalistically.

'I'm thinkin' it's wastin' your time you are, mo ghaoil, cleanin' your potatoes when there's showers about. You're no' givin' the weeds a chance to die.' Morag was standing by my potato patch assessing its chances of survival with much the same expression on her face as if she were standing by a deathbed. 'You should get at them when the ground's good and dry.'

The thought that much of my day's labour might have been in vain was a little deflating but I rallied when I remembered I had carried away most of the uprooted weeds to the dung heap behind the byre where they could revive or perish without harming my potatoes. Nevertheless it was with relief that I abandoned the hoe.

'Me an' Flora,' continued Morag, 'was thinkin' we'd go down to the shore an' see maybe will we get a wee bitty dulse. The tide's right for it now.'

We looked down at the sea-deserted, weed-covered rocks, assimilating the prospects of dulse picking.

'Oh, yes. It's pretty low tides this week,' I agreed, confident now of my knowledge of the sea and its movements.

Flora gave me a kipper-coloured glance. 'D'ye like yon?' she asked with a vigorous nod towards the sea.

'Dulse, do you mean?' I was constantly being nonplussed by Flora's haphazard 'yons'.

'Aye, yon.'

'No,' I confessed. 'I've never managed to acquire a taste for it.' To me dulse tasted like strips of rubber steeped in water that had been used for washing fishy plates.

'Och, yon's good, yon,' she commented ecstatically.

'Erchy brought us a skart just the other day and Flora has a fancy for a wee bitty dulse boiled along with it,' explained Morag.

'He gave me a skart, too,' I told her. 'He must have been feeling generous.'

'Generous?' echoed Morag. 'Did you not notice he's lost his teeths an' canna eat them himself?'

'Oh, of course,' I admitted, remembering Erchy's gummy embarrassment when he had come to bestow his gift and his subsequent hasty departure in spite of the tea I offered.

'It will be six months he'll need to wait till the dentist comes again unless he goes up to Inverness himself to get a new set,' Morag announced. 'An' six months is a long time to be without your teeths once you're used to havin' them,' she added.

'He told me he'd lost them overboard when they were fishing,' I said.

'Indeed it was the truth he was tellin' you,' agreed Morag with the flicker of a smile.

'Well, I wouldn't wish Erchy discomfort but they say it's an ill wind,' I said lightly. 'And it seems a long time since I last tasted skart.'

'An' had he yours skinned for you?' asked Morag.

'Oh, yes,' I replied. 'I doubt if I could have done that for myself.' A skart or shag is prepared for cooking not by plucking but by skinning it like a rabbit and then the thick red meat can be cut from its breast like steak. There was normally so much meat on one that, casseroled, a bird would provide me with four good meals and there would still be stock for soup. 'It was last Tuesday he gave me mine and I'm just about at the end of it now,' I told her.

'Aye, I believe it was Tuesday we got ours,' agreed Morag. 'I mind him sayin' he got three that day.'

'And you haven't cooked it yet?' I asked. It was now the following Monday and as Bruach boasted no such conveniences as refrigerators I doubted whether in such sultry weather a shot bird could be kept so long.

'But we've had it buried,' she retorted in a voice edged with compassion for my ignorance. 'Put in a poc an' buried in the ground a skart will keep for weeks. Surely you knew that, mo ghaoil?'

'Oh, I knew about burying them but never more than for two or three days. I wouldn't have expected it to keep as long as this,' I replied.

'It keeps,' asserted Morag. 'An' likely it will be tender enough when we come to eat it. Did you no find yours a bitty tough on the teeths, eatin' it so soon?'

I was about to deny that I had found it tough when Flora gave me a searching look. 'Ah, but yon's gey teeth, yon,' she asserted positively. 'Yon would crack bones like a dog, yon.' She was looking at me as if she expected me to confirm her assertion.

I smiled. 'I haven't been hungry enough to try,' I told her. 'Yet,' I added.

'We'd best away for our dulse, then,' Morag said.

'Oh, stay for a cup of tea,' I urged, starting to gather up my treasury of weeds. 'I'm so dry I could drink a potful.'

'I'm as dry as a crow myself,' confessed Morag. She treated the shore to a Canute-like glance. 'The tide will keep a whiley yet, I'm thinkin'.'

'The kettles's been at the side of the fire all afternoon so it won't take long to boil,' I told her.

'Ach, then I'll away to the house an' fuse the tea while you finish your clearin'. Flora will give you a hand.'

Flora gave me a hand, accompanying her labours with such loquacious unintelligibility that I had to judge from her expression or intonation where to smile or to nod or exclaim. It appeared to suffice. As we turned to go back to the cottage she paused and with both arms full of weeds contrived to jerk an elbow towards the still unweeded part of my potato plot.

'Yon's filthy, yon,' she commented with powerful disgust. I nodded rueful agreement. It deserved no more generous a criticism.

It was good to see Morag pouring out the tea as we entered the kitchen and while I rinsed the dirt off my hands with a dipper of cold water and emptied the earth and grit out of my shoes, Morag, who was as much at home in my kitchen as her own, unwrapped the tea-towel from the girdle scones I had baked that morning, spread them with butter and jam and placed one on top of each steaming cup. In Bruach where all water had to be carried one never used more crockery than was absolutely essential. A cup required no saucer; a scone could be balanced on a cup until it was taken in the fingers. It might mean slops on the table or crumbs on the floor but rough wood is soon mopped clean and hens are good gleaners.

We sat down, Morag on a hard-backed chair near the open door so that she should not miss anything that was happening; Flora on a coir boat's fender which I had found on the shore and now used as a pouffe, and I in my usual armchair.

'Tell me, did you have yon mannie to see you?' asked Morag, slewing round in her chair.

'Was it a man?' I countered with a chuckle. 'I wasn't sure what it was.' I turned to Flora. 'This figure,' I explained, 'just came to me out of the blue and asked, "Do you love the Lord?"'

Flora brayed with laughter. 'Yon's mad, yon,' she declared.

'It was sluicing with rain,' I went on, 'and the figure was in oilskins and sou-wester and it had a high-pitched voice . . .'

'An' long hair,' interrupted Morag. 'Though the Dear

only knows why a man would want to grow his hair long unless he had a disease or somethin'.'

'It was a "he", then? Are you sure?'

'Indeed, I couldn't be sure what he was myself unless I turned him upside down,' replied Morag. 'But no, mo ghaoil, that wasn't the one I was meanin'. There was another one came.'

'Was there? No, I didn't see him.'

'They were sayin' he was one of these Yanks.'

'A Yank? Oh, no, I haven't had any Americans calling on me,' I told her. 'Just the hermaphrodite.'

'Oh, is that what he was?' enquired Morag. 'I wondered what religion he had to make him grow his hair as long as that.' She threw a crumb of scone to a straying hen.

'Well, if you didn't have the Yank callin' you missed somethin', I'm tellin' you.' She wiped away a smile with the back of her hand. 'He was wearin' a kilt that near reached his ankles an' short white stockings an' a straw hat an' them dark glasses so you couldn't see if he had eyes or spider's webs behind them.'

Flora shrieked appreciation, and the laughter lines ploughed deep on Morag's wrinkled face.

'What did he want?' I asked.

'Am't I tellin' you?' reproved Morag. 'He comes to my house an' when I go to the door he asks will I take him into the cow byre an' show him my antics.'

'Your what!' I ejaculated.

'My antics,' she reiterated and seeing my expression added : 'He offered to pay me, true as I'm here.' She reached over to the table and put down her cup. 'I told him, says I, "A few years ago if you'd come then to me I could have shown you plenty of antics but ach, not now. Those days have passed." '

'What sort of antiques was he after?' I enquired soberly.

'Why, crusie lamps an' steelyards an' quern stones an' goffering irons—even the worm we had for the whisky he was wantin'.'

'I know what happened to the worm,' I said. (Morag had once told me that after receiving warning of an impending visit by the Customs man all the village's whisky-distilling apparatus had been dumped into the deepest well.) 'But did you find anything else for him?'

'I did not, then.' She rose and helped herself to another cup of tea. 'The quern stones I had right enough till Hector broke them up to use for his lobster creels, the wretch, an' the crusie lamp disappeared when he was short of somethin' to oil the engine of his boat.'

'But the goffering iron,' I reminded her. 'Your mother's goffering iron was still in the byre when I was with you. I remember your bringing it out to show me.'

Morag gave a snort of disgust. 'Indeed, mo ghaoil, but since Hector an' Behag's come to live with me what can I keep my hands on save my own breeks an' it's tight I have to hold on to them sometimes for fear Hector will snatch them for cleanin' his engine,' she complained bitterly. 'No, but didn't Behag take the gofferin' iron first for liftin' the crabs claws out of the fire when she'd toast them—as if she couldn't do that with her fingers—an' then the next I see is Hector's got hold of it an' usin' it for stirrin' the tar to put on his boat. The Dear knows where the iron is now,' she went on. 'I doubt it's at the bottom of the sea along with the boat he tarred.'

'What a pity,' I murmured. 'I remember your telling me how you used to love watching your mother sitting by the fire and crimping the lace on her bonnet with the hot iron.'

Morag stared reflectively through the doorway, a gentle smile hovering around her lips. 'Indeed, I remember it like yesterday,' she said with a wistful sigh.

Down on the shore Morag and Flora wrested brown dulse from the wet, limpet-stippled rocks until their bag was full when they came up to the tide's edge and joined me in the collection of driftwood. No matter how adequate one's store of driftwood might be it was impossible to resist taking home bundle after bundle rather than leave it for the tide to take away again. Morag looked up at the sky, assessing the degree of light.

'If we don't start back they'll be thinkin' the "Each Uisge" has got us,' said Morag. 'An' there'll be no milk for the tea if I don't away to the cow. Hector's awful heavy on the milk,' she explained.

We made our way towards the heather-fringed burn where a relatively easy path led up towards the crofts. By now it was time for the evening milking and we could hear, though we could not yet see, the milkers calling for their cattle over the echoing moors. From closer at hand came the bawling of frustrated calves which, recognising the calling and the clanging of milk pails as a portent of supper, would be cavorting within the limited circle of their tethers.

Beside the burn Erchy was working at his dinghy, gouging handfuls of thick yellow grease from a tin he had found washed up on the shore and ramming it between the gaping planks. Like all Bruachites he had a sublime faith in grease and tar for keeping out the sea.

'Are you gettin' good fishin'?' enquired Morag, surveying with unusual interest the floorboards of the dinghy which were speckled with fish scales.

'Aye. There's plenty of fish about now,' he admitted.

'The sea's hissin' with mackerel.' With his elbow he ges-
tured towards the outlying islands. 'There's a bit of
herrin' too. Tearlaich an' me, we brought home a nice
few herrin' last night.' He and Morag exchanged wary
glances.

Flora, still carrying her bundle of wood, leaned over the
boat. 'Yon's no herrin' scales, yon,' she stated flatly. 'No,
nor mackerel either.'

'Indeed they are so,' argued Erchy but with dwindling
defiance as he realised he was confronted by an expert. He
glanced again at Morag but she had turned away,
elaborately disinterested.

'Yon's salmon, yon!' accused Flora.

'Be quiet!' returned Erchy with a challenging gleam in
his eye but seeing Flora's conspiratorial smile he went on :
'What if they are salmon, anyway? It's pleased enough
you'd be if you found one waitin' for you in the mornin', I
doubt.'

'I would too,' agreed Flora with unusual lucidity. 'There's
nay harm in yon.'

'The Lord puts the salmon in the rivers like he puts the
berries on the trees,' said Morag piously. 'They're there for
all of us, no' just the laird.'

'Aye so,' concurred Flora and she might just as well have
said 'Amen'.

I did not need to express an opinion, having lived long
enough in Bruach to accept that poaching was not just a
means of obtaining trout or salmon for a tasty meal but a
daring and exciting pastime. To outwit the watchers or
evade the police was a game as compulsive as betting or
gambling might be to a townsman, with the added attrac-
tion that it yielded a repertoire of adventure and escape
stories for the participants to narrate at winter ceilidhs.

Nearly every able-bodied male in the village, whatever his occupation, poached or had poached at some time or another. Even the salmon watchers were reputed to engage in a little poaching when they were not on duty.

Sure of his audience's wholehearted support Erchy became expansive. 'Indeed I mind the old laird askin' me to poach his salmon for him more than once,' he told us.

'Go on!' taunted Flora.

'Damty sure he did. I was doin' watchin' for him then an' he was expectin' this house party to come an' wanted salmon for their dinner. He was up at the loch all day an' didn't get a bite so he comes to me an' he says will I put my net in the river that night an' make sure there'd be one or two nice fish for them.'

'An' you made sure,' put in Morag with a reminiscent smile.

'Aye, we got near a dozen so we picked out all the ones that had the marks of the net on them an' sent them up to the laird's house. The rest we kept for ourselves.'

'That wasn't right at all,' Morag chided him.

'Ach, the cook got a hold of then an' had them prepared before the guests could put an eye to them but the next time the laird asks me to poach a few for him he says, "An' mind you, Erchy, make sure there's no net marks on them this time. I cannot rely on this cook to make such a good job of them." '

'Is it true?' demanded Flora.

'As true as I'm here,' averred Erchy.

Flora shook her head. 'Yon's a mon, yon.'

'These are no' very fresh,' Morag declared, leaning over the boat and scraping at the scales adhering to the wood. 'Would these be the minister's scales?'

Flora and I exchanged amused glances. 'The minister's scales?' we said simultaneously.

'What I was meanin' was were they the scales left from the night he had the minister out poachin'.' She laughed 'The night Erchy spent in the gaol.'

'Never surely!' breathed Flora.

'Aye, we did,' Erchy confirmed. 'Him as well.'

'The minister?'

'Aye.' Erchy nodded smugly. 'An' it served him damty well right too.'

'What happened?' I asked.

'Well, you mind that Sassenach minister was over stayin' for a holiday last week?'

I nodded.

'Well him, it was. He mentioned more than once he'd like a nice salmon to take back with him so in the end I said I'd take him. We went to the river an' we'd got a couple of good salmon in the net when suddenly there's a shout an' a couple of pollis come out of the dark an' grab the net, salmon an' all. They couldn't see who we was an' I got away out of it quick but this daft minister shouts, "No, Erchy, it's no use. We're caught red-handed." God! I was that mad I could have hit him. If he'd had any sense he would have followed me an' they'd never have been able to prove it was our net. We could always have said we'd just noticed it there an' were havin' a look.'

'You'd have lost your net,' I pointed out.

'We could have got a new bit of net for the price of the fine,' returned Erchy.

'So they put you in gaol,' I sympathised.

'Aye, well, that fellow wouldn't be satisfied. "We must plead guilty, Erchy," he says to me. "No damty fear," says I "They've no proof, I tell you." "But, Erchy," says he, "if there's a case about it my name will be in the papers an' what will my congregation think if they see their minister's been caught poachin'?"'

'The man was right,' interrupted Morag. 'He has to think of his congregation.'

'Right for himself maybe but ministers should think about others as well,' returned Erchy. 'If he was goin' to plead guilty then I had to as well.'

'What difference does it make pleading guilty?' I enquired innocently.

'If you plead guilty you just spend the night in the cell an' in the mornin' you pay your fine an' get out an' nobody much the wiser,' he explained.

'So that's what they did. An' the minister didn't get his salmon to take back with him,' Morag said.

'No, but he had the cheek of the devil, that fellow,' Erchy disclosed. 'When the copper came to the cell the next mornin' he was mighty pleased with himself at havin' got the pair of us an' the two salmon as evidence. Oh, he was smilin' an' tellin' us it was a nice day, an' then he says, "What would you like for your breakfast, gentlemen?" as if it was a hotel we was stayin' at.

' "I fancy some bacon an' eggs," says I, thinkin' I'd be cheeky an' put them to as much trouble as I could.

' "An' what about you, minister?" he says. An' that minister looks at him as cool as I don't know what an' he says, "Oh, don't go to any trouble for me, boys, just give me the same as you had yourselves—a plate of poached salmon".'

Flora and I dissolved into laughter.

'We'd best be on our way,' said Morag. 'Oidhche mhath!' she called.

'Oidhche mhath!' responded Erchy. I had taken a couple

27

of steps in the wake of Morag and Flora when I realised that Erchy's farewell had been spoken with his normal clarity and I realised suddenly that he was equipped with a full set of teeth.

'Erchy!' I exclaimed, instantly recognising them as his own because of the broken eye tooth. 'You've got your teeth back again!'

'Aye, I have so,' he admitted.

'You were lucky to find them, weren't you? Didn't you tell me you dropped them in the sea?'

'I said I dropped them overboard,' corrected Erchy, and seeing my puzzled look elucidated: 'I dropped them overboard in the river the other night when I was poachin' an' I was certain I'd never see them again, but, aye, I was lucky. Somebody did find them. They got them in their net.'

'How extraordinary!' I said. 'Who got them?'

'I'm not sayin' who,' responded Erchy with an air of mystery, 'but this mornin' who should be at the door but the pollis an' when I asked him what he wanted he pulled out this handkerchief an' there was my teeths wrapped in it. "I hear you lost your teeths, Erchy," says he. "Well, I did so," says I. "I'm wonderin' if these are yours?" asks the pollis. Well, I knew fine anybody would know they're my teeths so I says, "Aye, they're mine, right enough."'

'But who would take them to the police?' I asked. 'Surely it would be tantamount to admitting they'd been poaching?'

'Who would take them to the pollis?' returned Erchy derisively. 'When I'm damty sure everyone in the village knew they was mine?'

'You mean . . .' I began and then paused as the full import of his words dawned slowly upon me. 'You mean the policeman himself was doing a spot of poaching and he caught them in his net?'

Erchy fixed me with an uncompromising stare. 'Now what damty fool would be askin' the pollis a question like that?' he demanded.

Hic Jacet!

ERCHY'S mother and I met down by the burn where I
had been looking for watercress and when I had first
spotted her standing barefoot in the peaty brown pool below the waterfall I stood captivated by the picture she made.
With sleeves rolled elbow high and skirts tucked well above
the knees she was carefully positioning two empty herring

barrels beneath a craggy rock over which a truant rivulet
of sparkling water poured gently enough to fill the barrels
without risk of bursting them. Satisfied at last she waded
about in the pool, selecting boulders to buttress the barrels
until finally, after a push or two to assure herself of their
rigidity, she waded back to the bank where she stood for a
moment assessing her handiwork while she shook stray drops
of water from her cotton bonnet. I marvelled at her tough-
ness. Erchy's mother was 'Seventy past'; I knew from experience how bitingly cold the water in the pool felt to bare
feet even in midsummer and guessed she had been enduring it for at least ten minutes. I continued watching while
she sat on the heathery bank, drying her feet on her long
skirts, pulling on a pair of thick black woollen stockings to
just above the knee and finally lacing up her sturdy
'tackety' boots. Not until then did I make my presence
known.

'He Breeah!'

'He Breeah!' She struggled up. 'Were you here long?'

'Oh, no,' I lied, fearing to embarrass her. 'I've just been
making my way along the burn.' I showed her my few sprigs
of watercress.

'Ach, the biolaire, as we have it in the Gaelic,' she commented and with a smile added, 'that's food for the wee
folk.'

'I've heard that.' I returned her smile.

'Aye, there's some folks hereabouts who'll swear to seein'
a wee mannie gatherin' it late at night but only the Dear
knows whether or not they were tellin' the truth.'

'I'm very fond of it.' I told her.

'Aye, an' so were some of the laird's folk in my mother's
day, I mind her tellin' me. But she had no likin' for it herself an' I daresay that's why I've never taken to it.' She

tucked stray wisps of white hair into her bonnet and tied the strings under her chin. Waking or sleeping Erchy's mother rarely left her head uncovered. Most of the year she wore knitted woollen helmets but on hot summer days it was always the old-fashioned but extremely becoming cotton bonnet.

'Seein' you're here you'll came an' take a wee strupach with me,' she informed me. 'It's an awful whiley since you were in my house.'

Already I had been out longer than I had intended but to have refused her invitation would have disconcerted us both. She turned to take a last glance at the two barrels now full and overflowing.

'How long will you leave them there?' I asked.

'Till Friday maybe,' she replied.

It was now Tuesday and I estimated that three full days under the waterfall would have cleaned the barrels better than any amount of scrubbing or scouring. To Bruachites whose homes were nearby the burn became merely an extension of their kitchens. There on the bank, supported by a couple of fire-blackened rocks and permanently in residence, Erchy's mother kept a large iron washing pot in which she boiled her linen, rinsing it afterwards in the fast-flowing burn; it was in the burn she did her annual blanket washing prior to draping them over high clumps of heather to dry in the sun. There she cleaned the insides of the sheep they killed each autumn and there she washed the meal-coated bowls and basins when she had finished baking.

As we drew near the cottage she shielded her eyes from the sun. 'There's the men busy at their bottoms,' she observed.

At the gable end of the house Erchy was thrusting a rusty gap-toothed saw through a plank of driftwood with the object of cutting it into lengths suitable for bottoms for lobster creels. The saw scrunched and jammed, scrunched and jammed again and again and Erchy swore and jounced, swore and jounced in retaliation. Nearby crouched Hector, chewing at a stalk of grass and watching the proceedings with cursory interest.

'I'm after tellin' Erchy he needs to take tsat saw to see a dentist,' he quipped as we paused to watch.

The saw, Erchy and his profanity jerked to a stop as he looked up. His face was red as a radish with exertion and a large bead of sweat dropped from his upper lip as he nodded acknowledgment of our presence.

'Indeed I'm thinkin' I could chew through it faster,' he confessed, dragging a tired arm across his glistening brow and giving the saw a long look of disgust. It was rare to see a well-kept tool in Bruach and it struck me that Erchy might have sawn wood more efficiently with a curry comb.

'It wouldn't be so bad if that bugger would take his turn at it.' Erchy nodded cheerfully at Hector.

'Ach, I'm no good wiss a saw,' Hector disclaimed hastily and giving Erchy a respectful look went on : 'Erchy's tsat good at it I believe if he had a mind he could make coffins as good as any undertaker.'

'I'll make one for you,' retorted Erchy searingly. 'An' I'll make it good an' strong. That's one job you won't wriggle out of.'

Hector smiled imperturbably. He turned to me. 'Me an' Erchy has a mind to go to Rhuna tsis evenin',' he disclosed. 'She'll stay calm enough, I reckon.' He stared with indolent optimism at the sunlit sea, frisked into sharp-edged ripples by a tease of afternoon breeze.

Erchy's mother turned on her son with mock indignation.

'How can you be goin' away to Rhuna when only this mornin' you were sayin' you hadn't the time to take from makin' the creels to bring home a load of peats just.'

'An' isn't it for the sake of the creels we have to go to Rhuna?' he exclaimed, glancing quickly at Hector, inviting endorsement of his statement. Hector's wide-eyed assent was very convincing.

'Ach!' The old woman's tone was explicit.

'It's true,' Erchy insisted. 'We need to go an' gather up the hazels we cut earlier this year. You canna make creels without hazels any more than you can make bannocks without meal.'

'I can see I'll be needin' to take home the peats myself, then,' his mother said with pretended resignation as she flexed her shoulders proudly.

'Aye, you will so,' agreed her son.

It seemed never to have occurred to Erchy and it would have been cruel to suggest to his mother that she was now too old to carry home heavy creels of peat from the moors. She had carried them since childhood and through the years her back had shaped itself to take the half-hundredweight or so of the loaded creels. Like her contemporaries she would continue to do so, insisting that stiff fingers could still grasp peats and a back rigid with rheumatism was still sound enough for burdens. Not until the day came when with only a token load of peats and making frequent stops for rest she found herself too breathless to totter to and from the moors would she give in. With a grunt that was acceptance of her son's remark and a warm 'thig a 's Tigh' to me she made for the cottage. However, I hung back for a moment.

'Does this trip to Rhuna mean there's likely to be a cruise?' I asked, looking appreciatively at the roan-coloured islands. 'It promises to be a perfect evening for a sail.'

'The sea makes no promises and breaks none,' Erchy rebuked me.

Hector contemplated his chewed stalk of grass, discarded it and chose another one. 'We're no likely to get away by ourselves, anyway,' he remarked philosophically. 'Tsere's always plenty folks keen enough to go to Rhuna on a nice evenin'. I daresay we'll get enough to sink tse boat.'

'I'll look out for you then?' I suggested.

'Aye, you'd best do that if you're comin',' said Erchy. 'At the back of eight or so.' He bent to resume his contest with the saw.

In the kitchen Erchy's mother was unwrapping crumbly oatcakes from a piece of bleached flour sack which in Bruach kitchens did duty as tea-towels. 'They're fresh-baked this mornin' an' left warm beside the fire,' she told me. In my larder at home were fresh mackerel fillets waiting only to be dipped in oatmeal and baked for my supper and I had eaten frugally all day so as to be able to indulge in what had now become my favourite dish. But Erchy's mother baked the most irresistible oatcakes in Bruach and I knew without doubt I should succumb. She cut a thick slice of home-made butter and placing it on the triangular cake offered it to me. In the Bruach idiom 'my teeths watered' as I watched the butter melting into a golden lake.

There was a footstep outside followed by a Gaelic greeting. I recognised Morag's voice.

'Ach, so this is where you are!' she said, coming inside and settling herself ready for the strupak which Erchy's mother immediately prepared for her.

I wiped the butter from my chin. 'Why, were you looking for me?' I asked.

'No, but seein' I was up at the Post Office Behag said

would I call in an' tell you she'll likely be down for a wee
ceilidh with you tonight. She sent away to the catalogue
for a new skirt an' she's wantin' you to gather her in round
the middle.'

'Not tonight,' I said. 'There's going to be a cruise. Have
you not heard?'

'A cruise!' she ejaculated. 'What way are you goin'?'

'To Rhuna,' I replied. 'Hector and Erchy have to go
over to collect some hazels to finish their creels.'

'If that's the way of it, mo ghaoil, I doubt you'll be seein'
Behag tonight except on the boat beside you,' Morag said.
'An' myself too, likely,' she added. 'I haven't set foot on
Rhuna these ten years since.'

'I was with you myself last time you were there, was I
not?' Erchy's mother reminded her.

'You were so,' Morag acknowledged.

'That man Hamish Beag was alive then. You mind the
one that played the bagpipes and wouldn't speak to a soul
save his horse.'

Morag nodded.

'He played his bagpipes the night we was there,' Erchy's
mother recalled.

'Indeed, that's true,' returned Morag. She turned to me.
'I'm tellin' you, Miss Peckwitt, that man stood in the door
of his house an' the minute he started to play his pipes all
the rats ran out an' hid themselves they was that feared of
the noise.' The two women chuckled reminiscently.

'They say he was forever blowin' his bagpipes,' said
Erchy's mother.

'An' they were right. That's what folks say killed him in
the end,' Morag told us.

'Not playing the bagpipes?' I protested.

'So they say.' Morag nodded slowly. 'Insanity of the lungs,

that's what he got with playin' the pipes so much, mo ghaoil, an' that's what killed him in the end.'

'Is there a strupach, cailleach?' Erchy sauntered into the kitchen followed by Hector and in their wake came Tearlaich who was carrying a slightly less disabled saw than the one Erchy had been using. Morag shot Tearlaich a disapproving glance. He was something of a non-conformist in Bruach and he came in now with his jacket slung over his shoulder and his shirt open to the waist revealing a fuzzy chest as broad and muscular as that of a champion plough horse.

'Are you no goin' to fasten up your shirt seein' there's ladies present,' she said to him, half jokingly. Tearlaich responded with a brazen smile but nevertheless began to do up his shirt buttons.

Erchy's mother's eyes grew bright with pleasure as her kitchen filled and she busied herself buttering oatcakes and pouring cups of tea. 'If the cows hadn't yet to be milked we could have a ceilidh,' she said wistfully.

The three men flopped down on the bench. I was sitting on an uneven stool and as I raised my overfull teacup to drink the stool wobbled and the hot tea slopped into my lap. I let out a startled exclamation and began mopping myself with a handkerchief. Tearlaich, who claimed to have acted as batman to a high-ranking officer during the war and who still retained a desultory interest in chivalry, immediately jumped up.

'What are we doing taking the best seats for ourselves,' he chided himself and the others. 'Come now, Miss Peckwitt, and take my seat and I will have that old stool,' he offered gallantly. Erchy and Hector flicked him the sort of glance that would have been merited by a potato that showed signs of blight.

'That's not goin' to do her any harm at her age,' Erchy said pitilessly.

I refused to give up my stool, knowing that if I sat near them neither Erchy nor Hector would be able to resist indulging in the time-honoured trick of leaving a teaspoon in their tea until it was really hot, then whipping it out and pressing it on to my bare arm. Tearlaich promptly resumed his seat on the bench. He offered his saw to Erchy.

'Here,' he said. 'Take a lend of this.'

Erchy took it without enthusiasm at first but then examining the handle more closely he exclaimed : 'Here, this is my own saw ! I know him by these three cuts on the handle.'

Tearlaich leaned over to inspect the notches. 'Aye,' he allowed. 'It's marked all right.'

'Where did you get him from then ?' Erchy demanded.

'From Johnny Mor Alistair.'

'Oh, that bugger !' commented Erchy, without venom. His mother darted him a reproving glance. No matter how much evidence she heard to the contrary she would undoubtedly go to her grave still cherishing the belief that her son never swore except in Gaelic.

'No wonder he didn't mind me gettin' the lend of it for you,' Tearlaich mused.

'Hell, no ! But it wasn't Johnny Mor Alistair that took him from me in the first place I believe it was Lachlan Beag that had him to make his wee hoosie when his brother was comin' home an' bringin' that fancy girl friend of his.'

'Oh, her,' responded Tearlaich derisively. 'The one that was too swanky to use the heather like the rest of us.' He grunted. 'It's a good thing he didn't marry that one. If she had to have a wee hoosie before she'd marry him God knows what she would have been askin' for next.'

'One of them Rolls-Royces to carry home the peats, likely,' submitted Hector with a smile.

Erchy still held the saw. 'He was a good saw when he was new,' he murmured sadly.

'Did you get it new?' asked Tearlaich incredulously.

'No, but my father did,' replied Erchy. 'He got him from the blacksmith after he died.'

'But the blacksmith died twenty years since,' Tearlaich expostulated.

'Aye, an' he was as good as new then.' Erchy ran his fingers along the toothed edge. 'He's still better than that one I was usin', anyway.' He put the saw on the floor under the bench. 'I'd like to know who Johnny Mor Alistair got him from all the same.'

'Who knows where any of the tools in this place comes from,' retorted Tearlaich, adding as an afterthought, 'From hell itself by the look of most of them.'

He took out a packet of cigarettes and extracting four pushed one behind his ear, gave one to Erchy, one to Hector and was about to bestow the fourth one on me when he suddenly changed his mind and pushed it back into the packet which he then held out to me. 'Sao,' he invited politely.

Hector stretched out his hand and helped himself to a piece of oatcake from the table. 'Indeed amn't I wishin' Behag could make tsem as good as tsese,' he said plaintively.

'Ach, but she was never born to it,' Morag defended. Behag's parents had both been crofters but as they were never married Behag herself had been adopted by a Glasgow couple and had visited Bruach only for occasional holidays until she met and married Hector.

'It's funny that,' observed Erchy with a puzzled frown.

'What's funny?' asked Hector.

'The way Behag was adopted. You'd think with her mother bein' from Bruach her own parents would have kept the child and been glad to do it.'

'It's always struck me as odd,' I interposed. I had lived there long enough now to know that any child born in Bruach was sure of a welcome.

'Indeed her mother's parents wanted her to keep the child!' exclaimed Morag indignantly. 'But Kate, that was Behag's mother, thought she could do better.'

'What happened, then?' I asked.

'It was like this, mo ghaoil,' began Morag. 'When Behag was no more than about two years old her mother went off to work in Glasgow an' she went an' got herself married to a man that lived in a nice house an' seemed to have plenty of money. He lived with his parents an' was brought up one of these Papists but ach, I suppose they were gettin' old so they made no fuss about havin' a nice girl like Kate to look after them in spite of her havin' a different religion. The husband must have been a decent man for all that, for he made no objection to Kate havin' Behag to live with them an' so they were all set up until he goes an' dies on them suddenly.'

'He was very smart about his dyin', I mind,' interpolated Erchy's mother.

'Smart!' echoed Morag. 'Indeed he was. He didn't have time to do whatever it is these Papists do before they die anyway, so Kate told me.'

'What happened to Kate then?' enquired Erchy.

'Didn't the daughter come home from abroad when her brother died an' say she'd look after the old folk now, an' Kate was told plainly either she'd change her religion or she'd get out an' take Behag with her.'

'The house an' the money belonged to the old folk all the time seemingly,' supplied Erchy's mother. 'Kate got nothin' but a few pounds out of it for all her work.'

'Did Kate get out?' I asked.

'She got out,' declared Hector grimly.

'Surely she got out.' Morag's tone made it plain there had been no alternative for a girl born and bred in Bruach. 'But Kate's parents were both dead by that time an' only her brother an' his wife in the croft. She didn't think much of the brother's wife so she had to take work herself an' get Behag adopted. It was lucky she did for she died soon after.' Morag shook her head. 'She had a sad life in a way, did Behag's mother. A sad life an' a short one.'

'This couple that adopted Behag,' pursued Erchy. 'Were they good to her?'

'Good enough,' said Hector.

'Why did they take her?' asked Tearlaich. 'Was it because they couldn't have bairns of their own?'

'Well, of course,' began Morag but Erchy cut her short.

'There's no of course about it,' he told her. 'Some of these folks that adopt children do it because they get paid more for havin' an adopted child than if it was one of their own.'

'That's true,' conceded Morag.

'An' that's as it should be,' put in Tearlaich. 'You'd expect to be paid more. After all if you've made your children you've had the fun as well.'

'Whisht now!' commanded Erchy's mother, with a glance at me.

'The shame about Behag is that she hasn't the Gaelic,' said Erchy, changing the subject.

'I don't care about her havin' tse Gaelic,' Hector responded. 'I can as well make her understand what I want of her in English as in Gaelic, but all tse same I wish she could learn to make oatcakes as good as tsese.' He broke off a large piece and stuffed it into his mouth.

'She tries,' Morag told him.

'Aye, she tries. But you know yourself tse ones she makes are tsat bitty most of tsem drops on tse floor for tse hens to eat.'

'Us girls had to learn,' Erchy's mother told him. 'If we wasted oatmeal it was our job to grind more on the quern stones an' that was hard work.' Leaning over the table and clasping her hands round an imaginary stick she strained, miming vividly the action of grinding the oats between the circular stones and her face became set into lines of remembered effort. She relaxed with a smile. 'How I hated havin' to do it,' she said.

'But the smell of it!' Morag reminded her. 'Did ever meal smell so good? Not like this stuff we get already ground these days.'

'To my mind nothin' smells as good these days as it once did,' Erchy's mother rejoined. 'I remember when I was young the way the flowers threw up their scent at you as you walked through the grass in the spring an' summer. An' in the autumn the tang of the heather would drift in of an evenin' over the crofts like a scented shawl.'

'An' the burn in spate,' Morag recalled. 'Once you turned your back on the sea you could smell the burn as surely as a fox smells a new lamb from afar off.'

'An' the honey! D'you mind the honey?' exclaimed Erchy's mother, her eyes glowing with reminiscence. 'The way it was that strong you could fairly taste the sweetness of it on your lips as you walked in the heather.'

'Aye, an' the hems of your skirt would be sticky with it when you came to take off your clothes at night.'

42

'It's funny you never smell such things now,' went on Erchy's mother. 'It's like as though the lovely smells of the place had been washed away with all the rain that's in it.'

'You're right,' agreed Morag. 'I've noticed that myself.'

Erchy seemed to be growing more and more uneasy as the recollections continued. 'Of course everythin' smells the same, you silly cailleachs,' he broke in. 'It's just you two gettin' old that's the trouble.'

Morag looked momentarily stricken but his mother smiled confidently. 'My nose is still above the ground,' she told him as she gathered up the cloth in which the oatcakes had been wrapped. Going to the doorway she flicked off the crumbs to a waiting cluster of hens.

'The trouble with the cailleach is she won't allow any-body to be old so long as they can stand on their own two feets just,' Erchy muttered with kindly understanding.

'When I was a girl,' said Erchy's mother as she came back into the kitchen, 'there was little ground oatmeal came into our house.'

Erchy fished a half-smoked cigarette from his trouser pocket and lit it. 'I mind my father bringing home meal that was already ground,' he said.

'Aye, but those were bad days indeed.' His mother's voice was unusually sharp.

I looked enquiringly from mother to son, sensing a story. 'How bad?' I asked.

'Ach, it was the laird that was here at the time. He was a bad man, Miss Peckwitt. A bad man indeed.' She took the kettle over to the water pail and refilled it.

'You'd best finish tellin' her now you've started,' Erchy encouraged her.

'Since you remember it you can tell her yourself,' his mother retorted.

'Ach, I was young at the time. I only mind my father tellin' me of it.'

'He'd be tellin' you the truth, then, so you can tell Miss Peckwitt the truth now.'

Contentedly Erchy embarked on his narrative. 'It was like my mother said. This laird that was here then was a hard man. A cruel man you could say an' when he wanted work doin' on the estate he'd drive round Bruach in his pony an' trap an' any man he'd put an eye on he'd point his whip at him an' say, "I've seen you." He never said a word more than "I've seen you" but once he'd pointed at the men then those men had to go the next day an' do a day's work for him. It didn't matter how much work they needed to do on their own crofts—they might have oats or hay to stack an' the weather like to break at any moment, but they had to leave it an' go at first light the next day to the laird's place and work right through till it was dark. All they got in payment was a measure of meal. Just that. No money.'

'But it was the measure that was wicked,' interrupted his mother.

'I was comin' to that,' he told her. 'This measure he had was a bit like a small herrin' barrel but it was divided into two across the middle.' He got up and going across to the dresser picked up an old-fashioned wooden egg-cup. 'The shape of it was a bit like this only bigger an' with this sort of waist in it so that the top half held a lot more meal than the bottom half. When the work was finished for the day the laird would make the men stand in two lines, the big men in one line an' the small ones in the other. They'd hold out their pocs an' the big men would get the big measure of meal tipped into it an' the small men would get the small measure.'

'All for the same day's work?' I asked.

'For the same day's work,' confirmed Erchy.

'What if the big man was a bachelor and the small man had a family to keep?' I pursued.

'Then that was the way of it,' was the reply. 'That's how they were paid no matter what family they had.'

It all sounded so medieval that I looked askance at Erchy, recalling that his father had still been alive when I had first come to Bruach.

'And all this happened in your father's time?' I could not keep the incredulity out of my voice.

'Aye. An' I mind it happenin', though I was young enough at the time.'

'Aye, he was young enough,' affirmed his mother. 'But if he didn't remember it he'd have heard the men speakin' of it for that they did often enough. They miscalled that man somethin' terrible, Miss Peckwitt, an' he deserved every bit of it.'

'And did this continue until the new laird took over?' I demanded, knowing that the crofters were eager enough now to be given work on the estate.

'It did not then.' Erchy's denial held a note of triumph. 'It was Big Ruari that put a stop to it.'

'Big Ruari?' I echoed. 'You mean . . . ?'

'No, not the Big Ruari that's alive today but his uncle,' Erchy corrected. 'He got the men together one day an' told them if they'd all stick by him they need never again work for the laird except for money or fair shares.'

'Big Ruari was my own father's cousin,' mused Hector.

'He was my own husband's cousin at that,' claimed Erchy's mother proudly.

'Wasn't he marrit to Anna Ruag that was an aunt of mine,' asserted Morag.

As everyone in Bruach appeared to be related in some

degree or other to everyone else I saw there was a danger that the story of Big Ruari's stratagem for overcoming the laird might be relinquished in favour of a prolonged delving into genealogies, so after a few minutes of simulated attention I put my question direct. 'How did Big Ruari stop them working for the laird?'

There was a hint of recoil and in the ensuing silence Erchy got up and made me wait while he searched in a drawer of the dresser for a crumpled packet of cigarettes. Outside two cockerels began to crow competitively.

'Well,' resumed Erchy, sitting down. 'The men was all agreed that next time the laird was seen comin' in his trap they'd make themselves scarce except for Big Ruari an' he'd stay workin' near the road so the laird couldn't help seein' him. Right enough, along comes the laird, points his whip at Big Ruari an' says, "I've seen you." Big Ruari touched his cap as he was supposed to but he didn't turn up for work the next day, no, nor the next. Back comes the laird an' by God! he's mad. There's Big Ruari again workin' beside the road but the rest of the men is hidden in his byre. "Why did you not come to do your day's work like you were told?" roars the laird. "See you come tomorrow, my man, or it'll be the worse for you." "I'm no' coming to work for you tomorrow nor any other day," Big Ruari tells him. "An' what's more there's no man in this place will ever work for you again except for fair wages." As soon as Big Ruari's done speakin' the laird ups with his whip an' gives him a mighty strike across the face so that the blood comes pouring out.'

'Oh, but he was a monster, that laird!' interjected Erchy's mother. 'An' him a Highlander!'

'Aye, he was so,' affirmed Erchy, gesturing his mother to remain silent. 'Big Ruari then, he steps up to the trap. "In that case, master, I'll do my day's work now," says he, an' he lifts the laird clean out of the trap an' throws him down on the ground. Then the rest of the men rushes out, un-hitches the horse and send it harin' away for home. They turn the trap right over on top of the laird so that it's like he's caught in a cage. An' there they left him an' went back to their own croft work.'

'An' no Bruach man ever did a day's work for that laird again,' said Morag dramatically.

'I suppose he sold up and left eventually,' I suggested, recalling that the only lairds I had heard spoken of had been Lowlanders.

'He did not, then. He died here in his own house,' Erchy refuted. 'Isn't that his grave in the woods you were askin' about yourself a good while back?'

'Oh, that's his grave, is it?' I said thoughtfully, and was glad that at last I had discovered the story of the lone grave. I had come upon it suddenly while blackberrying in a gentle birchwood not far from the laird's house. The surround-ing iron railings had fallen outwards and were partially em-bedded in the moist earth but the area of the grave was still clearly marked by an abundant growth of nettles impres-sively green in contrast with the pale spongy moss elsewhere; the roots of a young tree had shattered what must once have been a large headstone. I had not lived long in Bruach when I had made my find and doubtless I had asked too many questions for a stranger so that when I had enquired about the lone grave I had been told merely that its occupant had been a Roman Catholic and therefore could not be buried in the Bruach burial ground. In-stinctively I had suspected more of a story but I had had to wait several years to hear it fully.

'Aye, that's his grave,' Tearlaich agreed. 'And I'm telling you, Miss Peckwitt, that laird was so much hated, if any man from Bruach needed to have a pee and he was within a mile of that wood he'd hold on to himself till he could get there just so he could have the pleasure of defiling that grave.'

'Indeed I do it myself to this day,' boasted Erchy.

'Be quiet!' his mother admonished him. 'Miss Peckwitt won't like to hear you.'

I laughed heartily. 'I wondered why those nettles look so well fertilised,' I said.

In Search of Apples

IT was well after the 'back of eight' before the first potential passengers began to drift in twos and threes down to the shore but since there was no sign of either Erchy or Hector I occupied myself with tidying up the tiny flower garden behind my cottage while keeping an eye open for signs of activity aboard the boat. My garden had perforce to be a

tiny one since in Bruach adequate shelter had to be provided from the savage storms which constantly beset us
irrespective of the time of year. The only satisfactory
shelter was a dry-stone wall, the building of which is infinitely more complicated than it appears and though
initially I had planned a garden large enough to grow
shrubs and roses as well as annuals, as I had wrestled
throughout the winter months with craggy jumbo-sized
stones that perversely slid from their beds as soon as my
back was turned so had my plans contracted until finally I
was more than content with a plot that measured little more
than three strides by two. I was able to rejoice that I had
some shelter and when spring came I sowed the garden
prodigally with seed that the catalogues described as being
'the hardiest of hardy annuals' : marigolds, poppies, candy-
tuft, lavatera, and flax among them. I had tried to sow to
a preconceived pattern of colour but when the seedlings
appeared they did so in haphazard swirls acknowledging
the eddies of a vagrant breeze that had been loitering, too
stealthily for my wind-conditioned body to notice, around
the garden at the time of sowing. The seedlings had
flourished and now after a few days of calm and sunshine
the full-grown plants were exploding into bloom, making a
patch of colour on the drab croft like a brightly crocheted
cushion in a barren room. I sometimes asked myself why
I so much wanted a flower garden when, in their season,
there was such an abundance of wild flowers to delight the
eye. Celandines, primroses, red rattle, butterwort, St.
John's wort, corn marigold, orchis and countless other
gems studded the crofts and moors with their discreet
beauty until eclipsed by the autumnal glory of the heather,
but comely as they were they were all either tiny or tough-
stemmed plants and perversely I found myself missing the

long-stemmed elegance of garden flowers. I stood regarding my plot, revelling in its colour and dwelling on even more ambitious plans. A rose bush here—my eye marked the spot. And another one there. . . .

'Them's bloody lovely,' said an unctuous voice in my ear and I turned to see Tearlaich who had come up quietly behind me and was regarding the flowers with eye-bulging admiration. 'Bloody lovely!' he confirmed with a congratulatory nod. Tearlaich was convinced that he possessed a rare eye for beauty. 'I'd like to grow flowers myself,' he confided. 'Indeed I did try to grow some once or twice just to see what they'd look like.'

'And were you successful?' I asked.

'Ach! It was always the same. Either the cows got at them or the sheep ate them or the horses broke down the fence and let the hens into them.'

I sympathised with him. There was little enough encouragement for would-be gardeners, particularly flower gardeners, in Bruach, since even in summer with the moor gates closed against the cattle there were always straying animals eager to devastate any unfenced crops and traditionally once the hay and corn and potatoes were lifted and stacked the gates were thrown open again allowing the voracious cattle to rampage in and feast on the aftermath of grass. During their first few days on the crofts the air was filled with the noise of clashing horns, thumping bodies and bellows of aggression or agony as the half-wild cattle which had all summer been free to wander over the vast expanse of moorlands found themselves confined within the relatively small area of croftland and we, their owners, went about our daily chores with anxious eyes ranging over the cliffs and gullies near the shore and carrying hefty sticks ready to drive a beast away from danger or break up what might prove to be a disastrous encounter for one's own or someone else's cow. By the time the herds had amalgamated and were concentrating on feeding rather than fighting the crofts had been churned into morasses of mud by their hooves and only the most robust fences had withstood their blundering assaults.

I was fortunate in that my cottage and byre were enclosed by a sturdy dry-stone wall, or dyke as it was always called in Bruach, which so long as I assiduously replaced any fallen stones was an effective barrier against the cows while the horses, which were not allowed on the crofts until the cows had gleaned most of the grass, were too busy seeking for food to have the energy for anything but dragging themselves from one promising-looking patch to another. My henhouse was far enough away to discourage the poultry from too close an investigation of the cottage and its immediate surroundings but it was the sheep which were my enemies. Against these I had little defence save sharp eyes, a supply of small stones and a stentorian repetition of 'Halla!' whenever they came in sight.

'It's a pity there aren't more gardens in Bruach,' I observed to Tearlaich. 'If more people grew vegetables or flowers they might be keener to keep the cattle away from the crofts at night.' It was difficult enough maintaining a watch on one's garden during daylight : it was virtually impossible to do so once darkness had fallen.

'Ach, but there's always the slugs to spoil a garden,' responded Tearlaich nimbly. 'It's that damp on my croft the slugs are near as big as mice. I grew some cabbages last year and I could lie in my bed at night and listen to the slugs gnawing through them.'

I laughed.

'It's as true as I'm here,' he assured me with great

earnestness. 'Honest to God, those cabbages were as full of holes as a herring net by morning.

From the shore came the rattle of oars being shipped.

'Have Erchy and Hector gone down yet?' I asked.

'Aye, they're away. They told me to call in and tell you to be ready and for me to pick up that rope fender Erchy dropped over your dyke a while back.'

My croft being situated conveniently near was the repository for precious objects retrieved from the shore. There were times after a storm when my croft resembled a museum of flotsam.

'I'll go and get a coat,' I said. 'Don't let them go without me.'

Tearlaich still hung back, apparently unable to drag his attention away from the garden. 'Those things, there,' he pointed. 'Are those trees?'

'They're supposed to be,' I confessed with a rueful glance at the row of baby conifers which I had planted early in the spring in the hope they would thrive and eventually provide natural shelter.

'They don't look as if they'll like to live,' observed Tearlaich without optimism.

'I doubt it very much myself,' I agreed, assessing the miniature branches which still showed faint traces of green tips but otherwise looked as if they had been pressed and scorched with a hot iron.

'Where did you get them?' asked Tearlaich.

'From that tinker. You know, the one they always call "Buggy Duck". He promised me last year he'd bring some next time he was round and this spring he turned up with these.'

'Were they like this when you got them?'

I nodded.

53

'I hope you didn't give him money for them?'

I admitted that I had paid Buggy Duck the price he had asked.

'Ach, I could have got you a few from the laird's place if I'd known you wanted them. He'd never miss that many.'

'I don't want illicit trees in my garden,' I said firmly.

Tearlaich looked at me and there were both pity and amazement in his expression. 'Why then did you ask Buggy Duck to bring you some?' he demanded. 'Like as not they came from the laird's place anyway but not so fresh as you'd have got them from me.' He threw the conifers a final disdainful glance as he turned away. 'I doubt they'll live the winter,' he informed me. 'They've been too dry.'

'I told Buggy Duck when he brought them they looked too dry to survive but he got quite indignant. He said they couldn't possibly have got too dry because he'd been sleeping with them inside his bedding for the last three months.'

Tearlaich and I exchanged amused glances. 'If a tinker's been sleeping with them for three months I doubt you'll have a lot of other things growing in your garden supposing you don't get any trees,' he comforted.

Even standing on the shore I could see the boat was grossly overloaded and when we came alongside in the dinghy I estimated there was hardly more than eighteen inches of freeboard. There were coy screams from some of the young girls aboard as Tearlaich jumped heavily on the gunwale causing the boat to rock spectacularly.

'She's fairly ready to sink with the weight of folks in her,' Erchy told him with a touch of irritation.

'Ach, it's calm enough,' retorted Tearlaich and squeezing himself between two of the girls sat grinning cheerfully with an arm round each of them.

It was a lustrous evening of velvet calm with remnants

of the sunset still glowing behind the dark hill peaks and the unruffled sea reflecting the pale celadon of the sky save where the outlying islands cast sable shadows. Sea birds were everywhere, puffins, guillemots and razorbills, all bobbing and diving for late suppers while above them terns wheeled and dipped in flight.

Erchy assessed the number of heads aboard. 'Where's Johnny Mor?' he asked. 'He swore he was comin'.'

'I've seen no sign of him,' said Tearlaich. 'Ach, he was out on the hill today seein' to his sheep. Maybe he's fallen in a bog.'

'Well, if he has we're not waitin' till he gets out of it,' said Hector with a bland smile. He started the engine while Erchy attended to the mooring of the dinghy.

Are we no' takin' the dinghy?' asked Hector as the rope was cast off.

'No damty fear,' replied Erchy. 'If nobody comes to meet us at Rhuna Miss Peckwitt can swim ashore an' get a hold of one of their dinghies.' I gave him an arch glance. I am a poor swimmer but the fact that I could keep afloat in the water at all astonished the Bruachites. The skirl of compassionate murmurings directed at me from the female passengers gave way to small shrieks and squeaks of excitement as the bow of the boat cut a sweeping arc through the water and turned towards Rhuna. The postman soon produced a mouth-organ and gradually coaxed most of the passengers into the singing of Gaelic and Scottish songs, the mixed choir of voices surging and ebbing over the water while the throbbing of the engine and the strains of the mouth-organ compounded into a makeshift orchestra.

'When you're on the sea,' Erchy had once confided to me, 'you either want to sing or you want to swear.' I stole a glance at him as he stood with one hand on the tiller, his head raised and his mouth wide open as he sang lustily. I watched the receding shore, the feeding birds and the evening settling over the water.

'Oh, look! A seal!' I cried as a sleek dark head bobbed out of the sea about fifty yards behind us. The rest of the company turned to give the seal a moment or two of its attention and then the singers, whose voices had only wavered at my interruption, were at full volume again. It was sometimes difficult for me to remember that sights which thrilled me were to the Bruachites so regular as to be commonplace; that they were as used to the presence of seals around their shores as I had once been to the presence of hawkers in town.

'There's another of them been following us for the past twenty minutes if you're that keen to see them,' shouted Tearlaich. 'It's the singing that brings them.'

'I sing nearly every time I go out in a boat,' I yelled back, 'but I've never managed to lure a seal to follow me yet.'

From the stern of the boat Erchy's voice came piercingly. 'That's because you sing in English. It's only the Gaelic that attracts them.'

For some time the two seals accompanied us, submerging and re-emerging at varying distances from the boat but always it seemed keeping us under observation with such timid yearning in their large dark eyes I was reminded of pictures of hungry waifs locked out from a feast.

As we approached the dark mass of Rhuna the island slowly yielded up its secrets. The bastion-like cliffs revealed themselves as being riven into steep sea-washed caverns and tiny shingle coves; shadowy hollows betrayed the entrances to secret caves; craggy pillars of rock were tenanted by uneasy shags, while on the tumbled boulders, still wet from the retreating tide, stood confident gulls watching us with half-hearted interest. Erchy steered the boat toward the mouth of a burn where two dinghies were moored by ropes to the shore. While we watched two men came out from one of the cottages and began to pull in both dinghies preparatory to rowing out to meet us.

'It's Roddy an' Calum that's comin',' announced Erchy. Hector stopped the engine. 'Aye, an' seein' tsey're bringin' two dinghies they must know we have a good load,' he observed.

'They're no' blind, are they?' Tearlaich told him.

If the boat had been overloaded the dinghies were even more so, there being barely three inches of freeboard on either of them. But no one worried. It was a calm evening and a short row. We clambered out on to the shingle without mishap.

'The cailleach has a strupach ready,' said Roddy, thus obliquely conveying to us that whoever we might wish to visit during the evening the real ceilidh was to be at his mother's house. She had staked her claim to our company.

'We'd best away an' get our hazels first,' Erchy told him. 'We'll take a strupach when we get back.'

'I'll take a look in at her,' Morag promised. 'But I couldn't swallow a mouthful till I've undone myself from the knot I was in aboard that boat. Indeed my legs was that stiff I thought I'd have to leave them behind.' She rubbed her knuckles into the small of her back.

'I want to go and see that apple tree,' I said firmly.

Rhuna boasted an apple tree which was reputed to have been grown from the pips of apples washed ashore when an American schooner foundered off the island during the Great War and on a previous visit, late in the autumn, I had

discovered beneath the tree two rotting apples which I had
taken home and planted. Despite lavish attention, however,
the seeds had not germinated and, since I hoped to try again,
I wanted to go and inspect the tree to satisfy myself it was
still flourishing.

'I'll come along with you,' said Behag promptly. It
transpired that most of the party had friends they wished
to see or things they wished to do before gathering for a
final strupach so it was agreed that Roddy was to tell his
mother we would all return in about an hour's time for our
ceilidh with her. The party therefore split up into various
groups and went their different ways. Behag and I were joined by Tearlaich and by Roddy's brother, Calum, who, because he had spent much of his time at sea, was almost a
stranger to Behag and to me. We ambled along slowly and
Morag, who had nipped into the cottage to exchange
polite greetings with the 'cailleach', soon caught up with us.

'You didn't tell me your sister Marie was home,' she accused Calum.

'Aye, she's home. She's gettin' married at the back end
to some doctor or other so she's home for a rest first.'

'She'll need a rest first if she's goin' to marry a doctor,'
remarked Tearlaich with an obscure smile.

'To a doctor,' echoed Morag. 'Do I know of him?'

'Indeed I don't know him myself,' returned Calum, 'except that he's from some hospital in Glasgow where she was
once nursin'.'

'Aye, well, I've no doubt the girl will do well for herself,'
said Morag in much the same tone as I might have said,
'She could do worse, I suppose.'

We followed Calum along an erratic track that skirted
rags of crofts where tousled grass contested with drifts of
heather its right to grow among the innumerable out-

crops of stone. Calum stopped frequently to point out places of interest.

'It was just there my father dug up a barrel of salt butter when I was a boy,' he told us. 'An' it was still good.'

'An' how long would that have been there?' asked Morag.

'God knows,' replied Calum. 'Twenty-five years maybe. There was nobody livin' then who remembered it bein' put there.'

'That's most interesting,' I commented.

'I'd be more interested if you dug up a barrel of whisky,' countered Tearlaich wistfully.

'An' that was a fairy house, there,' said Calum at another juncture, indicating a smooth green mound covered with flat stones. 'An' this we're comin' to is what's always known as the "Red Burn".'

'Why red?' I asked.

'Because of all the blood that flowed in it.' His tone became grave. 'In days long ago, Miss Peckwitt, there was a wicked factor lived hereabouts an' once every year the crofters used to gather here to pay him their rents. Any man that couldn't pay was just murdered an' his body thrown into the burn. That's how it came to be known as the "Red Burn".' He looked at Morag. 'You'll surely have heard the story?'

'They say it was all true, right enough,' agreed Morag.

'It must have been,' asserted Calum. 'Why else would the cows refuse to drink from it, even to this day? No, nor walk through it, even.'

'Is that so?' asked Tearlaich with polite interest.

'It is so,' maintained Calum. 'I've seen a cow that's been tethered all day on the croft without water an' when she was loosed she made straight for the well on the moors sooner than go anywhere near that burn.'

'There must be the smell of murder in it yet,' declared Morag with apparent conviction.

'Aye, an' another thing,' continued Calum. 'Supposin' the cows are over this side of the island an' you need to drive them back to the crofts you can put half a dozen people an' dogs on to their tails but the beasts will never cross that burn. You'd have to walk a good mile out of your way an' beyond the loch before you'd get them home.'

We crossed the 'Red Burn' by the stepping stones and in doing so I noticed a promising-looking clump of watercress growing on one of its boggy banks.

'Look, watercress!' I pointed it out to Behag. I turned to Calum. 'Tell me,' I said, 'do the people of Rhuna believe like the Bruach people that watercress should be left for the fairies?'

'Aye, so they do.' He nodded back towards the burn. 'I seen a couple of them here the other night just, gatherin' great bunches of it.'

'Fairies?' I asked.

'Aye.'

'Did you see them yourself?' breathed Behag in an awe-struck whisper.

'I did. I was out after a rabbit an' I came back this way pretty late an' there they were. I saw them as plain as I'm seein' you.'

'How did you know they were fairies?' I asked in a steady voice.

'Who else would be wearin' little green jackets an' red caps,' he retorted with a trace of asperity. Behag and I exchanged quick glances.

Our path led us towards a lichen-patterned heap of stones which had once enclosed a small patch of ground and I was delighted to see the apple tree not only growing vigorously but bearing an abundant crop of sizable though still unripe fruit. Tearlaich picked one but after tasting it he threw it nonchalantly in the direction of a late lingering hoodie crow which was picking at an ancient cowpat. Calum volunteered to bring me over a creelful of apples as soon as they were ripe if the Lord spared him.

'Now you've seen your tree is it not time we got away back to the house?' asked Morag.

'Ach, there's plenty time,' argued Calum. 'If the tea's cold the kettle will boil again.'

Morag was looking curiously at a ruined house nearby. 'Is that not the place the filmies burned?' she asked Calum.

'Aye, that's it.'

'They really burned down a house for making a film here?' I questioned.

'They did, but it was a ruin before they burned it mostly. They got my Uncle Alistair an' my cousin John to build up the front of it an' put a bitty thatch on so that it looked all right to the cameras but it was no more than a ruin for all that.'

'Was it not your Uncle Alistair that let them have the house to burn?' pursued Morag.

'Aye, it was him.'

'I heard he got good money for it,' Tearlaich observed.

'I believe he did,' admitted Calum. 'Ach, an' why not?' he continued. 'Those filmies were right daft with their money.'

'That's what I was after hearin' myself,' said Morag enviously.

Calum chuckled. 'Right enough, at first Alistair was makin' out his own father was born in that ruin an' so the old place meant a lot to him still.'

'Was his father born there?' I asked.

'He was not. Alistair just wanted to push up the price he could put on it but the filmies were that convinced they started askin' around for men to build them just enough of a place to fool the cameras. Alistair got so scared they'd do it he went an' offered the ruin to the filmies for fifty pounds so long as he and his son got the job of building it up for them. I believe he had to have a good drink on him before he could pluck up courage to ask such a high price but the filmies jumped at it. When he got home he was as sick as a dog for not havin' asked double.'

'Were you home yourself the time the filmies were here?' asked Behag.

'I was. Indeed I was in the film myself,' Calum replied.

'You were?' exclaimed Behag admiringly.

'Aye. I played one of these extras, they call them. We all did at one time or another. They paid us well for it too. I tell you they was daft with their money. In the evenin' when we went to draw what was owin' to us they paid everybody that was in sight whether they'd been workin' for them or not. Hamish Beag came ashore in his boat one time, just, after bein' out fishin' but when he passed the place where the man was payin' out the money he was called over an' handed the same pay as the rest of us. I've never seen a man look as surprised as Hamish looked then, I can tell you.'

'Why would they do that?' asked Morag, puzzled.

'Ach, they didn't seem as if they could tell one from another of us no more than I can tell one black man from another.' He chuckled again reminiscently. 'We got a good laugh out of those filmies an' all.'

'An' good money,' Morag reminded him again. 'There was a few in Bruach would have come over to work for the filmies if they'd got the chance. Why, they tell me even old

Kenny Mor, him that was so religious he wouldn't so much
as boil a kettle on the Sabbath an' yet he was earnin'
money for himself makin' tea for them.'

'He was so,' agreed Calum. 'An' Kenny fairly enjoyed
himself doin' it until the missionary came over one Sunday
an' preached that films was sinful an' anybody that worked
for them would go straight to hell.'

'An' did anybody take any notice?' asked Morag.

'Only Kenny Mor,' rejoined Calum. 'He gave up the job
an' the money for fear of goin' to hell.'

'Ach, the missionary was just jealous,' summed up Tearlaich. 'I doubt he wanted to make the tea for them
himself.'

'Where are you takin' us to now?' demanded Morag as
Calum led us on through a narrow strath of swampy ground
so liberally tasselled with bog-cotton it looked as if an eiderdown had burst over it.

'Just a wee way yet,' he told her.

We followed, pushing our way through a tough little
corrie black with waist-high dead heather; over wide slabs
of weathered rock and then along a poachy path, rumpled
with hoof prints and leading into a miniature birchwood
which in turn petered out as it met the rocks and shingle
of the shore.

'Who can that be?' asked Morag, stopping in her tracks.
A man and a woman were coming away from the beach, the
woman bent under a burden of driftwood that was roped
to her shoulders while the man carried only a few short
lengths of wood under his left arm. In his right hand he
held a slim pole which he was using as a walking stick.

'That's Dolina an' Mata,' Calum told her.

Although it was impossible for our paths not to bring us
face to face, Morag immediately began to shout greetings in

strident Gaelic which diminished in volume as the distance between us decreased. By the time we did meet all the initial pleasantries were disposed of and they were ready to converse in English. Dolina, whose tall, utility-built body seemed to be packed full of bones, was obviously delighted to see us. With strong hands and in no way constrained by the load she carried she pulled first Morag, then Behag, then myself into a warm embrace which was intense enough to make me gasp, and in the brisk whisper that was her normal speaking voice she begged us to be sure to take a strupach with her before leaving the island. Here, however, Calum stepped in, jealously guarding his mother's privilege, and advised her of the proposed ceilidh, whereupon Dolina declared that nothing save a cow calving or the end of the world would keep her from joining the company. 'Is that not so, Mata?' she addressed her husband.

In contrast with Dolina, Mata looked as if he had been expertly filleted; his handshake was flabby and his bulging grey eyes looked about as ardent as two water blisters on the point of bursting, but he managed by a swift raising and lowering of his eyebrows to convey that he too would be coming to the ceilidh.

'We'd best not keep you back,' said Morag after a while and having been thus politely dismissed Dolina and Mata went on their way.

'I wish to goodness he'd carry her load for her,' I said as soon as they were out of earshot.

'Indeed Dolina wouldn't allow it,' stated Morag.

'He'd never have married her if he thought she'd let him,' added Tearlaich.

I murmured something about his being a shirker.

'But poor Mata doesn't enjoy good health,' Morag excused him.

'Damty sure he doesn't,' Tearlaich rejoined. 'That man only enjoys himself when he's sick.'

'Oh, whisht, now,' chided Morag, chuckling in spite of herself. 'All the same,' she added after a pause, 'there's somethin' about that man I canna help mislikin'.'

'I mislike him myself,' Tearlaich agreed and added, almost confidentially, 'I'll tell you, he's a disgustin' bugger that one.'

'I haven't seen him do anything positive enough to be disgusting,' I told him. 'Except, of course, leaving Dolina to do all the heavy work and he's not the only man around here who's guilty of that.'

'It's the way it's always been since I remember,' interpolated Morag. 'An' right enough that's the way many of the women want it to be.'

'I wasn't thinking of him being disgusting like that,' Tearlaich denied. 'But I was on the bus with him once and he started shouting he wanted to pee. He made the driver stop and he got out but instead of going some place where he wouldn't be seen he just stood and peed beside the bus like a tracehorse. Honest to God! And there was tourists aboard too. I didn't know where to look I was that ashamed of him.'

'That was ignorant of him,' Morag agreed. 'Poor Dolina would have died had she seen him.'

'I can't help feeling sorry for Dolina,' I said.

'I feel sorry for her myself,' concurred Tearlaich, 'but all the same I was near laughing when I saw her hugging you three as if you were children.'

'An' isn't it because she has no children of her own that makes her want to hug people,' Morag reproved him. 'A woman like Dolina ought by nature to have children at her skirts.'

'Aye, right enough, but not you three grown women.'

From his expression I guessed he had been about to say 'old women' and had only just caught himself in time. 'It's not Highland,' he added, much as an Englishman would have said 'It's not done'.

'Mata didn't marry Dolina to give her children,' asserted Calum. 'The reason he married her was to quiet his sister.'

'That's not what I heard then,' Morag rebutted his statement indignantly. 'Surely his sister was that jealous of Mata takin' a wife if it hadn't been for Dolina's good nature they would have quarrelled every day of the week—except the Sabbath,' she added.

'She was jealous all right,' confirmed Calum. 'But all the same it was her that made him take Dolina.'

'Why did she insist on his marrying?' I asked.

'Because she'd never in her life laid in a bed by herself till her mother died. She had another sister an' they slept together until that sister died. Then she moved into her mother's bed an' when she died there was no one to share her bed so she girned at Mata to find another woman to lie beside her.'

'But shouldn't she have got married herself or at least found someone to share her bed?' I asked. I could not seriously believe that a man would get married simply to provide a sleeping partner for his sister.

'Aye, but you see she claimed it was her home as much as Mata's, which is right enough seein' she was born there. Mata got the croft but the house belongs to those born in it, so she said. Anyway Mata's such a poor thing he just took a quick look around an' there was Dolina who'd have thrown herself into a bog for any man. It was easy as that an' it kept his sister quiet.'

'An' has Dolina never shared her man's bed?' expostulated Morag.

'Never,' averred Calum. 'Mata told me so himself.'

'He must have an orra chomais on him,' quipped Tearlaich, and we all laughed.

'He's a detestable fellow,' I commented.

'But Dolina loves him like the sun,' Morag reminded me simply.

'Aye an' that's why she's glad to do the heavy carryin' to save Mata doin' it,' said Calum. 'Seein' she's not allowed to do the little things for him that a wife likes to do for her man. The sister does the cookin' and washin' his clothes an' puttin' out his slippers in an evenin'. Dolina just washes the dishes an' does most of the work of the croft.'

'An' never a word of complaint on her lips, I doubt,' added Morag.

'St Dolina of Rhuna,' I murmured.

'Aye, if you believe in saints she must be one,' agreed Calum.

'Now we're here why have you brought us here?' Morag stood looking about her curiously.

'I have a thing to show you that I found down on the shore,' replied Calum. 'Wait you now till I get it.'

He made towards a pile of boulders and crouching he appeared to be extricating something from a deep crevice. Having retrieved it he came back to us. 'See this!' he said, holding up a small canister with a screw top.

We had all been expecting Calum to produce some really unusual or valuable find and our disappointment at seeing such an apparently uninteresting object was plain.

'What is it?' asked Tearlaich.

'It's a body!' announced Calum dramatically.

'A body?' Behag's question came out in an incredulous squeak.

'Aye, see this now. Can you read it?' Calum held the

canister nearer towards me as I backed away. 'That says somethin' about a crematorium, does it not? That's where they cremate bodies.'

Tearlaich took the canister and examined it. 'Aye, you're right,' he said. 'Did you open it yet?'

'I did,' Calum admitted. 'But open it yourself an' take a look at it.'

Tearlaich did as Calum suggested and tilted the canister so as to see inside it. 'It's full of stuff like that guano we had one year for the potatoes.' He handed the canister back to Calum who emptied out a little of its contents on to the palm of his hand.

'Are you sure it's a body?' asked Behag doubtfully.

'Sure it is,' declared Calum. He licked his forefinger and dipped it into the powder. 'Here,' he held his finger towards her. 'Taste it if you like,' he invited without the ghost of a smile.

Behag turned away and I was not sure whether she was giggling or vomiting.

'What are you goin' to do with it?' asked Morag.

'Damned if I know,' said Calum.

'Ach, give it to Miss Peckwitt for her garden,' Tearlaich proposed. 'It'll make good fertiliser.'

Calum screwed back the top and was about to hand me the canister but I recoiled away from it. 'D'you not want it?' he asked in surprise.

'I do not,' I said firmly. 'I'd never sleep at night if I thought someone's body was spread out among the flowers in my garden. I think you should throw it back in the sea,' I advised.

'It'll only get washed ashore again,' said Calum, shaking the canister with absent-minded vigour. 'Maybe you're right, though,' he continued after a few moments. 'I might

68

just as well throw it back seein' the tide's goin' out anyway. It'll maybe take it to someone else's beach.' He went down to the tide's edge and hurled the canister away into the sea.

'I don't know why you didn't take it for your garden,' Tearlaich rebuked me. 'Bone meal's one of the best manures you can get.' I tried to quell him with a look.

Calum rejoined us. 'I know a woman once whose husband was very fond of growin' roses,' he told us. 'When he died she had him cremated an' his ashes put on his favourite rose bushes.'

'Never!' Morag's voice was a disapproving groan.

'It's true,' he asseverated. 'She used to go out an' talk to them every night. Said it was like havin' her husband there out in the garden, an' when she used to prune them she used to pretend she was cuttin' his toenails for him like she always used to when he was alive.'

'She was mad, surely,' said Morag.

Calum raised his eyebrows in perfunctory agreement.

'Talking of such things brings to mind a story my commanding officer used to tell,' recalled Tearlaich. 'Seemingly at one time in India it used to be against the law for the natives to make their own salt. They were supposed to buy it from the government but some of the natives used to know where they could get earth that was full of salt and they'd wash it and then dry it in the sun till there was only salt left. If they were caught doing it they were up before the judge and one day the pollis got one old woman actually with a bag of this illegal salt in her possession, or so they claimed. Anyway, up she came before the court and the judge asked her what was in her bag but the old woman wouldn't say a word or plead one way or the other. The judge was just tellin' her he was goin' to fine her one rupee for disobeying the law when he suddenly thinks he'd best make sure it really was salt in the bag so he calls for a spoon and dips it in the bag and just as he's puttin' it into his mouth the old woman speaks for the first time. "This is a wicked court," she shouts, "not only do they fine me one rupee but they also eat the ashes of my dead husband." '

'Oh God,' murmured Behag with a feeble attempt at a giggle. Tearlaich gave her an arch look. 'It's true,' he insisted.

'True or not,' interrupted Morag firmly, 'that's enough of your stories for tonight. We'd best get back to the cailleach or she'll be thinkin' we're in a bog.'

Although it was after midnight there was only a little fuzzing of the light while among the dark hill peaks the afterglow still threaded itself like a bright scarf. It was impossible to know if the rosy rock pools were reflecting the sunset or the dawn. I recalled Masefield's lines:

> 'By an intense glow the evening falls,
> Bringing not darkness but a deeper light.'

and thought how perfectly they described the evening. Over the moors snipe drummed and closer at hand there were still sporadic trickles of birdsong.

'I wonder if Erchy and Hector are back with their hazels yet,' I mused.

'Their hazels?' echoed Tearlaich with some bewilderment.

'Yes. That's what they went for, isn't it?'

'Surely,' agreed Tearlaich, a little too eagerly. He and Calum exchanged cryptic glances. Morag avoided looking at me. I pinned my enquiring glance on Behag.

'You surely didn't think they came here just for the hazels?' she asked gently.

'But that's what they told me they were coming for,' I argued. 'That and to have a ceilidh at the same time.'

There was compassion and amusement in the four pairs of eyes that regarded me.

'Likely they will get their hazels seein' they'll soon be needin' them for the creels,' Behag admitted.

'Aye, an' everyone likes a wee bit of a ceilidh,' interposed Morag.

'But that's not what they came for?' I challenged, beginning to smile.

'Did you no' see the net under the seats of the boat?' asked Behag with an answering smile.

'How could she not see it when her own two feets was planted on it?' declared Morag.

I had indeed observed a net under the seats but I knew little about the type of net needed for the catching of different fish and in my ignorance I had thought it was an old herring net my feet rested on.

'It's a bit risky over there, isn't it?' I said. 'Didn't Erchy say the police are pretty keen to catch the poachers in that river?'

'Aye, they're keen,' agreed Tcarlaich fervently. 'They'll even go there on their nights off and hide themselves in the hope of catching a poacher's boat. Folks say that the sergeant gets a good salmon from the laird every time he catches a poacher.'

'And yet Erchy and Hector aren't afraid of getting caught?'

'They won't get caught,' asserted Morag confidently.

I gave her a sidelong glance but she only smiled.

'Erchy has a sign,' explained Tearlaich. 'He's arranged

with Jimmy's wife that lives in one of the houses near the shore that if there's a pair of long underpants on the clothes line then the pollis are hidin' somewhere about an' he mustn't go near. If the clothes line is empty he's safe.'

'An' Erchy will not get caught so long as Jimmy has a spare pair of underpants his wife can hang on the line,' observed Morag.

'Ach, if she's no spare underpants she'll just hang Jimmy on the clothes line,' said Tearlaich, and added after a moment's thought : 'Right enough, I believe she'd do that for Erchy.'

The Men who Played with the Fairies

THE window of Calum's mother's cottage was a token of light in the after-midnight dusk, and through the open door, interwoven with the murmur of voices, swooned the vague strains of the postie's mouth-organ. Calum left us abruptly and disappeared round the back of the house and Morag and Behag, panting for tea, hurried inside. As they entered, Erchy emerged carrying a cup of tea in one hand and the remains of a thick wad of dumpling in the other. He sat himself down on an upturned tub beneath the window.

'Any luck?' enquired Tearlaich.

One side of Erchy's face bulged as he cached a large bite of dumpling in order to reply.

'Plenty of luck,' he said thickly. His eyes glistened with excitement. 'You should have been there I'm tellin' you.'

'How could I be when I was keepin' the women out of the way?' returned Tearlaich reasonably.

'Aye, but you'd best have come with us,' reiterated Erchy.

'Aye?' Tearlaich's voice was sharp with interest.

Erchy nodded emphatically. 'There was one of the monsters went clean through the net. The biggest salmon I've seen yet,' he added impressively. He took a gulp of tea. 'We got a good laugh out of it all, I can tell you.'

'You got a good laugh out of losin' a big salmon an' gettin' a hole in your net? It's a queer comic you are, then,' Tearlaich commented.

'Not out of that just but out of Hector,' Erchy elucidated. 'He was that mad when we lost the big fellow he jumped into the river himself an' tried to stop the rest gettin' through. There was about a dozen fish in the net then an' Hector was so feared they'd get away he threw his arms round the biggest one an' held on to it. He'd barely caught hold of it when he got his foot caught in the net an' he sat down on his bottom in the river still clutchin' this huge fish an' it jumpin' an' twistin' like a serpent.' Erchy slopped tea as he used his arms to illustrate Hector's predicament. ' "Hit it! Hit it! Erchy!" he shouts at me.

Well I was seein' if I could close the net first but I managed to grab hold of a stick at the same time. "Hit it, you fool!" yells Hector, gettin' awful wild with me because he thought I wasn't helpin' him. "How can I hit it when it's first your head an' then the salmon's where the stick would land?" says I. It was one of them big male salmon with the huge jaw an' that great hook they have on it.' Erchy put down both cup and dumpling on the window-sill and spread his arms to indicate the size of the salmon. 'My God! there was some power in it too. The beast kept leapin' up an' Hector kept pullin' it down hand over hand like a man climbin' a rope. "Get your jersey over it!' I shouted to him, so he pulls up his jersey an' wraps the salmon in it while I see to the net. I went to help him then but God! if only you'd seen him gettin' to the shore with the fish still jumpin' up an' down inside his jersey an' him fightin' it an' swearin' an' stumblin' over the rocks you would have laughed fit to cry.' Erchy shook his head slowly. 'You should have been there.'

'Did he manage to get his salmon ashore?' I asked.

'Aye, he did. An' most of the rest. We were lucky. We got eight altogether,' he replied with deep satisfaction. 'That's a good night's work for any two men.'

'And you holed your net,' Tearlaich reminded him. 'Was it in much of a state?'

'Not as much of a state as was Hector's jersey,' responded Erchy. 'That's why I came out here. I'm best out of the way for when Behag catches sight of it. She only finished knittin' it for him last week just.'

I left the two men talking and went into the cottage where already round about twenty people were compressed into the small room. It was obvious that some more sophisticated hand had been at work on the old croft

75

kitchen; the floor was covered with tile-patterned linoleum; the wooden walls and the dresser were a glossy apple
green; the dignified wall clock looked a little surprised to
find its frame painted in bright yellow and indeed the whole
room though it looked fresh and cheerful struck me as
having the faintly startled air of a tramp who has been
compelled to wear a smart new suit.

Calum's mother greeted me with a lengthy handshake
and the rest, all of whom I knew by sight, acknowledged me
with grins or nods or murmurs of welcome according to
their degree of shyness. Morag tried to make room for me
to sit beside her on the crowded bench but I selected a more
comfortable seat on the floor where, within minutes, I was
joined by Behag who brought me a cup of tea.

'I don't see anyone here who could be Calum's sister
Marie,' I whispered. Behag looked blank. 'You know, the
one who's going to marry a doctor.'

'Oh!' Behag glanced round. 'I believe she's just away
for a pail of water,' she told me. 'They're needin' more,
likely, seein' there's been a few fillin's of the kettle already
an' I daresay there'll be more before the night's over.'

There came from outside the clink of pails followed by
some male chaffing to which everyone strained to listen, then
a laughing retort in a female voice that sounded as
melodious as a harp. A tall, strongly built woman, gum-
booted and wearing a sad old skirt and an overtight jersey,
entered the room followed by Erchy gallantly carrying two
slopping pails of water. The woman cleared a small table
beside the door for Erchy to put down the pails and turned
to smile a confident greeting. Although Calum's mother
was in her eighties and Calum himself was nudging fifty I
had foolishly been expecting the prospective bride to be a
younger woman, forgetting that in Bruach a spinster is re-

ferred to as a girl be she seventeen or seventy. Marie, I
estimated after a brief appraisal, was probably in her forties
but she was still a strikingly handsome woman. Her skin
was smooth and white as a dawn-picked mushroom; her
bee-tawny eyes were wide and lively; her abundant russet-
coloured hair swathed her head in soft waves until it was
caught by a crocheted wool snood. She came forward and
shaking my hand made me welcome in so attractive a voice
it would have made scurrility sound like a serenade.

'We're awful quiet, are we not?' she observed after a
few moments. 'Hector, now! What about you givin' us a
song?'

Hector looked pleased but shook his head. "I've swallowed tsat much of tse river tonight I'd only gargle,' he
replied. 'What about a song from you yourself, Marie?'

'Oh, I can't sing,' denied Marie firmly, and to my surprise there was not even a polite contradiction. She turned
to Morag. 'Morag here's good at the singin'. What about
you? Give us a song now an' the rest will join in.'

Whether or not Morag would have complied I do not
know for just at that moment a tall, fair-haired man pushed
his way through the men clustered around the doorway.
He was wearing a cap and what was undoubtedly his best
raincoat. In his hand was a folded sack tied with string
which he carried like a shopping bag. Immediately he appeared there were screams of expectant laughter and everyone settled down to enjoy themselves. Putting his sack on
the table the man extracted from it a crescent of wire
attached to a length of thin rope. He beckoned one of the
young girls to sit down beside him and since everyone knew
what was about to happen the girl quickly complied. Pretending the wire and the piece of rope were his stethoscope
he set about examining the girl's chest, back and head and

77

while the girl giggled the man listened and groaned, hunted in his bag for more instruments, mimed swabbing and surgery, stitching and bandaging and with silent gesticulation kept his hilarious audience informed of what the various ailments were and how he proposed to treat them. Though, like the rest, this was by no means the first time I had witnessed his act, I laughed and applauded along with them. But my enjoyment was feigned. Undoubtedly the mime was good and the performer delighted by our appreciation but I would have enjoyed it more had I not known that the actor was not only deaf and dumb but also mentally retarded; that mime was indeed his sole means of communication. Known as 'the Dummy', he was a gentle soul, glum when he observed others to be glum; happy when he saw them happy; and having once discovered that some of his attempts to communicate brought smiles to people's faces he had exaggerated his mime until their smiles had erupted into laughter. It was all he asked. He had made people happy and consequently he insisted on performing at every ceilidh on the island. Since the doctor-and-patient mime made people laugh he saw no reason to change it though it had continued for the ten years since the doctor had last visited the island.

'Not that one grows tired of it,' confided one of 'the Dummy's' neighbours. 'But you sometimes wish somebody more interesting than a doctor would visit the island to give the poor man something else to imitate.'

'What about the filmies?' I asked.

'Ah, he was only a poor thing then,' she explained. 'He hadn't discovered his gift.'

When 'the Dummy's' performance was over Erchy spoke up. 'Marie's goin' to give us the sword dance,' he announced, and treated the company to a heavy wink. He put his arm around Marie's waist and tickled her vigorously. She pushed him away.

'Indeed I will do nothing of the kind,' she declined but the pleading that she should dance for us became so clamorous—'maybe for the last time, seein' you're to get yourself married'—that she was finally persuaded. We squeezed ourselves even more tightly back against the wall so as to make sufficient space in the centre of the room. The shuffling revealed the presence of a child of about four years who had previously been hidden by his mother's skirts but who now peeped out timidly from among them like a chick peeping from among the feathers of the mother hen. It also revealed that behind the legs of the people seated on the bench lay a sheepdog watching the proceedings with eyes that in the lamplight glowed large and round as gold medals. There was some discussion as to what could be used for swords but Erchy was soon flourishing four brass rods taken from the linoleum stair runner and handing them to Marie to arrange into a cross on the floor. The postman retrieved his mouth-organ from the lad who had been blowing into it unskilfully and began to play. Marie kicked off her gumboots and barefooted commenced the intricate dance in and out of the 'swords', slowly at first but as the postman increased the tempo of the music so did her pace quicken until her feet appeared to be fluttering above the floor rather than touching it. It was an impressive performance and young and old shrieked and stamped their admiration until Marie, declaring herself to be utterly out of breath, abruptly ceased dancing to a chorus of disappointed 'Ahs'.

'I could do with watchin' that all over again,' said Erchy.

'Oh, help!' gasped Marie and snatching off her snood shook her head so that her hair cascaded soft and springy as a child's around her shoulders. I noticed Tearlaich staring at her with wide-eyed adulation.

'That's made me as dry as a stick!' she exclaimed and picking up the teapot she poured herself a cup of tea.

'I'll be takin' anotser myself,' said Hector, and by handing her his empty cup started a chain reaction so that there was suddenly a flurry of cups all being passed for refilling. It appeared that the dancing had induced a great thirst among the onlookers also. The room quietened as they sipped.

Calum spoke. 'I was after tellin' Miss Peckwitt I'd seen the fairies gatherin' the biolaire by the Red Burn the other evenin',' he informed the company in general. 'I doubt she wasn't believin' me,' he added dispassionately.

Calum's uncle, a seared old man with a raised furrow of white hair that ran like a partition across his otherwise close-cropped head, was slumped in a wooden chair beside the fire. At Calum's remark he sat up and shot me a glance from sharp black eyes that were set deep in a face as brown and rutted as a peach stone. He drew his pipe from his mouth and fondled it in a calloused hand. 'Ach, but she's from the town, is she not?' he excused me gently. 'There's no use speakin' to some about the wee folk. No use at all.' He shook his head sadly. 'But there's plenty round these parts that's seen them an' there's some that's been the better of it an' some that has not.'

I looked at him steadily but his eyes were fixed on the bowl of his pipe.

'Like the men who played with the fairies,' interposed Calum's mother in a low voice.

'Just that,' agreed the old man with a nod.

'I've heard of them before but just who were they?' I interposed.

'Wasn't one of them my own father's cousin's child,' he replied.

'You should have taken Miss Peckwitt to see the men who played with the fairies,' Calum's mother turned to Hector. 'It's not so long since they passed on. No more than three years I doubt.'

'Five,' corrected Calum.

'Well, five,' his mother allowed. 'But Miss Peckwitt's been in Bruach for more years than that, surely?'

'I have indeed,' I replied. 'But whenever I've heard them spoken of I always assumed they'd been dead for some time. Was it really only five years ago that they died?'

'No more than that,' confirmed Calum's uncle, shifting his gaze to the coloured plates on the dresser.

I was intrigued. The 'men who played with the fairies' had been mentioned more than once at the Bruach ceilidhs but I had always assumed them to be as remote as legend.

'These two men,' I pressed. 'I understood they were twins?'

'No, they were not then. Didn't I say one of them was my own father's cousin's child.'

'And who was the other one, then?'

'Yes, who was he?' The question came from the postie.

It became obvious that some of the younger Bruachites were not completely familiar with the story of the two men and their adventures and after one or two questions Calum's mother said: 'You'd best tell them the way of it as you know it yourself, for it's right that the truth should be known about these things.'

Obediently, putting his pipe on the hob, Calum's uncle settled himself for the story. 'I mind seein' the boys just before it happened,' he told us. 'My father took me with him over to the island where they lived to try would he find a good spot for gatherin' the whelks. Seein' his cousin was there we left the boat an' went up to have a wee crack with him. The both boys was there then: a few years younger than myself they were but I mind they were fine healthy-lookin' lads though wee rascals I believe, the pair of them, and always playin' tricks on folks as though it was Hallowe'en all the year round. Robbie, that was my father's cousin's child, an' Euan, that was the son of Hamish the Seanachaidh, was about the same age within a month or two an' when they weren't needed to help on their parents' crofts they'd go off fishin' together or seekin' gulls' eggs or maybe settin' a snare or two for the rabbits.' The old man paused and standing up helped himself to a spoonful of baking soda from the tin on the mantleshelf. 'The next time I went with my father to the island,' he resumed as he sat down again, 'I was maybe in my fifteenth year an' like we did before we went to have a crack with my father's cousin. We didn't see either of the boys an' so my father asked after them, sayin' he hoped they were well. That's how we came to know the story.

His body tautened; he gave a loud belch and relaxed again. I slid a surreptitious glance around the room and saw that except for Marie, who appeared to be asleep with her head resting against the wall, and her mother, who was gazing into her lap, everyone's attention was concentrated on the old man willing him, it seemed, to go on with his tale.

'Aye,' he said unhurriedly, leaning back and tucking his thumbs into the armholes of his waistcoat. 'We had the story of it there on the spot where it all came to pass.'

'What was it that happened?' I could not be sure who had spoken but the voice sounded young and impatient.

'What happened,' went on Calum's uncle, 'was that they went together off fishin' one day just the same as they'd

gone before, but when the evenin' was darkenin' there came
no word of either of them. They were about nine years old
at the time an' good at playin' tricks as I've said before, an'
nobody worried a great deal at first, thinkin' the boys was
well able to look after themselves, but when it came to midnight an' past an' there was still no word of them the men
set out to look for them. They went to all the places they
knew the boys liked to go an' they shouted but never a
whisper came back to them. The next day every able-
bodied man an' woman an' child in the place went lookin'
for them over the moors, up an' down the cliffs an' along
the shore thinkin' they might have fallen into the sea. But
no. They looked till there was no place they could look and
still there was no trace of Robbie an' Euan. On the fourth
day they gave them up for lost when suddenly that same
evenin' they see the two boys comin' down the hill towards
the houses. At first folks thought it was ghosts they were
seein', for the boys were walkin' that steady an' close to
each other like they'd never done before; holdin' hands like
little girls. "It's never them!" people said to one another
but it was them right enough though there was such a
change in them people looked at them like strangers. Their
faces were white as if they'd been shut in the dark for a
while an' the merry eyes of them had got grey an' dull like
empty pails. They didn't look at their parents when they
rushed to meet them but only stared in front of them without speakin' a word. It was just like they were blind an' yet
they knew where they were goin', for they both made for
Euan's house an' there they got into bed together as if they'd
been sharin' a bed since they were wee. They slept without food or wakin' for near three more days an' their
parents, thinkin' the boys would come to their senses after
a good sleep, left them alone. But they never did. When they

woke they still stared at their folks as if they were strangers an' they never spoke save in whispers to each other. They never smiled either an' when they moved they stayed that close to each other Robbie's father said it was like as if you were seein' one man with three legs walkin' about. He took it badly did Robbie's father but try as he would there was no doin' any good with either of the boys any more. He told us it was like lookin' at one man carryin' a mirror they copied each other so much.'

'Did they never say what happened to them during those four days?' asked the young Bruach schoolteacher.

'Never a word. No, they were useless. They wouldn't work on the crofts any more an' no one dared to try to force them. They knew then, d'you see, that the boys had played with the fairies an' until the wee folk lifted the spell they'd put on them they'd have to allow the boys to do as they pleased.'

'What did they do with themselves, then?' Behag enquired softly

'Ach they just roamed the moors, gatherin' all sorts of plants an' flowers or they wandered along the shore collecting coloured pebbles an' pieces of wood an' things they showed no interest in before.' The old man belched again and picked up his pipe. 'An' that's the way they were for many a long year,' he told us.

'Did you ever see them again?' I asked.

'I saw them once more,' replied the old man. 'An' I'm tellin' you I was that taken back I didn't know what to say. They was middle-aged by then an' they'd grown so alike you'd have sworn it was a pair of twins they were.' He looked at me. 'That's how you would be hearin' they were twins,' he explained. 'I didn't remember there bein' any likeness between them when they were younger but now I couldn't tell one from the other. Where one had red hair the other was black but now they were both white as old fleece.'

'Did they still hold hands and move together?' asked the schoolteacher.

'Indeed they did,' replied the old man. 'Still fittin' their steps to each other's like soldiers on parade an' with such a strange look on them I didn't feel I wanted to stay near them.'

'I suppose they didn't recognise you,' someone said.

'It seemed like they didn't know anyone or want to know anyone. Euan's parents had died but he didn't seem to notice. His sister stayed lookin' after them though even she saw little enough of them.'

'Did Robbie never return to his own home?' Again it was I who put the question.

'Never. Not from the day the two boys came back an' got into bed together. It was as if Robbie had forgotten he'd ever had a home.'

'An' did they never go off again?' I could not tell whether Morag was making a statement or asking a question.

'No, they never did. But as soon as they were old enough they built themselves a shed at the back of the house an' that's where they spent most of their time.'

'What did they do in there?'

'Indeed for a long time no one knew what they did but seemingly the sister found out they'd taken to carving wood. Wee boats like toys with oars an' sails an' wee chairs an' tables no bigger than if they were for a doll's house. Not that they let people see them if they could help it. They worked on their own an' they kept the shed locked but the sister managed to get a peep in every now an' then an' tell of what she saw. An' that went on for years.'

'They must have made a good few things in that time, then,' someone observed. 'What did they do with them all?'

'What indeed?' replied Calum's uncle. 'No one knows except that once Robbie's sister was seekin' driftwood on the shore an' she came across one of their wee boats wedged among some rocks. It was smashed to pieces but all the same she took it home an' put it beside their shed. She said when they found it they were so upset she wished she'd left it where it was.'

'What happened eventually,' I prompted.

'They died,' said the old man. 'An' they was as queer about their dyin' as their livin'. It was like this, y'see. Euan's sister was after havin' these fly peeps from time to time into their shed an' she saw they were buildin' a far bigger boat than she'd seen before. It was small enough still but carved an' decorated so much she wondered how hands could be gentle enough to do it. They were busy at it for a year or more an' then one day they seemed to be so much happier, more like they should be, so while they were out she went for another peep an' saw the boat was finished. She wondered what would happen an' that night she heard them go off after dark as they sometimes did an' it was near daylight when she heard the house door close. In the mornin' she heard moans comin' from the bedroom an' when she went in she found Euan lying alone in the bed. He looked straight at her an' spoke her name for the first time in years, an' asked her for a drink of water. She took it to him an' he drank it an' seemed as though he would sleep again, but when she went back a whiley later he was dead, just.'

Ever since he had taken his pipe from the hob the old man had been fondling it but now he filled it and picking a blazing peat from the fire puffed it alight. Having sharpened our eagerness by the deliberate pause he resumed : 'An' where was Robbie, you'll be wantin' to know. Robbie was back in his own home an' his own bed as if he'd suddenly remembered it was his. His parents were old then an' they didn't know what to say but he was that hot an' lay tossin' an' turnin' an' bletherin' away like the wild geese passin' over, though they couldn't make out a word of what he was sayin', they told the nurse to come. She said he had pneumonia an' she tried to get hold of a doctor but before he could get over Robbie was dead too. They buried them together an' I went with my father to the funeral.'

'What happened about the boat they'd been buildin'?' asked Behag.

'Now that's the strange way of it,' replied Calum's uncle. 'When the sister got hold of the key of the shed an' opened it after the funeral the boat had gone. All that was left of their toys at all was the little wrecked boat she'd found and brought back to give them. Just that in a corner of the shed an' near covered with sawdust.'

'Surely someone must have found the boat?' I said.

'No one ever did.' The old man's voice was firm. 'An' from what the sister was sayin' it was a great shame indeed, because it was beautiful just an' somethin' a body would like to keep in memory.'

'I wonder what happened to it,' mused Behag. But no one suggested an answer.

The postie blew suddenly on his mouth-organ a long chord that could almost have been a raspberry.

Calum's uncle got up stiffly, stretched himself and went to stand at the open door. 'The light is awakenin',' he proclaimed, coming back to resume his seat.

Erchy, who appeared to have been dozing through much of the old man's tale, pulled himself up from the floor. 'One more song an' then we must be away,' he declared. 'Come on, everybody.' The postman began to play 'My ain Folk' and we belted it out with sad enthusiasm before we trouped down to the shore in time to a lilting version of 'Mairi's Wedding'. We said our goodbyes and thank yous for a 'grand ceilidh' and were rowed out to the boat which was already loaded with its additional cargo of hazels and illicit salmon. The night was quiet except for a few muted gull cries and the water was still, though patterned as if it was covered with wire netting.

'Where's that bundle of cordite you found on the shore?' Marie's voice came clearly and we saw her run to the byre and return with a bundle which she hastily distributed among the crowd gathered to see us off. They lit the bundles and waved flaring farewells. To the strains of 'Will ye no come back again' echoing from the shore the boat chugged Bruachwards through a sea that was the colour of smoked glass. It was cold on the water and I was glad that lack of space necessitated our huddling together. Tearlaich's breadth was on one side of me and Behag's comfortable rotundity on the other. Erchy, who was again at the tiller, crouched behind us.

'I'm thinkin' that Marie's a big woman to be as light on her feet as she was,' observed Behag thoughtfully.

'Mmm,' I agreed. 'They often are, these big women. She's good-looking though, isn't she?' I went on. 'And her voice was beautiful and so was her hair . . .'

'Aye, her hair,' interrupted Tearlaich eagerly. 'Now Marie's hair's the sort of hair I'd want a woman of mine to have. An' did you see when she snatched off that net she had on the way it all fell as soon as it was loosed?'

'I saw,' I told him. 'And I noticed how overcome with admiration you were.'

'Indeed that's true,' he agreed fervently. 'I'll never forget the way it just dropped round her shoulders as soft and brown and easy as shit from a mare's behind. Bloody lovely it was.' He mistook my expression. 'Honest,' he repeated earnestly. His eyes closed but his own expression remained ecstatic as he apparently dozed off to sleep.

'Well, are you glad you came on the trip?' demanded Erchy from behind us.

'I wouldn't have missed it for the world,' I assured him. 'Meeting Marie and hearing all Calum's stories. It's been a wonderful evening altogether.'

'Indeed I don't know when I've enjoyed myself so much,' corroborated Behag.

'I've fairly enjoyed myself too,' Erchy admitted. 'But I'm thinkin' I'll be best pleased with it when I come to eat my dinner.' He nodded to where the box of salmon was hidden under a sack.

Behag said, 'I wonder will Calum remember to bring you the apples from that tree?'

At the mention of Calum's name Tearlaich became alert again. 'Calum?' he repeated. 'He'll not be remembering tomorrow what he's said today.'

'He has a good enough memory for some things,' I pointed out. 'All those stories he told us tonight. I loved listening to them.'

'Aye, I noticed that,' he murmured non-comittally. There was a glint in his eyes which I put down to my use of the word 'loved'. Bruachites 'like fine' something. The word 'loved' in such a context they looked upon as amusing exaggeration.

'He seemed pretty certain he'd seen those fairies, too,' I said. 'Did you believe him about that?' I taxed him.

'Believe him? What, that fellow? I'd as soon believe a

89

drunken tinker,' he scoffed. 'Ach, you mustn't believe any story Calum tells you,' he added half seriously.

'Not any?' I repeated with a slight feeling of dismay.

'Not a one,' reiterated Tearlaich. 'That man!' His face broke into a broad approbatory smile. 'I'm tellin' you, Miss Peckwitt, he's the most beautiful liar God ever put two boots on.'

Family Silver

FERGUS BEAG (Little Fergus) had died suddenly at the age of eighty-two and, as was customary, the women of the village were calling at varying times before the burial to condole with the widow, Ina. Morag, her niece, Behag, and I went together after the chores were done and evening was beginning to soften what had been one of the summer's really hot days.

'Hector was girnin' again about him goin' so sudden,' confided Behag with a hint of apology. 'He was sayin' Fergus will be one of the heaviest corpses they've had yet to carry to the burial ground an' him havin' no illness to weaken him first.'

Little Fergus had in his prime been one of the biggest men in the village—over six foot tall and with shoulders as broad as a door. Even at eighty-two he had been no lightweight but because his father had been 'Fergus Mor' (Big Fergus) the son naturally had been dubbed 'Little Fergus' and 'Little Fergus' he had remained despite the subsequent inaptness of the description.

'Ach, Hector will soon stop his girnin' once they have the grave dug an' a good dram for their pains,' Morag comforted with a sly smile at me.

'If they ever have it dug,' murmured Behag dubiously.

Morag gave her a searching glance. 'An' why will they no'?'

'Did you not hear Hector complainin' this mornin' that his leg was troublin' him?' asked Behag.

'Which leg was that?' demanded Morag as if Hector had a selection. 'The one he left behind him in the boat when he twisted his foot?'

A baffled expression flitted across Behag's face. 'I believe that was the one,' she admitted.

'What happened?' I asked.

'Ach, Hector was steppin' out from his boat to the dinghy with his hands full of fishes,' scoffed Morag. 'He had one of his legs over the side when didn't a floorboard slip an' jam his foot under it. It was no more than if a cow had stepped on it but to hear Hector shoutin' you'd think it was on crutches he'd be for the rest of his life.'

'But his ankle was as big as a haggis for a day or two an' sore right up his leg,' defended Behag.

'But that was more than a week ago,' protested Morag.

'It was so but he was feelin' it again this mornin'. Did you not hear him sayin' that?'

'I did,' responded Morag with a grim smile. 'An' I heard Erchy swearin' he'd make sure Hector dug his share of the grave supposin' he has to stand on his head to do it.' Behag sighed acceptance.

Bruach graves were dug not by an official grave digger but by any relatives of the deceased fit enough to accomplish the task and Hector and Erchy, being Fergus Beag's two nearest male relatives in the village, had been called upon to do their duty. Erchy could always be relied upon but Hector's aversion to physical labour and his habit of developing agonising back or stomach pains or even disappearing altogether for a day or two whenever there was a chance of his being compelled to wield a spade was so well known in Bruach that even the loyal Behag was at times hard put to it to find excuses for her husband.

Our path to the late Fergus's cottage wound sinuously over the heather-covered moors and was wide enough for only two people to walk abreast so that Behag and I, who were barelegged and wearing shoes, had appropriated it for ourselves, while Morag, who persisted whatever the weather in wearing gumboots on weekdays, scuffed her way through the bristly heather, scattering drifts of moths as if she were scuffing her way through autumn leaves.

'I'm thinkin' it's no' like Fergus to die so sudden,' she observed. 'But ach, he was always the queer one right enough.'

'What took him d'you think?' asked Behag.

'His heart, likely,' returned Morag. 'The doctor was

sayin' that people livin' in hilly places like this always has hearts.'

'He was a good age, after all,' I pointed out.

'Aye,' Morag allowed, 'he was a good age but indeed I never seem to mind that Fergus was ever young. Not to my way of thinkin'.'

'Why do you say that?' Behag asked.

'Well he was that religious an' that ages a man,' Morag explained. 'An' another thing, even as a child he used to have a lot of these premunitions. That always made him seem older than he was.'

'Premunitions?' echoed Behag. 'What sort of premunitions?'

'Did you never hear how he knew Old Farquhar's house was to go on fire weeks, but no, months, before it happened?' demanded Morag in an incredulous voice.

'No, I never did,' denied Behag. I also shook my head.

'Nor of him premunising the death of his daughter?'

'I did not,' said Behag, sounding as indignant as if she had been denied food at a banquet.

'I remember your telling me his daugher had been killed in an accident but I didn't know there'd been any warning of it beforehand,' I disclosed.

Morag was so astonished at our admissions that she stopped in her tracks, staring at us as if trying to divine some reason for our imperfect tuition. 'Well, indeed, it was so,' she reiterated as she started walking again.

'Tell us about it,' I coaxed. We still had the best part of a mile to walk and I knew from experience that if Morag would regale us with stories of past happenings in Bruach the journey would not seem half so long.

She needed little encouragement. 'Fergus an' Ina, now,

they had none but this one child, Alex they used to call her.
Aye, an' she was always a queer kind of lassie too, to my
way of thinkin'; not what you'd expect from folks like Fergus an' Ina, for though Fergus was queer himself he was a
good man for his work an' for his church. Indeed,' she
added parenthetically, 'maybe she wasn't rightly Fergus's
child at all for he was often away at sea an' Ina was always
one for the lads. Alex grew up hatin' the croft an' wouldn't
settle so she left home when she was gey young an' went to be
a servant. Folks were after sayin' it was Fergus's religion
that drove her away an' I doubt myself that was the reason.'
She permitted herself a small sigh. 'Ach, right enough he
was awful hard on the girl.'

'Did she not come home at all?' asked Behag.

'Aye, she'd come home maybe for a holiday now an' then,
an' for her mother to make a great fuss of her but she never
stayed long. A week or two an' then she was away again.
Fergus used to grumble. A "gogaid"—that's a flighty one—
he would say she was for he was wantin' she should stay
an' help her mother on the croft, though she'd have none
of it. As she got older she came home less an' less an' she
hadn't been home for a while when one evenin', an' it was
an evenin' like this one.' Morag waved an arm at the quiet
moors and the lustrous sky. 'Fergus was comin' home from
the moor after milkin' the cow an' suddenly he hears the
sound of weepin' comin' seemingly from behind a peat
stack. He goes to look but there's no sound nor sight of a
thing an' he's just makin' back to the path when the weepin' begins again, only louder, an' he's sure it's his own
daughter an' she pourin' her grief on to the heather. He's
that upset he stands still an' calls, "Alex, is it yourself?"
At that the weepin' grows fainter an' more far away till
he can hear it no more.'

'An' was that when she was killed?' asked Behag, awe-struck.

Morag tossed the interruption aside. 'Fergus found he was shiverin' so much he made for home as quick as he could an' when he got inside, though it was a warm night, he piled wood an' peats on the fire till Ina thought the flames would be comin' out of the chimney an' she so hot she had to go an' sit in the door. "Whatever ails you?" she asks him. "You'll know soon enough," says he, an' gets a blanket off the bed an' wraps it round his shoulders an' sits as close to the fire as if he'd been all day at the back of the hills in a snowstorm.'

'Did he not tell Ina about hearing their daughter's voice?' This time the interruption was mine.

'He did not,' confirmed Morag. 'He told no one then, but Ina says she knew he'd had one of his premunitions to make him turn like that. Sure enough the next day there came a wire tellin' them their daughter had been killed in an accident. Then it was that Fergus told Ina what had happened to him while he was out on the moors.'

'Did they ever find out when was the accident?' Behag's tone was meek.

'They did,' replied Morag. 'An' it was just about the time Fergus must have been comin' back from the cow.' Morag turned to see how deeply her story had affected us. 'Now will you believe that!' she enjoined us.

Neither Behag nor I made any reply. Behag was the most credulous woman in Bruach and on a lonely moor in the company of Gaels I could shed logic as easily as I could shed a wet shawl.

'An' another time I mind,' continued Morag, warming to her subject. 'There was the time he was skipper of a boat for a rich man.' She paused. 'You knew he was a skipper when he was young?' she asked us. We acknowledged that this fact we did know.

'Aye well, the owner had decided they was to spend the night at moorings; strong, new moorings they were,' she emphasised, 'an' they'd cost him a deal of money gettin' them laid specially by the firm that made them. But Fergus wasn't happy. He could sense a storm comin' an' though they'd all gone to their beds an' it wasn't his turn to be on duty he couldn't seem to settle. He was that worried he went an' woke the engineer an' told him to get up a good head of steam an' keep her at the ready. Fergus said the engineer was none too pleased to be got out of his bed since everyone had been sayin' the new moorings was strong enough to hold a battleship in a hurricane, but he did as he was told. When the storm broke it wasn't such a bad one as storms at sea go but they hadn't been ridin' it more than half an hour before those strong new moorings broke just as Fergus knew they would.'

'That was a lucky one,' I murmured.

'Lucky?' echoed Morag. 'Indeed if Fergus hadn't made the man get steam up it's likely the ship an' all their lives would have been lost.'

'What did the owner have to say?' asked Behag. 'You'd have expected him to give Fergus a good pound for that.'

'Indeed the owner wouldn't believe it at first when Fergus woke him to tell him but he believed it all right afterwards when he saw it for himself. They got some divers down to inspect the moorings an' they found somethin' wrong with them that had caused them to part. Fergus said the owner took the firm who'd made them to the law over it an' won his case.'

'Did he ever ask Fergus why he'd made sure they had steam up?' I asked.

'He did,' declared Morag. 'An' when Fergus told him he shakes hands with him. "Fergus," says he, "I've always laughed at your premunitions before but I never will again." He never did an' that's the truth. He never forgot that night, either, an' when he died he left Fergus a pension for the rest of his life.'

'It's nice to hear of that,' I remarked.

'Aye, there's some of these rich folk that do right by people,' admitted Morag grudgingly.

'I wouldn't care to see the future,' said Behag with a slight shudder.

'Well, Fergus could without a doubt,' Morag told her. 'An' that's what folks will best remember him for when they're speakin' of him. Aye,' she repeated, 'they'll remember his premunitions.'

I did not divulge then it was in no supersensory way that I should best remember Fergus. I had been living with Morag for some time before starting to look around for a house and croft of my own and hearing of one which had been empty for years and might possibly be bought I set out one day to find it. I knew roughly where it was situated but I knew also that if I kept to the road it was going to be a long trek and as it was winter with short hours of daylight I took what I thought to be a short cut. Morag has assured me there was such a path but her instructions, always more colourful than correct, had led me into a deep, boggy valley. At that early stage of my initiation bogs terrified me and in mounting panic, visualising myself being sucked rapidly into miry mud with darkness coming on and no one to see my plight, I tried repeatedly to find a path back to firm ground but drew back each time as I went ankle deep in treacly mire. Common sense told me my panic was foolish. The day was mild for the time of year; the sun indicated it was around midday and except for one or two historic and easily identifiable bogs none was reputed to be dangerous except to cows and horses with their small feet and heavy bodies. All the same I was immensely relieved to see Fergus coming over the hill in my direction carrying a creel of peats. I hailed him and, still with the heavy creel on his back, he came towards me, testing the ground at every few steps. He guided me back to the path and asked me where I was making for. I told him and begged for directions.

'You've lost yourself, have you?' he said with mockery in his voice.

I grinned and acknowledged I was a little lost.

'Aye, aye, I thought that must be the way of it.' With a hand that was as hard as a cricket bat on my shoulder he turned me in the direction I was to go. He raised his right arm. 'Now look along the length of that,' he instructed. Obediently I looked along the length of his arm. 'Now you'll see that,' he went on, holding up a sturdy thumb that was as dark and wrinkled as oak bark. I assured him I could see it. 'Now, Miss Peckwitt,' he told me, wedging each word into the sentence as carefully as a mason wedging stones into a wall, 'you'll just take a line from the black of my thumbnail,' he commanded. Heedfully I had done so.

The three of us were now approaching the croft land as distinct from the moor and the ever-elusive corncrakes were croaking in the unscythed grass down towards the burn.

'I mind my father always used to say those birds made him think of the angels,' observed Morag as I stopped to listen.

I looked at her. The rasping of the corncrake might be music to the ear of an ornithologist but it was hardly what one would expect to hear from angels.

'Aye, he'd say they're all around you an' yet you scarcely ever saw one,' she explained.

When we were within a few paces of Fergus's cottage two women emerged wearing suitably staid expressions.

'How is she?' asked Morag.

'Ach, she's no' bad. No' bad at all,' replied one of the women.

'She's frettin' more about gettin' her cow to the bull before her season's over,' added the other. 'She's wonderin' if Angy will get here in time or will one of the men come an' do it for her.'

Angy, being Fergus's nephew, was now Ina's closest relative and was confidently expected to come from the mainland and take over both his great aunt and the small croft.

'He'll surely be here for the funeral,' Morag asserted. 'They'll need him for the carryin'.'

'The more the better,' agreed one of the women.

'I'm thinkin' the men will be awful dry if the weather stays as hot as this,' commented Behag.

The sombre expressions on the faces of the women were wiped off as easily as dust from a mirror as we all turned to assess a setting sun so fiery that one expected the sea's rim to hiss and bubble as they touched. The hills were clear except for a crumpled bunch of cloud behind their peak which looked as if it might have been a coverlet hastily thrown aside.

'I believe this weather will stay with us for a whiley yet,' predicted Morag with satisfaction. 'Surely carryin' Fergus is goin' to make the men sweat worse than carryin' a load of hay.' A gloating smile creased her face. 'Mind you,' she went on, 'I believe they'd as soon he died now as wait till they're busy at the hay.'

The murmurs of agreement from the two women were

cut short by a croaking voice calling from inside the cottage.

'She's hearin' us,' whispered Morag. 'You two had best away an' we'll go in to her.'

Despite the warm perfection of the evening Old Ina, Fergus's widow, was sitting in a chair drawn close to the hearth, cherishing the fire as if, now that Fergus had gone, it was destined to become her mate. Behag and I settled ourselves on the bench and mumbled trite commiserations while Morag, going immediately to the old woman, laid a hand on her shoulder and crooned comfortingly in the infinitely more expressive Gaelic. Ina shook her head or nodded, making whispered denials and acquiescence and after a few minutes Morag came and sat on the bench beside us. Her voice became more matter-of-fact.

'Would you say he had a premunition about it?' she asked.

'Indeed, I'm sure now that was the way of it,' replied Ina. We leaned forward avidly. 'Aye, an' I should have known it,' continued the widow, 'for when he came in that evening for his potatoes he ate three sooyan along with them before he pushed his plate at me for more. "That's a meal enough for a ploughman you've taken already," says I. "Right enough," says he, "but I don't wish to go my way hungry." "Go?" I asks him. "Go which way?" But he doesn't say a word an' just goes through to the room an' lies on the bed an' that's the last speech I had with him till I went to tell him it was time to go to the milkin' an' found him gone.' Her voice faltered and she struck her forehead with the back of her hand.

'It's sad, mo ghaoil,' Morag sympathised when the widow had recovered herself. 'An' him such a strong healthy man all his life.'

'Indeed he was so,' agreed Ina, wiping the sleeve of her cardigan across her eyes.

'An' always so good to eat,' prompted Morag.

'Good to eat an' good to sleep,' the widow confirmed.

'An' never seein' a doctor.'

'He saw a doctor only once in these twenty years past,' Ina replied, 'an' that was only to see how he was wearin'.'

'Aye, aye,' commented Morag. 'An' nothin' artificial about him,' she added.

'Nothin' but his teeths,' corrected Ina.

'Did he have his teeths?' Morag's voice was sharp with surprise. 'I never saw them, then.'

'Indeed they never came out of that little box you see there on the chimney shelf,' confided the widow. 'Never once but when he took them out to polish them.' I glanced up at the exquisite little lacquered box which sat between what I had discovered on a previous visit to Ina to be a Georgian silver salt-cellar and pepper-shaker.

'He polished them?' asked Morag with a touch of scepticism.

'He did so. The same time as he polished the other ornaments there with some stuff he got from the van. There should be a tin of it there now.' She indicated a tin of a well-known brand of metal polish which stood tied in a duster at the end of the mantelpiece. 'He liked to see things shine,' she explained. 'I daresay it was the boat in him still.'

Ina picked up a pair of tongs roughly fashioned out of fencing wire and added a couple of peats to the fire.

'You'll take a cup of tea,' she stated with shaky-voiced emphasis and shifted the kettle from the hob to the hook above the fire. While the kettle boiled and the other three women talked pious trivialities I studied Ina's kitchen with

its wood walls tanned by peat smoke; its bare wood floor
dark as lichen with age and wear. Apart from the long
wooden bench on which we sat there were two roughly made
upright chairs, a table obviously knocked up from driftwood
and a varnished dresser which occupied almost the whole of
the wall opposite the window. The lower shelves of the
dresser were loaded with plain earthenware basins of uni-
form size; brown glazed jugs of varying sizes, and an
assortment of stone jam jars, while on the top shelf sat
three fat brown teapots interspersed with such oddments as a
pewter tankard, sporting an engraved coat of arms; a silver
sauce-boat, and one of a pair of elegant silver candlesticks.
The last time I had been in Ina's house both candlesticks
had been on display, as had also a pair of silver meat-dish
covers which had hung on the wall on either side of the
dresser.

'Useless things!' Ina had said when I had admired them.

I glanced about me, trying to locate the missing items,
and soon found the candlestick which was propping open
the tiny window to allow the slight evening breeze to drift
into the over-warm room. The meat-dish covers I could see
nowhere and I sighed for Ina's indifference to her
treasures, wondering if Morag's 'anticsman' had paid her
a visit or if some travelling tinker had cast a covetous eye
on them and had exchanged them for a couple of milk pails
or even tin water dippers. It was so unusual to see such
treasures in a crofter's kitchen that I had once asked Morag
how the old woman had come by them, imagining that perhaps Ina was descended from some once wealthy family and
these were the remaining heirlooms or perhaps that at some
time in her youth she had acquired a taste for fine things
and had saved up her money and bought them on rare visits
to the mainland. Admittedly neither theory fitted Ina's

present attitude towards her valuables but that could always be put down to age or the bludgeoning effect of a harsh crofting life.

'An' hasn't she a box full of other things under her bed in the room?' demanded Morag. 'Dishes an' spoons an' little ornaments, all wrapped in pieces of blanket. She showed them to me one time.'

'It seems so odd,' I began, but Morag cut me short.

'Ach, Ina doesn't know they're valuable,' she said. 'Nobody's told her an' it's best if no one does.'

'Why ever not?' I asked, puzzled.

'Well, you see, mo ghaoil, when Ina's daughter was alive she used to travel about the country takin' jobs as a servant in these big houses. She never seemed to stay in any place for long but she was always sendin' her mother home some little keepsake or other. Ina thought she was buyin' them an' sendin' them for her to keep till the girl got married.'

'Oh,' I said expressively.

'Aye,' agreed Morag. 'So there they are an' where they rightly belong the Dear only knows but it's certain it's not in Ina's kitchen or under her bed.'

The tea was brewed, the girdle scones handed round. Ina was not eating and Morag began questioning the old woman as to what food she had taken that day.

Ina shook her head. 'I have no hunger,' she said.

'That's no way to be,' Morag told her severely. 'Wait you now while I just switch you up an egg in a bitty milk an' supposin' you take nothin' else till the mornin' you'll not starve.' Bending down she extracted a pan from under the dresser and poured in some milk from the pail. She peered in various basins.

'Where do you keep your eggs?' She turned to Ina.

'Indeed if there's none in the basin there's none in the

house,' replied Ina. 'I mind now I didn't gather them yet today,' she added plaintively.

'Did you feed your hens?' enquired Morag.

'Kirsty did that for me while she was here,' admitted Ina. I volunteered to go to the hen-house to look for eggs.

'You'll take this an' see an' just lift the clocky hens while you're at it,' said Ina, showing signs of animation. From beside the fireplace she picked up a bowl of meal in which reposed a long-handled serving ladle. 'You'll just lift up the hens an' throw them into the air,' she instructed me. 'They've been sittin' that tight the last four or five days an' they're needin' to come off or they'll get stuck.'

I assured her I knew how to deal with broody hens and, picking up the basin and ladle, went out towards the hen-house, casually inspecting the ladle on my way. It was heavy and dull but as I had expected the hall marks on the handle were plainly visible.

There was a cluster of hens outside the hen-house all obviously questioning and counselling one another as to whether it was time to go and roost. I shooed them aside and bending down entered the tiny, strong-smelling shed where the two clocky hens sat, screened by pieces of sacking, one at either side in nests only slightly raised from the floor. The first hen tried to peck me as I lifted her out and when I threw her into the air she came down with such a squalling and shrieking that the rest of the hens scattered in panic. The second clocky reacted similarly and I watched until they had muted which was what was required of them and then threw down ladles of food, fending off the other hens until the clockies had eaten their fill. Only then did I go back into the hen-house and after collecting the eggs from half a dozen laying boxes I crouched down to check that there were no broken hatching eggs in the two snug hay-lined nests near the floor. The neat shape of the nests intrigued me and pulling aside a little of the hay to inspect them I found my fingernail was scratching on metal. I lifted a little more hay, then sat back on my heels, shaken with a mixture of disbelief and laughter. I had found the two silver meat-dish covers. They were tarnished and speckled with excreta but undoubtedly they made excellent nests for the two clocky hens and their expected progeny.

Wild Wander

I AWOKE with the first flurry of wind around the house and lay drowsily listening and wondering if this was just an exploratory thrust of a breeze attendant upon the turn of the tide or whether it was in the nature of a rehearsal for a gale which, gaining proficiency, would stampede the calm spell that had been lulling us during the past few days.

The flurry died briefly then came again, still indecisive. I tried to guess at the time. It had been day bright when I had gone to bed at my usual time and it was day bright now and I felt as if I had slept no more than an hour. I gave up guessing and stretched out an arm to pick up the alarm clock. It was a crippled clock; both its feet had gone so that it had to lie prone and the minute hand had broken off, but as nearly all Bruach clocks were either crippled or wildly eccentric I saw no reason to waste money on a new one. Except for the postmistress, the schoolteacher and the bus driver 'mechanical time' was of little importance. In winter, day began with the very first glimmer of light which told the mothers of school-age children that there was time only for them to make a quick bowl of brose and murmur a bible reading before rushing the children off to school. It told the rest of us that though there might be time for a more leisurely breakfast this must be followed by a few brief hours crammed with disciplined comings and goings; carrying hay for the outwintered cattle; milking; mucking out and renewing bedding; bringing water from the well and peats from the stack; feeding hens, and yet more hay carrying until it was dark and we could recuperate with a long evening beside the fire until one decided for oneself that it was time for the day to end. During the spring and early summer when nights were transient enough to pass almost unnoticed the working day was not so easily definable. The children took their cue for school by the smoke which appeared from the schoolhouse chimney (the peat fire burned all the year round) and their mothers knew it was time to put on the potatoes for the evening meal when the returning scholars were sighted climbing the homeward path, but though these two daily events served as useful reminders to the rest of us no one appeared to notice the lack of them when the school was closed for the holidays. We would say, 'It is time to milk the cows', or, 'It is time to feed the hens', or, 'It is time to take my dinner', and even I, novice that I was, rarely glanced at a clock for guidance. Time became instinctive: a sense that developed with the constant observation of the sky and sun shadows and the behaviour of animals and birds whose promptings were less arbitrary and more reliable than clocks and watches.

Confused now by sleep I stared at the clock. The hour hand had crept fractionally past four showing me that it was some three hours before my usual waking time. My body felt as if it was roped to the bed with the need for sleep but nevertheless I continued listening, trying to gauge the strength of the wind and almost whimpering a prayer that it would die away for just three or four hours so that I could finish my rest when, I promised, it could blow for weeks and I should not grumble. Since coming to live in Bruach I had found I was inclined to sleep less deeply on nights of calm and quiet than on nights of bustling storm, wind and rain being the characteristic pattern of our weather and calm spells merely an interruption. Like everyone else I rejoiced in the respite from the interminable battles with the wind but I was conscious that if they lasted more than a day or two they became seductive, luring me into negligence. Perhaps into leaving an empty wheelbarrow out on the croft; into forgetting a feeding bowl or some garden tool that a strong gust could snatch up and hurl against a window; into omitting the extra tie on a barn door which, if the door were blown open, could result in the loss of the roof and though I might go to bed happily exhausted by all the extra work the calm spell had enabled me to accomplish there was always this subconscious aware-

ness of more elementary chores neglected so that I was inclined to sleep fitfully, one ear alert for the first threaten-
ing rushes of a rising wind.

The flurries were undoubtedly gaining strength, punching at the windows and the roof. A pail rattled over the
cobblestones and a tub went bumping after it reminding
me of yesterday's big wash of sheets still on the clothes-line
I jumped out of bed and slid into some clothes. As soon as I
opened the door I could hear the noise of the sheets crack-
ing like whips as they streamed in the wind and I hastened
to rescue them. Some of the pegs had gone and the hems
were already beginning to fray with long cottons plagued
into tangles but I was relieved to see they were still whole.
Once before when I had been slow to take in sheets left out
in a gale I had found only the top hems still pegged to the
clothes-line; the rest were white remnants clinging to
clumps of spiky heather and decorating the barbed wire and
netting fence around the haystack. At that time it had been
a near disaster since my linen cupboard was not well stocked
and I was expecting a succession of visitors. My only re-
course had been to buy sheets from 'Aberdeen Angus', the
cheerful Asian tinker, whose entire stock I discovered to
have become stained along the folds with a most persistent
brown dye which had leaked from the cheap and inevitably
sodden portmanteaus in which he always carried round his
wares.

As soon as I grasped the sheets the remaining pegs flew
out and I fought the wind for possession of my bundle,
crushing it against me as I trotted back to the house. Dump-
ing it on the table I sped back to the croft, retrieving anything that might be blown away : a bundle of potato sacks
washed in the burn and left to dry on the stone dyke; odd
pieces of driftwood; a half-gallon tin of paint which I had

been using to paint the barn door; a shovel; a broom, and a couple of pails. Even a creel of peats had to be taken to the safety of the shed since it had already been nudged over and some of the peats scattered thus making the creel light enough to be tumbled about and perhaps become airborne should the wind increase to a gale. Satisfied at last I returned to the cottage and while I folded the sheets, cool and fresh-smelling as the dawn wind itself, I debated whether it was worth while going back to bed. My sorties into the brisk morning had driven away the yearning for sleep and I wondered whether after a quick cup of coffee I should turn my back on work and make the most of the enforced early rising by indulging in what I liked to call a 'wild wander'. Several times during the kindlier months of the year I liked to make these early-morning expeditions either along the shore or over the moors before there was much risk of other people being about and rarely did I return without the reward of having glimpsed some shy, wild creature or witnessed a thrilling example of animal behaviour the memory of which I knew would remain with me for the rest of my life. I had seen the elusive wild cat slinking among the bracken; I had observed at close quarters a family of otters playing like puppies at the mouth of a cave until, presumably winding me, they slid lithe as snakes across the rocks and into the sea. I had come at low tide within forty yards of a party of seals, lying out on the rocks and rolling and flopping their great bodies into first one position and then another while they expressed their satisfaction or otherwise by noises that were half belches, half groans. I had been puzzled by a gathering of weasels, I counted seven in all, which appeared to be playing a game of 'In and out of the bluebells' on a mossy bank near the shore, and I had watched enchanted while a magnificent stag had led his party of hinds across a swollen burn, turning every now and then it seemed to re-assure the more apprehensive among them. At almost any time there was a variety of wild life to be observed in and around Bruach but in the early mornings when it felt as if the day itself had only just begun to breathe there was more chance of surprising the more wily or more timid creatures which, once discerning the slightest stir of human activity, speedily retreated to the security of the hills or took refuge on unscaleable cliffs. Admittedly there were mornings when I saw nothing more unusual than a stag silhouetted against the skyline; a buzzard swooping on a rabbit, or a patient heron being attacked by a couple of gulls which coveted his fresh-caught breakfast, but no matter how common the sight for me the wonder and the rapture were always there. I had come straight to Bruach from the town and though the ensuing years had moulded me into a countrywoman they had not lessened my excitement on seeing creatures of the wild. So far as they were concerned I knew I should remain in a perpetual state of wonder.

I opened the door and studied the great soft clouds that were moving serenely across the sky to join those already in ambush behind the hills. With this wind I should have expected them to be racing across the sky and I seemed to recollect that according to Bruach weather lore when there was 'more wind low than high' it was a sign that the wind would not last long. The morning was inviting. I made my cup of coffee and refused to think of work. As yet I could see no threat of rain in the sky but all the same I pulled on an oilskin, tied it round my waist with a length of rope and pushed a sou'wester into the pocket. In Bruach it was usually raining, had just ceased raining or was threaten-ing to rain so it was as well to be prepared. In any case there was nothing so good as an oilskin for defence against the wind. Discarding my heavy workaday gumboots I slipped into a pair of shiny, thin-soled rubber boots, bought in an English town and kept exclusively for 'wild wanders'. Ordinary gumboots had to be heavyweight to withstand the rough stony ground and had to be several sizes too big to allow for heavy socks in winter which resulted in their clumping noisily as one walked, warning anything within a hundred yards of one's approach, but these lightweight boots, though I could feel every pebble through the thin soles, were excellent in that they kept my feet dry and yet trod as quietly as a pair of tennis pumps. Slinging my binoculars round my neck I closed the door and stood once more to assess the weather and decide which way I should go. The tide was well in and throwing great plumes of spray, wetter than any rain, over the shore so I made for the moors. As I passed the hen-run the hens came racing towards me with an expectancy that changed to puzzled murmurings as I ignored them. A feed at this hour of the morning would have upset their routine and might have affected their egg-laying. They would have to wait until I returned in about three hours' time. Crossing the stepping stones of the burn I climbed into the wind and followed one of the sheep-tracks that would take me around the shoulder of the hill and eventually into a small corrie where I could peer down into a vast chasm of tumbled rocks, reputed to be a favourite haunt of hill foxes. In all my years in Bruach I had never glimpsed a hill fox yet I was constantly hearing the shepherd grumbling at the number of sheep they took and hearing the gamekeeper boast of the number he had shot. The shepherd claimed that hill foxes were far wilier than other foxes and described almost with admiration how one of them had got the better of him at lambing time. The shepherd had gone to check up on his ewes and found one in a sheltered corrie all by herself with newly born twin lambs. He noticed that the ewe seemed agitated and looking round for the reason soon spotted the fox stealing towards her. The ewe turned to face her enemy, backing away and try-ing to keep her lambs behind her but it was obvious that one of the lambs was much weaker than the other. Before the shepherd could get near enough to do anything about it the fox had nipped in and taken the weaker lamb. The shepherd scrambled quickly down into the corrie, throwing stones and shouting at the fox until it dropped its catch and made off, but he was too late. When he reached the lamb it was already dead. Just as he made his discovery he heard a sharp bleat from the ewe and turning round was in time to see the same fox slinking rapidly out of sight with the remaining lamb in its jaws. It had merely circled the corrie and while his back was turned had swiftly taken the other lamb. 'If only,' the shephered chided himself, 'I'd had the sense to let it get away with the weaker lamb I would have been able to get the strong one to safety, but ach, he was just too clever for me I doubt.'

The shepherd told too of his experience with an old dog fox. He had been out on the hills one day looking for white heather for some friends of his and feeling rather warm he took off his jacket and left it on a small knoll while he made his way down to the burn for a drink. Having refreshed himself he was about to retrace his path to the knoll when looking up he saw the old dog fox was there pawing at something. Realising it was his own jacket he shouted and waved his arms at the fox trying to scare it off but the animal only looked at him before resuming his attack on the jacket, pulling it about the knoll until the shepherd was afraid it would be torn. He hurried forward to rescue it and just as he reached the knoll he saw the fox extract a bar of chocolate from one of the pockets. It gave him another leisurely look before loping away with the chocolate still held in its mouth. 'The look that beast gave me as it went off with my chocolate was kind of uncanny,' he used to add when he told the story.

For another mile or so I trudged on, disturbing nothing more exciting than a flock of drowsy sheep and a trio of hill ponies contentedly grazing the short grass while the wind combed their long manes. The ponies pranced away, full of summer energy and sweet mountain grass. It was while I was negotiating a skintight little path between two bastions of cliff which led to a miniature plaeau that I came upon the wild goats. Several times previously I had glimpsed the goats but never at such close quarters and from the concealment of the cliffs I was able to observe them without their seeing me. The herd was clustered around the entrance to a cave, the old grey billy to the fore but still fast asleep lying half curled with his nose resting on his flank like a dog. Behind him two young nannies stood steadily cudding and staring out at the sea with tranquil yellow eyes. Behind them again three more elderly nannies lay with the relaxed air of those who are enjoying a morning lie-in while two leggy kids sniffed at each other's ears and seemed to be consulting with each other as to whether they should lie down again with their elders or begin the day's gambolling.

It was said in Bruach that this herd of goats were the descendants of domesticated animals left behind by the crofters during the terrible evictions of the last century when homes and possessions were burned and pillaged by avaricious landlords but whatever their history the goats looked wild enough now with their strong horns and their long shaggy coats so matted and bramble-threaded that the wind could scarcely hustle a way through. I edged back along the path, not wishing to disturb them, and clambered up a rocky gully which brought me to an even loftier sheep-track so that when I came out at last above the corrie I had to slide and scramble down into it. I approached the rock edge cautiously expecting a snatch of wind to buffet me as I came into the open, but I was pleasantly surprised. I had been too engrossed to notice how the wind was dropping and now as I looked towards the sea I realised it was only a stiff breeze that was turning the white bellies of the waves towards the wink of silver above the mainland hills and that the gale I had prepared for would prove to be no more than a morning prank. I lay down, peering hopefully into the deep abyss, impressed as always by the sheer desolation and size of the havoc of barren rocks severed so cleanly from the rest of the land by steep, sharp cliffs that provided footholds for nothing larger than a raven. It was an eerie place and if it was true that there were many fox earths among the boulders I imagined the foxes would continue to live there without fear of molestation.

For about an hour I lay there enjoying the solitude and silence while ranging the abyss hopefully with my binoculars, without once detecting even a suggestion of movement. Any foxes were either still asleep or already out prospecting for their breakfast. I gave up, aware that I was hungry for my own breakfast and that even if I hurried by the time I reached home again my poultry would be protesting that their feed was overdue. Not wishing to risk meeting or disturbing the wild goats I began to climb, zig-zagging my way towards the higher track through mossy gullies that provided easy footholds and over projecting boulders which did not. I was standing on a ledge of rock about to pull myself up and over it when glancing carelessly to my right something caught my eye. Instinctively I froze. For a fleeting second I imagined the tawny, gold shape perched on the plinth of rock above me to be headless but as my excited thoughts steadied I realised I was looking at an enormous golden eagle standing with its head turned away from me and tucked under its wing. It looked to be about three feet high and except for the golden feathers on its back which were being gently lifted by the breeze it was as still as a carving. I gaped at it, astounded by its size and by the great talons, bigger than my own hand, which gripped the rock and I think I forgot to breathe for so long that I must eventually have let out a gasp. At any rate, some noise I made disturbed the eagle which turned its head quickly and looked straight at me with piercing yellow eyes. 'You beauty!' I raved silently. 'You stupendous, unbelievable beauty!' My heart thumped as we stared at each other with what seemed like equal incredulity until the eagle spread its great wings, poised itself for a second and without haste allowed the wind to lift it from its perch. I wanted to cry out to it to stay but I could only stand dumbly watching its trance-like descent on the wind out towards the sea where, levelling off and still without discernible movement of its magnificent wings, it glided on and on until it merged into the mainland hills and no matter how much I peered I could see it no more.

I pulled myself on to the ledge and walked to where the eagle had stood. I counted only five of my paces. It was staggering! I had actually stood within five paces of a golden eagle and I wanted to scream the fact into the wind if only to convince myself it was really true. I stood leaning against the rock, overwhelmed by my phenomenal good luck and conscious of the deep soul-satisfying elation that filled me and would, I knew, surge through me whenever I recollected my morning's adventures. 'People will never believe me,' I thought and with something of a shock realised that this was perfectly true. No one would believe me. If I mentioned my experience to my neighbours they would undoubtedly appear to accept my story but I knew myself it would sound too implausible. To have got within fifty paces of a resting golden eagle they might just have accepted but a claim to have got within five they would have regarded as pure exaggeration. It would be better to say nothing, I thought, and tried to make the thought a resolution, reminding myself that there were idiots with guns in Bruach who were the avowed enemies of eagles because of their reputation for taking new-born lambs. 'Say nothing,' I told myself firmly as I left the place of the eagle's perch. 'Say nothing,' I repeated to myself again and again. And all the time I was bursting with the urge to tell somebody. Just one other person if only to see their reaction.

Once safely past the goats' cave I dropped down again to the lower path and as I reached the corrie where I had encountered the hill ponies I saw a figure in cap and oilskins seated comfortably on a boulder and staring out to sea through binoculars. I recognised Donald, Bruach's shyest bachelor, and would have skirted the corrie so as to keep out of his way had he not appeared to sense my presence the moment I spotted him. Perhaps for a space I had been visible on the skyline while I was on the high path and he had expected me to make for the corrie. He turned and we greeted each other with stiff smiles.

'You're out early,' he observed.

I was surprised. He had always evaded addressing me directly and I had gained the impression he resented me as an intruder in Bruach. This morning, however, he appeared distinctly affable so I told him what had led me to take such an early-morning walk.

'Ach, but that was what we call a tide wind, just,' he replied, confirming what by this time I already knew. 'Even this bitty breeze will be away before the tide's been gone back for more than an hour.' He looked up at me. 'You'd best be tryin' to learn the ways of the wind.'

I gave a rueful little laugh. 'I try,' I told him, 'and I know more of its ways now than when I first came to Bruach but these, what you call "tide winds", usually manage to fox me.' His expression became faintly superior. 'You're out early yourself,' I observed.

'Aye.' He rose deliberately. 'I'd best be away back to my house or the cailleach will be shoutin' I'm starvin' her hens.' Donald lived with his testy, chair-bound old mother and did all the housework and cooking as well as the croft work. He seemed disposed to accept my company for the walk home and for once I was at a loss to know whether I should attempt to start a conversation or whether he would prefer it if we continued on our way virtually in silence. For a time I left the initiative to him although I wanted to talk to him very much. Apart from the fact that Donald was supposed to know more than anyone else about the wild life of the area I wanted to ask him why, when he had the reputation of being by far the best shot in the village, he had suddenly and without explanation put away his gun and taken to using binoculars and a camera to observe wild life rather than to destroy it indiscriminately as he once had. He bent, picked up a pebble, and aimed it at a clump of heather below the path. A surprised rabbit peered above the clump and loped unhurriedly away. Donald grunted.

'Did you know it was there?' I asked him.

'I didn't know for sure but I felt as if there should be

one there.' He darted a glance at me. 'If you'd had a gun now that would have made a dinner for you.'

'I don't shoot,' I told him.

'No, I don't myself now.'

'Not at all?' I queried.

'Ach, I might get a rabbit if they're takin' too much of the corn or if the cailleach takes a fancy for one but I scarcely ever take the gun down from the wall now.'

'And yet people tell me you are easily the best shot in Bruach,' I encouraged.

'Aye, I believe I might have been once,' he acknowledged. He tweaked a stalk of grass from beside the path and stuck it in his mouth. I thought it signified the end of the subject but after we had walked another little distance in silence he turned to me, slowing his pace almost to a standstill.

'There was a time once when I'd shoot at almost anythin' that moved : rabbits, hares, grouse, hoodies, gulls, ach, any bird you'd name an' just think myself the fine fellow that I had the skill to do it but then the day came, an' it came all of a sudden, that I was brought to my senses. I grew up as you might say.'

He flushed and his yellow uneven teeth were bared in an embarrassed smile but he was still walking slowly. I reasoned that if he wanted me not to pursue the subject he would have quickened his pace again so I prompted :

'You say the day came quite suddenly?'

'Aye.' He took the stalk of grass from his mouth and started to pull it into tiny pieces between his fingers. 'Did you ever see a newly dead grouse?' he asked, looking at me searchingly.

'Yes.'

'An' did you ever notice the markings on its feathers; all its feathers, I mean, not just the wings an' the brighter coloured ones?' He moved his fingers as if he were riffling them through the feathers on a bird's breast.

'Not specially,' I confirmed.

He nodded. 'I'd shot this grouse one day an' I was just bendin' down to pick it up when suddenly the sun comes through the clouds like a pointing finger an' a wee breeze tickled at the bird's feathers, liftin' them so that it made me notice the markin's on them. Beautiful it was, beautiful just. No man could have made a thing like it. I've never been able to explain it, least of all to myself, but it was as though somethin' was behind my shoulder forcin' me to see what I'd been blind to before an' what a fearful waste it was to destroy it. I took home the grouse an' we ate it but for the first time in my life I didn't enjoy it an' when I came to put the feathers at the back of the fire an' I saw their lovely patterns goin' up in smoke I knew I didn't want to destroy another living creature. I cleaned the gun that night an' I put it up on the wall an' I doubt I've taken it down more than two or maybe three times since an' that's a good few years back.' His pace quickened. 'Ach, I daresay I was daft but that's the way of it just.'

I tried to give him an understanding smile but he kept his face averted. All the same I knew now that here was some-one with whom I could safely share my secret.

'I don't suppose you'll believe me,' I began, trying to keep the excitement out of my voice, 'but up there on the crag I've just stood within five paces of a golden eagle. It was asleep with its head under its wing.'

He turned to face me. 'Why wouldn't I believe you?' he demanded. There was a wry twist to his mouth.

'Oh, it just sounds too impossible. I'd decided not to mention it at all but I was dying to tell someone. You won't let it go any further, will you?' I asked hastily. There was something about the tightening of his lips that made it unnecessary for him to answer.

'Indeed not long before you found me I was watchin' a golden eagle makin' over towards the mainland. Likely it would be the one you disturbed.'

'Oh, yes!' I exclaimed, glad of some corroboration of my story.

'You were lucky all the same,' he congratulated me. 'There's not more than one other person hereabouts that I mind ever got that close to an eagle.'

'You know of someone else?' I asked tensely.

'Aye, an' he was my own father.'

'Your father?'

'Indeed. He was salmon watchin' at the time, livin' in the bothy, an' he was comin' over to collect some fresh milk an' food. It was about midday, an' sunny an' calm. Seein' he was keepin' an eye open for his sheep at the same time he didn't stay on the path. He climbed up to a crag an' found himself almost on a level with the eagle an' so close he could touch it. Like the one you saw it had it's head under its wing so that it didn't see him. My father was a very honest man, you understand, Miss Peckwitt?' He looked at me and I nodded. 'There's nothin' that upset him more than bein' disbelieved but all the same he knew if he came back to the village tellin' nothin' but the truth about what he'd seen people wouldn't be able to bring themselves to believe him just. So, quick as a flash he slipped off his jacket an' threw it over the eagle an' held it in his arms. He lifted it an' carried it all the way down to the village an' there he started shoutin' for folks to come an' see what he had. When he thought there was enough witnesses he lifted his jacket off the eagle an' let it go.' He grinned. 'They had to believe him then.'

'He must have been even closer than I was,' I remarked.

'Aye, but I doubt you wouldn't have had the strength to carry it back even supposin' you were able to throw your jacket over it,' he replied. 'They're big birds with some weight in them.'

I laughed. 'It wouldn't have occurred to me to try,' I retorted. 'It looked enormous and its talons were really fearsome.'

He grunted again. 'You'd best be careful who you mention the eagle to,' he warned. 'There's one or two here would be out with the gun if they heard of it.'

'I've already decided I'm going to keep quiet about it,' I assured him. 'It's enough that I've seen it.'

We were coming in sight of the village now and he began to move away, gradually making for a track that would take him to the far moor gate. I guessed that he had no wish to be seen in my company.

'Aye, well,' he said, throwing the words over his shoulder, 'I'd best go an' make some breakfast.'

'D'you know,' I told him, 'I recall feeling quite hungry for my breakfast before I saw the eagle but since then the thought of food hasn't crossed my mind.'

He paused and looked at me with a gentle understanding smile.

'Ach, Miss Peckwitt,' he pronounced, 'when anyone has seen such a sight as you have seen this morning they have had food and drink for the day.' He turned his back on me and we went our separate ways.

Pears in Brine

'WELL, that's us near ready,' announced Erchy, indicating the forty or so lobster creels spread on the cobbled
ground at the side of the house. 'This is the last one.' He
was tying a flat stone to a creel bottom and beside him sat
Hector expertly plying a netting needle which, being a sed-
entary occupation, was the only one he cared to undertake.

'When Hector's finished that net we'll have forty-two creels for tarrin' tomorrow an' if the weather holds they'll be in the water by Wednesday surely.'

'It's a pity you have to put in the stones before you net them,' I said, lifting one of the creels. 'It makes them terribly heavy to carry.' I picked up another creel. 'Two of them balance quite well, though,' I observed, weighing one against the other. 'Would you like me to take these two down to the shore for you, seeing I'm going down anyway.'

I thought Erchy was about to refuse my offer but Hector interrupted quickly. 'Aye, let her,' he said magnanimously. 'It'll be two less for us to carry.'

'Aye.' Erchy's voice was dubious. 'So long as she doesn't fall an' break them.' He finished tying the stone. 'Where did you put your own creel?' he asked me.

I nodded towards the house. 'Beside the door,' I told him.

'Aye, well you'd best fetch it here. I'll be ready to sort it for you just now.'

I brought him my one creel which he had promised to mend for me. He inspected it with a disgruntled air. 'Ach, you'd best have a new creel. This one is like matchwood.'

'It will do me,' I argued, knowing that if this one was not repaired I should be without a creel for the rest of the season and I dearly fancied a fresh lobster.

Erchy sat down and began tearing off the old net which was like a ravel of dirty string.

'If you boys hasn't got your creels in the sea yet you'd be best leavin' them on the shore!' Angy, who had forsaken his job as a fisherman to come and take over the deceased Fergus's croft, appeared from the direction of the house. He was a small man with a thin, bouncy figure, red hair and sea-blue eyes. He looked at my creel. 'You're surely not thinkin' of puttin' that in the water?' he asked contemptuously. 'Surely the lobster would be walkin' in an out of it as if it was its own kitchen.'

'That's what I've been sayin' to her myself,' agreed Erchy. 'But she's that thrawn. She'll no' listen.'

Hector smiled impishly. 'You'd best be careful what you're sayin',' he jested. 'She might be catchin' more wiss her one than us wiss our forty.'

'Indeed an' that will be the way of it unless we get ours into the water pretty soon,' returned Erchy.

I ought to have left them to their work and their chat but Erchy's mother had made me promise to await her return from the well so that she could give me a pat of home-made butter for my supper and it was pleasant outside in the silky breeze with the bright sun gentled by drifts of clouds that looked soft and white as a rabbit's belly.

'Are you tarrin' them here or down at the shore?' asked Angy.

'On the shore,' Erchy replied.

Hands in pockets, cigarette in the side of his mouth, Angy studied the assembled creels. 'How will you get this lot down anyway? You'll need to hire a lorry.'

'We're hirin' no lorry,' retorted Erchy.

'You'll surely not be thinkin' of carryin' them down yourself?' Angy, having been a professional fisherman, was inclined to be scornful of Bruach's part-timers. 'You'll need help if you are.'

'We're carryin' them down but we'll have help all right.' There was a combative look in Erchy's eyes.

'I'm taking two on my way home,' I interpolated. 'And I expect there'll be others willing.'

'I'm no meanin' that sort of help,' exclaimed Erchy. 'What we'll do is wait till it gets a wee bit dark an' then we'll take the bier from the church an' carry them down on that.'

'The funeral bier?' I echoed.

'Aye,' affirmed Erchy, 'it will hold a good few creels at a time will that.'

'People won't like it,' I pointed out.

'Why should they complain?' asked Erchy. 'It's not as if we're tarrin' the creels first. Right enough I wouldn't think it right to get the bier all covered in tar,' he added virtuously.

Angy's eyes sparkled. He was already beginning to get the reputation of being a practical joker and now he nodded appreciatively. 'By God! I wish I'd thought of that myself,' he said.

'I'm sure some people are going to be offended,' I repeated.

'Not more than a couple of fresh lobsters will cure,' declared Erchy confidently. He turned to me. 'You'd best not let on you know anythin', all the same,' he warned. 'Just keep your eyes an' your door tight shut if you hear some strange noises near the place tonight.'

'You're aimin' to take them down this night?' asked Angy.

'We are so,' responded Erchy. 'We're meanin' to spend the day tarrin' them tomorrow.'

Angy looked downcast. 'You're not wantin' the job I spoke about, then?'

'We are not,' replied Erchy. 'Like you said, if we don't get these creels into the water soon we're as well leavin' them ashore.' His voice became emphatic. 'We're tarrin' them tomorrow an' puttin' them into the sea the next day if we're spared. There'll be no time to do any job save that.'

'There'll be good money in it,' said Angy persuasively.

At the mention of money Hector evinced a mild interest in the conversation. 'How much?' he asked.

'Ach, I couldn't say for sure, but plenty. The family's rich enough anyway.'

'How would you know that?' demanded Erchy.

'They must be,' asserted Angy. 'They pay income tax anyway.'

Hector enveloped the three of us in his broad guileful smile. 'If tsey pay income tax tsey must be daft as well as rich, I'm tsinkin',' he commented.

'I cannot see why the boat you were on yourself doesn't drop it off,' suggested Erchy. 'Do they not pass near to the island most every day?'

'With herrin' the price it is how would they take time off from the fishin' just to deliver a corpse?' argued Angy. 'Anyway, fishermen don't take to coffins aboard their boats. They say it brings bad luck.'

'An' aren't we expectin' to be fishermen?' responded Erchy.

Angy hastily pushed another cigarette between his lips. 'Not herrin' fishermen, you're not,' he replied. 'I believe corpses only affect herrin'. I don't believe the lobsters mind them at all.'

I had pricked up my ears at the mention of a corpse but deemed it wiser to ask no questions and there was an appreciable silence before anyone spoke again.

'It would set us back wiss tse creels, right enough,' remarked Hector. 'We'd need a good pound for tsat.'

'Well, I'm gettin' nothin' out of it,' said Angy offhandedly. 'I only said I'd ask you seein' they weren't findin' it easy to get a boat an' I thought you'd be keen on the money.'

'Not that keen,' muttered Erchy.

'Ach, then, I'll away to the Post Office an' telephone to say you're not comin', will I?' said Angy.

At that moment Erchy's mother returned and I went with her into the house. When I left there was no sign of any of the three men but the next morning Hector and Erchy's boat had gone from its moorings and the untarred creels were piled in a mound on the shore.

'Where have they gone?' I asked Morag.

'Ach, they're away to take a corpse to one of the islands, though the Dear knows why,' she replied.

'I heard them discussing it yesterday and they seemed determined they weren't going to take it,' I told her.

'They were not indeed but, ach, I think it was the money tempted them in the end,' she explained.

Later in the day whilst I was repairing the stone dyke which surrounded my cottage I was surprised to see a fishing boat come into the bay and drop anchor. The sound of a klaxon horn hit the village followed some time later by the noise of booted feet clumping down the brae. It was Angy and I guessed that this was the boat on which he had worked. I watched him row out and climb aboard.

'You're a hardy!' Behag's voice startled me momentarily and one of my carefully placed stones rolled out of position. 'That's Angy's friends come for a ceilidh with him,' she enlightened me, shielding her eyes as she studied the boat. Under her arm Behag had the new skirt which she wished me to 'gather her in round the middle' so I left my dyke mending and went with her back to the cottage where she slipped out of her old skirt and tried on the new one. I was just pinning in some darts when we heard heavy footsteps approaching.

'Who can it be?' gasped Behag and sooner than risk having her skirt fall down and despite all the pins I had inserted she promptly sat on the nearest chair, pulling her jersey well down over her waistline. Angy stood in the doorway.

'It's my mates that was,' he explained after the preliminary greetings had been exchanged. 'They're sayin' all their bread's gone mouldy on them an' they're thinkin' maybe they'd get a loaf from you. Just what will do them till mornin' when they'll be back in port.'

'They've no bread at the shop,' interjected Behag. 'I was up there this mornin' an' there's none till the bus comes this evenin'.'

'Ach, you wouldn't expect the shop to have bread at this time of day,' scoffed Angy.

'I've no bread either,' I told him. 'But I've plenty of oatcakes and it won't take me a minute to bake them some girdle scones.'

'Aye, that will do them fine,' Angy accepted and sat down to wait.

I heated the girdle over the fire and tipped flour into a basin. 'Behag,' I said, 'will you brew the tea? The kettle is boiling and I daresay Angy will be glad of a cup.' She did not move and when I glanced at her enquiringly I saw she was biting her lip and looking rather coyly distressed. I remembered her predicament with the pinned skirt and wondered if I dared ask Angy to make the tea.

'Angy! How about brewing the tea?'

'Eh?' His voice was pained and he looked uncomprehendingly from me to Behag and back to me again.

'Well, you'll either have to brew the tea yourself or go outside while Behag changes her skirt. My hands are thick with flour,' I told him.

Angy got up. 'It's a damty fine thing when a woman has first to change her skirt before she can make the tea,' he re-

marked sourly as he went outside. Behag slipped into my
bedroom and returned her respectable self. Angy, whistling
loudly as if to warn us of his reappearance, ambled in and
sat down again.

'So you managed to persuade Hector and Erchy to go for
the coffin?' I taxed him.

'Ach, there was no persuadin' in it at all,' he replied.
'They were keen enough to go all the time, I could see that.'

I raised my eyebrows. 'They didn't sound in the least
keen to me,' I observed.

'Indeed, only the devil himself knows what those two are
keen on.' Angy loaded his tea with several spoonfuls of
sugar.

'You did!' Behag challenged. Angy responded with a mis-
chievous grin.

'I hope the weather stays calm for them,' I said.

'Indeed I hope so too,' murmured Behag. 'I was hearin'
them sayin' the boat was leakin' a good bit since they
scraped that rock a week or two back.'

'They'll be safe enough anyway with a coffin aboard,'
Angy told her cheerfully.

'What do you mean?' I asked.

'Well, with a coffin aboard supposin' the boat sinks under
them they'd still be all right.' He saw my bewilderment.
'Coffins float,' he explained. 'If the boat sinks they'd get
into the coffin. It stands to reason for with a couple of oars
they'd make land sure enough.'

'It's not an empty coffin,' I reminded him.

Angy shot me a withering glance. 'Aye but two live men's
not goin' to drown to save a dead one, are they?' he said
reasonably.

As soon as the scones were browned on both sides I
wrapped them and a few oatcakes in a teacloth and handed

them to Angy. 'You could take some fresh milk for their tea,' I suggested. 'I've plenty and I know fishing boats don't see fresh milk from one week-end to another. I poured some from the setting bowl into a can. 'Bring me back my cloth and my can,' I called to him as he set off for the shore.

Behag was just being pinned up for the second time when we heard what sounded like the same footsteps again approaching the cottage. Sure enough it was Angy.

'They're sayin' why don't you come aboard an' take a wee strupach with them?' he invited. 'They've just taken their meal an' they're goin' to have a cup of tea and a bite to chase it down.'

'Are you sure?' I asked, pleasantly surprised.

'Aye, that's what they said.'

'I thought they didn't like women on fishing boats,' I demurred. 'Don't women bring bad luck the same as corpses?'

'Not while the boat's moored,' Angy retorted. 'No indeed they're keen enough you should come. See, they don't wish to feel obliged to you for the milk an' the scones. If they had a fry of herrin' aboard now you'd get that instead.'

I understood, and turned to Behag. 'Shall we go?' I asked.

Her expression was eager. 'I believe my cousin's wife's brother is in the crew, is he not?' she asked. 'Him they call "Dodo"?'

'Aye, he's there,' replied Angy. 'At least, the pieces of him are,' he added obscurely.

'I'd love to come,' I admitted. 'I've never been on a real working fishing boat.'

'You'd best hurry then,' instructed Angy. He went outside and Behag again rushed into my bedroom to change.

The skipper and crew hauled Behag and me aboard their boat with awkward gallantry and the cook came up on deck to show us the grey-green loaf which he had taken from its wrapper only that morning. 'Not that the fresh stuff we get is much better,' he complained. 'It's that soft an' doughy you'd think the pollis could use it for takin' finger-prints.' With an expression of disgust he tossed the loaf into the sea.

He invited us into the fo'c'sle where a dusty grey, hot-smelling iron stove was almost covered with kettles and metal teapots. 'Sit you down,' he commanded hospitably and Behag and I inserted ourselves into position on the narrow bench between the bunks and the table. Angy sat beside Behag and the skipper and the two members of the crew took the opposite bench. The cook remained standing, pouring out black tea into permanently tanned mugs and sliding them one at a time along to us.

'I see Hector's boat's away,' observed the skipper in a voice that 'glugged' as if it was being poured out from a bottle.

'Aye, they're takin' that corpse from the mainland,' Angy told him.

'They're takin' it?' The skipper sounded astonished. 'I never thought a Bruach boat would take on a Roman Catholic corpse,' he remarked, stirring his tea perfunctorily before passing on the spoon to his crew.

'Do they know it's a Roman Catholic?' I asked, thinking of Bruach's rabid presbyterianism and abhorrence of 'Papists'.

Angy nodded.

'So that's why they were so reluctant,' I said.

'Ach, they wouldn't have taken it except for bein' paid double,' replied Angy with a smile.

'Oh, that's terrible,' said Behag, trying hard to disguise her approval for the deal.

'It would be the same if it was the other way round,' said Angy.

I smiled. 'You know,' I told them, 'I've always thought of Bruach people as being some of the most tolerant in the world and yet they have this fearful prejudice against Roman Catholics. I just don't understand it at all.'

'Are you a Papist?' asked Dodo suspiciously.

'No,' I replied, 'but some of my friends are.'

'An' can you trust them?'

'Of course,' I replied, chuckling.

'Aye well,' summed up the skipper. 'It's just the way they have hereabouts. I get on all right myself with them but all the same, there's a somethin'.' He nodded towards one of the lockers. 'Come on, Sammy, with that stuff,' he said.

The cook opened the locker and took out a large tin of pears which he opened.

'You'll take a wee bitty fruit?' he asked me.

At that moment I was not really feeling much like eating anything let alone sweet tinned fruit since the boat was rolling steadily and the fo'c'sle was at the same time both draughty and fuggy. It felt as if someone was packing round my feet with ice cubes while swathing my head in hot towels. However, I smiled acceptance, and the cook carefully slid the tin of pears along the table towards me along with a spoon and a tin of evaporated milk.

'Help yourself,' he invited.

I waited for the expected bowl or plate but to my surprise saw that the cook was opening another large tin of pears which he slid along the table, again with a tin of milk and a spoon, to Behag. Next the skipper was pre-

sented with his tins, then the crew and Angy. Finally the
cook was able to sit down with his own allotment in front
of him. I felt shaken. Seven large tins of pears and seven tins
of milk for seven people. The skipper's eye was on me. 'Go
on, don't be waitin' for everybody else,' he urged, mistak-
ing my hesitation for politeness. He tipped milk into his
tin of pears and began spooning the fruit into his mouth.

'Look, I can't possibly eat all this,' I protested. 'Couldn't
I put some out into a dish first to save wasting the rest?'
Beside me Behag murmured that she too could never cope
with such a quantity.

'Ach, just leave what you don't want,' instructed the
skipper, loftily. 'Sammy will get rid of what's left over the
side.'

I felt guilty about leaving so many of the pears and more
than two-thirds of the tin of milk and would have felt even
more guilty had I not observed that only Angy and the
cook had managed to dispose of the whole contents of their
tins. The skipper and the other two crew had eaten only
about half of theirs before pushing the tins away.

The cook picked up a bucket with a rope in its handle.
'Are you sure you can no' eat just a wee bit more?' he enquired, looking solicitously at Behag and me and when we
shook our heads he swept all the remaining tins higgledy-
piggledy into the bucket and whistling nonchalantly
climbed up on to the deck. I had always been brought up on
the old adage 'Waste not, want not', and I winced as I
heard all that good food splashing into the sea. The cook
came back into the fo'c'sle with the pail rinsed clean. Behag
and I exchanged dismayed glances.

'Aye, it's good to have fresh milk for a change.' said the
skipper, gulping tea from his mug. 'I fairly enjoy the taste
of fresh milk in my tea.' He winked at me, the diffident

fisherman's method of saying thank you to a strange woman.

Behag addressed her cousin's wife's brother, Dodo, who was sporting a large piece of sticking plaster behind his right ear, a colourful bruise on his jaw and a deep ruddy scar on the back of one hand.

'Were you in an accident?' she asked him.

'Some accident!' snorted the cook and Dodo's face split into a bashful grin.

'What were you doin'?' pursued Behag.

'I fell down one of these manhole things,' Dodo told her in tones that implied it had been a pleasant experience.

'How did you come to do that?' she pressed anxiously.

'He was drunk,' supplied the skipper. 'Go on, Dodo, tell her the rest of it while you're about it.'

'Ach, right enough we had a good drink on us,' admitted Dodo sheepishly. 'It was on Saturday night when me an' some of my pals were at a dance. We didn't think much of the lassies there so when a gang of strange fellows came in we started tormentin' them. It turned out they were Irish an' it ended up by us bashin' one another about a bit. The next thing we know is somebody's got the pollis so me an' my pals start to run before they can get a hold of us.'

'Only they didn't run fast enough,' interjected the cook.

'Was it run?' echoed Dodo indignantly. 'We ran like tinker's ponies. "You lead the way, Dodo", my pals shout to me seein' I know this place as well as I know the deck of this boat, so I dodged down this dark entry but by God! hadn't some damty fool left open one of those manhole covers an' plump! down I went into it an' plump! plump! plump! down came my three pals on top of me. If they'd kept quiet we would have been all right even then but they were swearin' at me so much for takin' them there the pollis heard an' that's how they found us. They carted us off to the station then.'

To me it sounded just like a description of a scene from one of the old 'Keystone Cops' films.

'Did they put you in the cells?' questioned Behag in a horrified voice.

'Aye, until the Monday mornin' an' they charged us five pounds apiece to get out again.' Dodo shook his head regretfully. 'I took ten pounds of good money to go an' enjoy myself on Saturday night an' when I got out of the cells I hadn't a penny in my pocket.'

'But you had five pounds' worth of whisky inside your stomach,' the skipper reminded him.

'Aye,' admitted Dodo. 'You can say it cost me five pounds to get in an' five pounds to get out.'

The skipper drained his cup and pushed it towards the cook for refilling. 'Right enough, the Irish are the ones for fightin',' he opined. 'I believe myself if an Irishman was on a deserted island an' he couldn't find another body to attack he'd have his left hand fightin' his right before he'd be satisfied.'

'When I was in hospital we had an Irish cleaner in the wards,' I recalled with a smile. 'She had rather badly fitting false teeth and one of the patients used to say that even without hearing the cleaner speak she could tell she was Irish because her top set of teeth were always fighting the bottom set.'

'I'll tell you this much,' declared Angy with some ferocity, 'it's not just the humans but even the bloody Irish lobsters fight.'

I could not repress a smile.

'It's true,' reiterated Angy. 'I was workin' on a lobster

boat for a time fishin' off the Irish coast so I know what I'm talkin' about.'

'Aye?' said the skipper with a wry smile.

'Well, skipper, you know yourself I've fished lobsters off the coasts of England, Scotland an' Wales in my time an' in the ordinary way when you take the beasts out of the creels an' put them on the deck they'll stay quiet enough till you can tie their claws. But you try doin' that with the Irish lobsters. By God! The minute you put them on the deck the buggers are starin' round with them stalky eyes of theirs an' as soon as one spots another it's straight across the deck they are and tearin' one another to pieces before you can bait a creel. No, if you're fishin' off Ireland you need an extra man to tie the claws of every lobster as it comes out of the creel,' he concluded.

The skipper stood up, glancing at the clock on the bulkhead. I pushed Behag and Behag pushed Angy along the bench.

'We must go back ashore,' we said, and soon we were out on deck.

'I'm right sorry we hadn't a fry to give you,' the skipper apologised. 'But next time we're in maybe.'

'We have plenty of bree,' offered the cook generously. 'D'you care for bree?'

'Bree?' I echoed and shook my head emphatically. 'Bree is the mixture of blood and salt and fish oil left in the barrel after fresh herring have been salted and kept for about six months. It looks and smells revolting.

'What are you doin' with bree aboard?' asked Angy.

'Ach, we met up with a Norwegian fishing boat last week an' they said would we bring them some bree if we could get a hold of it. We took it for them but we didn't see them so we still have it,' explained the skipper.

'What do they do with it?' I asked.

'Drink it,' replied the skipper and seeing my expression added, 'they nearly come to blows over it they're that keen on it.'

'Great bowls of it they'll drink,' volunteered the cook. 'Honest, they just tilt back their heads, open their mouths an' pour the stuff down their gullets. They'll pay for it if you'll let them.'

Behag and I grimaced at each other.

'They reckon it cures cancer in humans an' foot-an'-mouth in cattle,' said the cook, 'so it must be true there's goodness in it.'

We let ourselves down into the dinghy, the crew dismissing us with enthusiastic promises of a 'good fry' next time they came in.

'Oh, how terrible it was to see all that lovely fruit an' milk goin' over the side,' moaned Behag. 'I felt like jumpin' in after it.'

'That's our skipper,' said Angy proudly. 'Unless there's food to throw over the side he thinks his men aren't bein' well enough fed. He's not a great eater himself, mind, but unless he sees food left on the men's plates he tells the cook to be sure an' provide more next time.'

I had from time to time heard of the prodigality of the catering on some fishing boats: the dictum that there should be 'double helpings for single appetites and all gash straight over the side', but I had never expected to witness it for myself.

'But all those pears!' I expostulated. 'I doubt if we ate more than three tins among the seven of us and yet seven tins were opened. Anyway,' I added, 'surely there was no need to ditch what was left. They would have kept for another meal?'

'It's easy to see you're no' used to boats,' retorted Angy. 'How would you keep opened tins of fruit an' milk an' stuff on a boat that's likely to be jumpin' all over the sea an' over one side then the other when the nets are hauled in?'

'Well,' I began lamely but he cut me short.

'No, it's not "well" at all,' he insisted. 'A man would be comin' down below for a sleep after a heavy night's fishin' an' maybe find tins of milk drippin' into his bunk, or sticky fruit juice all over the fo'c'sle. Indeed, any fisherman findin' that's as likely to throw the cook overboard as the food. No,' he repeated. 'Eat what you want at the time an' dump the rest, that's the only way on a fishin' boat.'

'But,' I persisted, 'if we'd been given plates or bowls we could have taken out only what pears we wanted. There would have been no need to open all seven tins of pears and seven tins of milk.'

'The skipper would have been feared you were stintin' yourselves to be polite,' explained Angy. He back-watered with the oars as we came in close to the shore. 'Anyway,' he added, 'that would have meant there was seven bowls to wash up an' you'd have to have a woman aboard to want to do that.'

Not their Funeral

ALL day the village had been swathed in mist and silence and fine silky rain that trilled reassuringly from the roof gutter into the half-empty water butts. It had been the sort of day when, since it was impossible to work in the hay, Bruach women felt justified in catching up with their washing or in baking a mountain of scones and oatcakes; a day when Bruach men, anxious to get away from such activity, chose to foregather in the doorway of a neighbour's barn or byre in the hope of being able to pass the time by watching someone else at work. For me it had been a relatively lazy day which, now that evening was thickening the mist, was going, I suspected, to leave me as tired at the end of it as if I had spent it raking and carrying hay. I had finished my evening meal and had put the sewing machine on the cleared table intending to put 'sides to middle' a sheet which had worn thin, but so dim was the light in the kitchen I had to use a magnifying glass to thread the needle. For over two months now I had not needed to light a lamp in the evenings and I felt if I lit one now it would be like betraying what was left of the summer. I decided to leave the sheet mending for another evening and go to call on Janet at whose house there would undoubtedly be some sort of ceilidh in progress.

'Well, an' here's me thinkin' only this mornin' you were makin' yourself a stranger,' Janet greeted me as I apologised for not having looked in on her for nearly two weeks. 'Come away in, mo ghaoil.' Janet's kitchen was a shade or two darker than my own but like me she had resisted lighting a lamp although on the dresser behind her brother's chair a swaling candle lit a smoked patch on the painted wall and gave him light enough to peer at the previous day's paper. Already in addition to Janet, her brother and myself there were seven other people in the room. Morag was one of them. I had apparently interrupted some story she was telling and punctuating it with a nod to me she continued: 'An' I mind old Ina keepin' them in a drawer till Fergus came home. She showed them to me once. "Fergus keeps on sendin' me these bills or recipits," she grumbled. "An' why should he do that when he's never done it before?"

"Ina," says I, "these are neither bills nor recipits. These are five-pound notes." She had more than twenty of them there, just pushed into the drawer of the dresser along with old envelopes an' paper an' bits of string an' postcards. "Five-pound notes?" says she. "I cannot believe those things are worth five pence. Why, there's not a bit of colour on them at all to give them a nice look," she says, starin' at them as if they was no more use than election forms she'd throw at the back of the fire. "That's what they are, Ina," I tell her, but ach, she would not believe me till Fergus came home an' took her up to the Post Office to get a book sayin' it was money he was payin' into it.'

'Ina never did take to readin',' commented old Murdoch. 'I was at school with her an' she was always the dunce, was Ina.'

The door opened and Angy came in, his homespun jacket misted with rain.

'I was just tellin' them about your old aunt Ina,' said Morag, drawing him into the conversation. 'The way she didn't know the recipits Fergus was sendin' were five-pound notes.'

'Aye, I mind hearin' about that,' said Angy, fishing out a damp cigarette. 'I'm thinkin' it's a good thing she never went to Glasgow. The poor old cailleach would have been robbed of everythin' she had.' He went over to the fire and lit his cigarette with a flaming peat. 'Well, Hector an' Erchy are well pleased with the pocketful of five-pound notes they got for doin' their little job,' he announced.

'Are they back?' I asked, and added, 'I didn't see their boat at the mooring.'

'How would you be seein' it in this mist, woman?' Murdoch derided.

'They got back this mornin',' Angy reported. 'An' they

would have been back yesterday but for havin' to wait for their money, so they tell me.'

'Did they know who was the corpse?' asked the shepherd.

'Surely they did,' replied Morag and went on to detail the dead man's family tree.

'Aye, aye, I knew the father,' said Murdoch. 'Four sons he had, was it not?'

'Four,' affirmed Morag.

'An' bad luck with all of them, I'm thinkin',' said Murdoch.

'How would that be?' demanded the shepherd.

'Well wasn't the first born deaf an' dumb an' the second died of his lungs an' didn't the third one turn into one of these psychiatrisses?' supplied Murdoch.

'An' now the fourth one has been drowned,' said Morag.

'Drowned, was he?' asked the shepherd and added, 'He'd be drunk likely?'

'No, he was not drunk,' replied Morag. 'They inquested him an' they found no alkali in his body.'

Murdoch rasped disbelief. 'Comin' from that family he was bound to be drunk,' he insisted. 'Why, I never saw the like of it. There was as many bottles of whisky went into that house in a week as come into Bruach in a year.' The old man paused as there came hoots of laughter and muttered accusations of exaggeration. 'Indeed but it's as true as I'm here,' he averred. 'I was workin' on a boat that used to deliver the stuff to them an' I saw it with my own eyes. When the old father of them died I was stuck on the island with the weather while they had his funeral an' I was told by one of the man's own relations that it took thirty-four bottles of whisky to bury him.'

'Thirty-four?' gasped Janet.

'Aye, thirty-four,' repeated Murdoch. 'An' that's a terrible lot of whisky just to put one man in his grave. Mind you,' he added, 'I believe some of the mourners went two or three times to the house to give their condolences as they say, hopin' everybody would be too upset or too drunk to notice them. I heard the widow herself complainin' of that.'

'That was some funeral,' said Angy admiringly.

'What some folks will do for a dram,' said Janet with a sorrowful shake of her head.

'Folks say this one that's been drowned was a queer one when he was home,' said the shepherd. 'I never knew him myself but that's what I've heard folks say.'

'Aye, right enough he was queer,' agreed Morag, who when it came to the inhabitants of the Hebrides was a *Who's Who*. 'I didn't know him either but I knew a woman who lived on the same island. She told me he used to make people gey angry he was that queer in his ways.'

'What sort of things did he do?' I asked.

'Ach well, mo ghaoil, daft things like payin' the income tax when they asked him an' puttin' his clocks backwards and forwards just whenever the government told him to,' she explained.

'That would upset folks right enough,' murmured the shepherd understandingly.

'People reckoned it was him that took the tax mannie to the island,' disclosed Murdoch. 'Seein' one was payin' tax they thought the rest must be cheatin'.'

I was intrigued. 'What happened?' I asked.

'I was there at the time,' he replied. 'An' I saw it for myself.' His eyes glinted. 'Ach, he was only a wee mannie this fellow an' he was that sick on the boat comin' over an' that pale he looked as if he'd been left out in the rain for a long time. He was waitin' on the pier to see the men when they came in from the fishin' an' as soon as the men got word of it they started shoutin' at one another. "There's some tax bugger over there waitin' for us," says one. "Ach, throw him down the fish hold," says another, makin' out they was feelin' right savage, d'you see? Then one of the boats that was unloadin' swung its derrick over an' tipped the whole basketful of fish on top of the poor mannie.' Murdoch wheezed at the memory. 'While he was cleanin' himself up from that they started peltin' him with fish guts. He didn't stay after that but went back to the boat that brought him over. "Take me back to the mainland," he tells the boat-man. "There's wild men in this place an' I've suffered enough for the government. If they want taxes from this island they'll need to send the army." ' Murdoch probed at the bowl of his pipe with a sharp splinter of wood. 'Right enough, the boatman told us the poor mannie did suffer for he was sick all the way back as well.'

'And did the tax people send anyone else?' I enquired.

'I don't believe they ever did another thing about it except maybe send letters that would go at the back of the fire,' responded Murdoch. 'Ach,' he added, 'the government's plenty of money, why should they give it to the likes of us else?'

'I'm thinkin' the rest of the folks on that island must have been glad when this one that was drowned took himself off to foreign parts to work,' said the shepherd.

'Aye.' Murdoch smiled roguishly. 'I'm thinkin' maybe he would have been drowned a lot sooner in his life if he'd stayed.' He turned to Trina, one of the village girls who had recently completed a teacher-training course. 'You watch the Education don't send you to that island,' he warned her.

'Why, what's wrong with it?' Trina challenged him with a smile.

'You'd have to teach Papists an' Presbyterians together, that's what's wrong with it,' Murdoch told her. 'There's two religions there but only one school.'

'I've never heard that they quarrel about it,' said Trina. 'There was a girl from there at college the same time as myself and she said they were as friendly as folks on any other island.'

'They're friendly enough,' conceded Murdoch, 'except when it comes to the schoolin'. That's when they start their girnin'.'

'Why?' asked Trina.

'D'you not see, lassie,' explained Murdoch patiently, 'they have only one teacher an' the way they've agreed is that if there's more Papist scholars than Presbyterian then the teacher has to be a Papist. If it's the other way round then the teacher has to be a Presbyterian.'

'That sounds fair enough,' said Trina. 'What happens if it's equal numbers?'

'They keep the teacher they have. But if there's one more Papist scholar than Presbyterian then the Papists are pesterin' the education for their own teacher an' the Presbyterians are just as bad if it's the other way round.'

'I'm not surprised the women on that island spend most of their time havin' babies,' observed Angy.

'I believe once there was a teacher there that didn't want to leave the place an' she took a hand in it herself,' Murdoch said.

'It must be a sort of competition,' submitted the shepherd.

'It sounds more like a production drive to me,' said Angy.

Throughout the evening the door had been opening and closing as more people entered the room and insinuated themselves into the company. Now Tearlaich burst in, full of confidence and wearing a town raincoat and a trilby hat.

'Were you away!' exclaimed Janet, eyeing his clothes.

'Aye.' Tearlaich returned her glance with mock surprise. 'Did you not know I got a lift from the carrier when he was over with Donny Beag's fencing? I've been to the mainland,' he added.

Except for me probably everyone in the village knew of Tearlaich's journey. What they didn't know was how he had spent his time between then and now.

'Where did you go?' asked Morag, who reasoned that if people did not wish to be asked questions as to their whereabouts or their activities they would take care that nothing they said or did invited them. Tearlaich's attire alone positively cried out for comment.

'I went over to the mainland,' he repeated. 'The carrier was telling me there was to be a big roup on next week so seeing the train was there I got on it an' went to have a look.'

'A roup?' asked Behag with sudden interest.

'Aye, all the furniture and stuff from some old castle,' replied Tearlaich. 'I believe they're going to auction the whole lot of it and the carrier reckons some will go pretty cheap if it's true what he's hearing.'

'Did you get to see any of it?' asked Murdoch.

'Aye, that's why I went.'

'What would you be after wantin' with furniture from a castle?' demanded Morag.

'I'm wantin' a new bed,' returned Tearlaich and smiled at the evident surprise his statement caused.

'The bed you have was good enough for your father,' Murdoch declared. 'Why would it not be good enough for you?'

'It's no' me I'm thinking about,' said Tearlaich. 'But

what if I was to take home a wife some day?' He spoke of
the possibility of taking home a wife someday as if he might
bid for her too at the auction sale. 'I wouldn't want her to
sleep in the bed I have,' he resumed. 'She'd be as well
sleeping on a dyke.'

'If you took home a wife she wouldn't get much chance to
sleep anyway,' Murdoch told him and Tearlaich looked
boldly across at Trina who blushed and shook her long
hair over her face.

'An' did you see any beds?' enquired Morag.

'Hundreds of them,' answered Tearlaich. 'Honest! You
could have slept an army in that castle with the number of
beds they had.'

'They possibly did,' I murmured.

'There was one bed though that I couldn't make out at
all.' He turned to me. 'Maybe Miss Peckwitt knows more
about funny beds than us and she can tell us.'

'Why should I know about funny beds?' I parried.

Tearlaich went on. 'This bed was about seven feet long
and about eight feet wide and it had two mattresses on it.
One was about five feet wide and the other near enough to
three feet. Now why would they have two mattresses on
the same bed like that?'

I tried to think of a suitable reason. 'It could be because
a single mattress eight foot by seven foot would be difficult
to turn regularly,' I hazarded.

'But wouldn't they have the two mattresses the same size
then?' suggested Tearlaich.

'That's what I should have thought,' I agreed. 'No, I
can't think of a good reason for their being two like that,'
I added.

For the first time that evening Janet's brother spoke.
'I've seen one of those beds an' I can tell you the reason for

it,' he offered. We looked at him expectantly. 'You mind Dolina across on Rhuna there?' He jerked a thumb towards the seaward wall of the kitchen. 'Now if Mata had a bed like that the three of them would be able to sleep together, the sister in her part of the bed an' Mata an' Dolina in their part. Well, that was the way of it in some of these big castles, only it wasn't the sister that slept with the couple, it was the old mother just so she wouldn't be lonely.'

'Is that true?' asked Janet.

'It's what I was told long ago, that's what they did. You see, they had their separate bedclothes so it wasn't as if they were really sharin' a bed.'

'That was a funny way of doing things,' said Tearlaich.

Old Murdoch took out his pipe. 'Indeed they do funnier things than that in some of these old castles,' he stated profoundly and returned his pipe to his mouth.

'Was there anything interesting at the auction?' I asked, turning to Tearlaich.

'Hundreds of things,' he enthused. 'Furniture and rugs and musical instruments and pails and dishes and bowls, indeed every sort of thing you could mention.'

'A piano?' I asked.

'Aye, two of them at least. Why, were you wanting a piano?'

I was about to tell him that I very much wanted a piano when the door was slammed back against the wall and Hector and Erchy came in.

'Well, here's the undertakers,' announced Tearlaich.

Erchy ignored him. 'We're wantin' somebody to give us a hand with the dinghy up the shore,' he announced. 'The wireless says it's goin' to blow a gale by mornin'.'

'What wireless?' asked Murdoch indignantly. 'That's not

what the wireless at the Post Office said. Force four to five, they said, an' makin' southerly.'

'It doesn't agree with what we've just heard, then,' Erchy told him. 'Force six to gale eight an' veerin' westerly.' He turned to Hector. 'Is that not right, Hector?'

'Aye,' Hector agreed.

'Ach, you cannot expect wirelesses to agree all the time any more than people,' observed Morag soothingly.

Janet's brother got up and going over to the barometer rapped it imperiously. 'The glass is droppin',' he reported.

'Well you don't need to pull your dinghy just yet,' Janet told Erchy. 'Sit you down an' tell us how your trip went.'

'Oh God!' said Erchy and sat down on the floor as if the request had sapped what strength he had left. Hector smiled at the young schoolteacher and she made room for him beside her.

'Knowin' that family I daresay you got a good dram out of it,' said Murdoch.

'Not a dram did we get,' said Erchy. 'Not so much as a look at a bottle of whisky except for what we had with us in the boat.'

'Oh my!' Murdoch was staggered.

'An' the state of that corpse,' grumbled Erchy. 'We needed a barrel of whisky never mind a bottle.' He sighed. 'I'm damty sick of funerals,' he said.

'What happened?' asked Janet curiously.

'Well, we got to the pier,' began Erchy, 'an' there was the coffin ready for loadin' but when we went to get it aboard we was near sick with the smell of him. He'd been coffined in one of these foreign places an' they hadn't done it properly so he'd gone rotten. The men on the pier agreed with us that nobody was goin' to carry it aboard like a coffin should be by rights. "Get the derrick," they told us.

So we went to see the man with the crane an' asked him would he load it on board for us. "I'm not supposed to lift coffins with the crane," he says. "Coffins are supposed to be treated with respect." "Well, we're no' carryin' him," says I. "He's too rotten." Anyway, the crane fastens on to him an' hoists up the coffin an' one of the pier men shouts to the crane driver, "Hey, Ronny, don't tilt him now or he'll spill out." '

'Oh here !' murmured Janet with a shudder.

'That's what they said. An' we had to put the bloody coffin on the stern so that the smell would blow away from us. Ach, it was terrible !' He gave a snort of disgust.

'An' did none of the man's friends come along with the coffin ?' asked Morag.

'Aye, three of them,' replied Erchy. 'But they had a good drink on them before they came aboard an' they just lay down an' slept all the way.'

'An' what happened when you got to the island ?' pursued Janet. 'Did you have to carry the coffin then ?'

'We did not,' said Erchy. 'Ach, there was seven or eight folks waitin' there an' with the three we had there was plenty.'

'Was there no priest ?'

'Aye, he was down too, fussin' around like a hen on a hot girdle, an' before they'd lift the coffin off the boat he took them all up to the chapel with him. They was there about half an hour an' they all came back wipin' their mouths an' smellin' of whisky.'

'An' you didn't get a dram yourselves ?' interrupted Murdoch.

'None but the smell of theirs,' reiterated Erchy. 'Maybe if we'd followed them up to their chapel we would have got one but there's some things you can't do even for whisky.'

He looked around the company, confident of their approbation.

' "Men meet but the hills do not",' quoted Murdoch.

'So they unloaded the coffin themselves,' prompted Janet.

'They did so. An' there was the priest wavin' his hands an' tellin' them, "Be careful boys, now," and "Gently, boys," an' them afraid would they jolt it an' have the priest swearin' at them for bein' careless.' He looked across at Hector. 'Was that not the way of it?' he asked.

Hector looked up and smiled wide-eyed confirmation. 'Indeed it was so,' he said. 'Tsey took tsat much care carryin' it ashore you'd think it was a case of whisky tsey was handlin', not a coffin.'

'Angy was sayin' you had to stay the night before you could get your money,' Morag said.

'Aye.'

'That was no' right,' said Morag. 'When a job has been done a man shouldn't have to wait to be paid for it.'

'Why was that?' asked Tearlaich. 'They'd agreed to pay what you'd asked, hadn't they?'

'They had, but when it came to actually handin' over the money they started sayin' it was too much.'

'Ach!' sneered Murdoch. 'Gettin' money out of them Papists is like gettin' butter out of a dog's throat.'

'But you got it in the end?' enquired Angy.

'We got it. An' we told them they was lucky we didn't charge them extra for the smell.'

There came a sudden puff of smoke down the chimney. Erchy stood up. 'We'd best away an' pull that dinghy,' he said. 'That's the wind on its way already.' He went out, followed by all the younger men.

'I must go too,' I told Janet. Behag followed me to the

door and we stepped out into a moonlit night with no trace of mist.

'I would like fine to go to the roup,' she confided wistfully.

'Why not go then?' I asked, avoiding her glance.

'Would you be thinkin' of goin' yourself?' she enquired diffidently. 'I hate travellin' on my own.'

When Tearlaich had mentioned the pianos at the sale the idea of going to the auction had indeed crossed my mind but it was immediately followed by the thought of haymaking, the arrangements I should have to make before I could leave my cow and poultry and by a mental review of the difficulty of getting a piano over to Bruach and eventually into my cottage. Much as I yearned for a piano I had let the idea slip away into the limbo of all the other ideas I had at times become enraptured with, but Behag's remark made me think again. Perhaps I could arrange to get to the roup and perhaps I could even bring a piano back with me. 'I'll let you know tomorrow,' I told her as we said good night.

The sky was clear, wiped clean by wind, and I walked thoughtfully homewards, almost hearing the notes of a Chopin nocturne and aware that my fingers ached to run over the keys of a piano. On reaching my cottage I stood looking up at the full moon tossed in the branches of the rowan tree and the evening star blinking over the hills, and worked out how long I could spare away from the croft and who would look after Bonny and the hens whilst I was away. Morag would, I was certain, but with Behag away also would it be too much for her to cope with? I went to bed and slept on my project. No doubt it would sort itself out by the morning.

Going to the Roup

By morning the forecast gale was strafing the village, flattening the uncut grass, tearing at the windows and bombarding the hay already cocked and rough-tied with grass ropes. As soon as I woke I rushed outside to inspect the damage to my own cocks and was agreeably surprised to find that only three out of the nine I had so industriously

stooked and tied two days earlier had been ravaged by the
wind. I blessed the mist and rain of the previous day which
had dampened down the outside of the cocks so that they
had settled into snug igloo shapes, trimmed to resist the as-
sault of the gale. As I gathered up the hay which the wind
had peeled off and slid into the lee of the damaged cocks
I had cause to be grateful once again to Morag for her
instructions on how to weave the traditional hay ropes which
undoubtedly had been responsible for saving much of my
hay. The hay rope was a simple but effective device for se-
curing cocks and it was achieved by gathering strands of
grass from the top on the windward side of the cock, twist-
ing them and at the same time drawing in more hay as you
worked downwards until with a final twist you tucked the
rope in firmly under the base of the cock, being careful
that you did not let the wind in so that the whole thing
blew away. Then you did the same on the lee side. I repaired
the three cocks, tucked in the ropes on the other six more
firmly and started back towards the cottage. The sea was
swirling white, the horizon a jumble of watery peaks, but
although the crofts were being lashed by sea spray there
was no rain. I recited to myself the weather lore I had
learned in rhyme:

> 'If the wind before the rain,
> Hoist your topsails up again',

which, so the old sailors explained, meant that it would
probably be a short blow with the rain coming in later to
quell the wind. On the other hand:

> 'If the rain before the wind,
> Your topsail halyards you must mind',

which again being interpreted meant the wind would be

strong enough to drive away any threatened rain. In other words, it foretold a long, strong blow. I looked up at the thick grey clouds racing across the sky, unsure whether or not I hoped they would soon burst. If they did it would probably result in there being constant rain for the next few days which would not improve the hay but if they did not and the wind continued unabated I doubted if my cocks would withstand its onslaught. Haymaking was always a worry and because of the malicious weather and the dishevelled terrain it was a worry that lasted a long time. Though cutting might be commenced at the end of July even in a good season it was likely to be well into October before the hay was finally stacked for the winter. I debated whether to take proper ropes and stones to tie and weight down the cocks but if I did that and the rain came the weighted ropes would make neat channels in the hay which would direct the rain deep into the cock, sending it mouldy and rotten. Back at my cottage, I stood in front of my barometer. It had dropped but not dramatically and when I tapped it the needle stayed steady. I decided to do nothing more about my hay until I had talked to some of my neighbours and listened to their predictions.

The rain came when I was out on the moor looking for Bonny. While I milked her the rain dribbled from her flanks and from the sleeves of my oilskin into the pail so that the milk took on a muddy-greyish look. I smiled to myself, recalling how horrified I would have been in my pre-Bruach days had I been expected to drink milk produced under such conditions. Now I knew that dribble from cows' flanks, oilskins and even from less salutary sources made no noticeable difference to the flavour of the milk and so far as hygiene was concerned I preferred fresh Highland germs to those that could be expected in the vicinity of a town or factory dairy. I gave Bonny the remainder of her potach, thanked her and sent her away with a gesture—she was too wet to pat—and turned into the wind and rain, making for home. Even with the lid tightly clamped down the milk splashed out as the wind buffeted the pail, lifting it and at times almost wresting it from my grasp; the rain was drumming on my sou'wester, streaming down my oilskin and running into my boots. It was stinging my face and filling my eyes so that I was constantly blinking to see where I was going and when, after taking advantage of the shelter offered by a narrow strath between two outcrops of rock, I came out again into the teeth of the storm the wind spun me round, whisking away my breath and making me feel like a chattel of the storm, seeing nothing but rain; no sea, no sky, with only occasional glimpses of the moors to help me find my way home.

After lunch I started to make bread and teacakes and the kitchen was full of the yeasty, floury smell of bread baking when the door banged open to admit Morag. She pushed the door closed with a practised shoulder and let down the latch.

'My, but it's a coarse wind you catch here,' she informed me as she slid out of the top layer of coats she was wearing. 'I thought my own house was the bad one for the wind but I'm thinkin' your own is worse.'

'It depends on the direction,' I reminded her. 'Yours gets the north-easterly pretty badly but this one is the wind I'm most exposed to. It has one advantage, though.' I nodded at the wire tray where the bread was cooling. 'My oven is always much hotter when the wind is from this direction.'

'Aye, an' you make good use of it, mo ghaoil. Indeed, there's nobody like the English for bakin' in an oven,' she told me.

I split and buttered some teacakes and we ate them while they were warm and doughy and swimming in butter. Morag was just helping herself to her third piece when the door opened again but with more violence this time and Erchy came in.

'I was just down seein' if there was anythin' worth while comin' ashore,' he announced in reply to our enquiring looks. 'We got a letter a night or two ago from my cousin that's workin' on a timber boat. He reckoned they'd be passin' through the channel out there yesterday an' he always tries to throw some good planks over the side thinkin' they might wash ashore here.'

Bruach had its share of beachcombers, ranging from the regulars who went daily to search for anything that might conceivably be of use, to the dilettantes like myself who went only when the weather was fine enough, but during gales when the men of the village could find little else to do they rushed down to appropriate for themselves stretches of shore, just as fishermen select stretches of a river, and there they crouched in the indifferent protection of a boulder, straining to be the first to spot any loot the sea might bring in. The most dedicated—some said the greediest—stayed out all night, the rest stayed for perhaps four or five hours before they gave in and returned to their own or someone else's home where they could be sure of a hot drink and a bite to eat.

'An' did you get anythin' for your trouble?' asked Morag.

'Only a couple of trawl bobbins an' a few fish boxes,' confessed Erchy. 'But there's time enough. Maybe I'll get down in the mornin' at first light an' get a hold of somethin' good.'

'You didn't by any chance get any of those glass net

floats?' I asked. I was collecting the coloured glass floats to edge a border in my flower garden.

'Aye, I got two,' Erchy replied. 'They're outside.' He eyed the teacakes. 'You'll get them for a couple of those scones you have there.'

I laughed and started to split and butter more teacakes.

'Eating them hot like this is probably going to give you terrible indigestion,' I warned. 'But I don't suppose that will put you off, will it?'

He winked. 'Indeed I wouldn't be put off supposin' you told me they'd give me the terrible plague,' he assured me and clamping the two halves together he disposed of the first teacake in two bites. I continued splitting and buttering.

'I hear you're away to the roup next week,' he observed, halfway through his second teacake.

'Am I?' I asked.

'Behag's expectin' you to go,' put in Morag. 'She's after makin' all her plans.'

'I didn't say I'd go,' I repudiated and chided myself for having forgotten that in Bruach anything less than an emphatic refusal was taken as acquiescence. 'I don't know if I can get away,' I went on. 'I've still to find someone to see to Bonny and the hens and with the day being so wild and wet I haven't got round to asking anyone yet.'

'An' do you need to ask?' Morag reproached me. 'Can I no' see to your cow for you the same as I have many a time before now.'

'But Behag will be away too,' I reminded her 'Otherwise I should have come straight to you.'

'An' when would Behag be any use milkin' a cow?' she demanded scornfully.

'I was just thinking of all the extra work for you,' I pointed out.

'But isn't my cousin comin' tomorrow on the bus to stay with me from Glasgow,' she told me.

'Which one's that?' asked Erchy.

'The one that was in hospital a while back,' replied Morag.

'Is she better, then?'

'She's better,' acknowledged Morag. 'Though I believe they were still givin' her egyptians for the pain for a week or two after she came out.'

'Well, she's not going to be of any help to you, is she?' I argued. 'Surely having a convalescent on your hands is going to make even more work for you?'

'Not at all,' denied Morag. 'She can see to the boilin' of the potatoes an' she can feed the hens an' she'll be glad to do it.'

'But if she's not well,' I began.

'Indeed there's nothin' wrong with her at all,' refuted Morag, who, possibly because of her experience with Hector, was disinclined to believe reports of ill health from any other of her relatives. 'Nothin' that a month or two in Bruach won't cure.' She put down her empty cup. 'I'll milk your cow for you an' willingly,' she repeated. 'An' seein' my own cow's startin' to go dry I'll be well pleased to get the extra milk for a whiley.'

I thanked her and pointed out that I still had to get some-one to come and feed my poultry. Even had Morag offered I could not have allowed her to take on this extra task. The milking was not so demanding since she would be going out to the moors to milk her own cow but feeding the hens would entail her coming down to my croft in the early morning and again in the evening.

Erchy said: 'I'd feed your hens for you if I'm about but if the weather clears I'll be at the lobsters the best part of the day.' He looked slightly distressed. 'I couldn't promise,' he added.

'If the weather clears I ought not to be away from home anyway,' I told him. 'Not with all that hay out in cocks.'

'They're sayin' this rain's on for a week or more,' asserted Morag. 'They're expectin' the wind to drop shortly but without the wind they say there'll be nothin' but rain an' mist an' rain again till the moon changes an' that's ten days away yet.'

'They' were the elders of the village. The pipe-smoking, pontificating old men whose weather predictions were at least as reliable as more official ones.

'That's some consolation, anyway,' I said. 'I shan't feel too guilty about the hay.'

'There's no need to feel guilty about anythin',' comforted Morag. 'Sheena was sayin' she'd be pleased enough to come an' feed your hens for you if she'd get the eggs. She has her brother an' his family with her an' she's girnin' that they swallow eggs as fast as gulls swallow fish guts.'

'That's splendid!' I said. 'My hens are laying well just now so I shan't be ashamed to go and ask her.'

'I don't believe there's any need to ask her,' Morag informed me. 'I believe she's made up her mind to it already.' She got up and started to put on her coat. 'Will I tell Behag you'll be goin', then?' she asked, adding in a lower voice, 'If the Lord spares you.'

'Yes,' I replied. 'I'll be going.'

As soon as word got around that Behag and I were going to drive in my car to the roup first Tearlaich and then Angy announced they would be bestowing their company on us.

'There won't be much room,' I told them. 'And it's a long drive.'

'Ach, we'd sooner be uncomfortable than lonely,' they replied and so it was arranged we should all cram into 'Joanna' and leave first thing on the following Tuesday morning.

As the old men had forecast the rain had continued and though the wind had dropped it was still harrying the sea enough to throw clouds of spray over the ferry as we crossed to the mainland. It poured over the car roof and coursed down the windscreen.

'If we'd gone by train, now, we wouldn't have the car to give us shelter,' Behag commented, indicating the two or three foot passengers who were seeking shelter behind the car.

'Poor things,' I said. 'I hope they're not going on the train. If they are they'll stay wet until lunchtime at least.'

'Ach, they won't mind,' retorted Tearlaich. 'On this ferry they don't take your fare if you get wet.'

We bounced off the ferry, up the mainland slip and drove for a couple of hours without seeing another moving thing. Occasionally we glimpsed a burn in spate tumbling and foaming under the bridge over which we were driving; occasionally there was a straggle of stunted trees, occasionally a dwelling of some sort but most of the time the rain enclosed us, taxing the efficiency of the windscreen-wipers. The car grew so stuffy that Behag had continually to wipe the windscreen clear of mist.

'Anyone know where we might get a bite to eat?' I asked.

Tearlaich responded immediately. 'I know a hotel not far from here. I used to know one of the waitresses.' There could hardly have been a hotel in the whole of the Highlands where Tearlaich did not claim to know one of the waitresses, and admittedly his knowledge appeared to serve him well. He frequently told tales of how he had got himself stranded

at various times, 'and if it hadn't been for this waitress I
knew I would have had to spend the night out on the hill
and without a bite to eat'.

'It's a wonder these waitresses don't get into trouble sometimes the way they look after you,' observed Behag and
added hurriedly, 'I mean, from their bosses.'

'Ach, I'm always away before the bosses appear in the
morning,' replied Tearlaich. 'Except for once when I had
to sleep under the table in the kitchen.'

'How was that?' asked Angy.

'This hotel had gone kind of swanky and they'd got in one
of these foreigners to manage it. Well, he comes down in the
night to get something from the kitchen an' he finds me
there . . .'

'By yourself?' interrupted Angy incredulously.

'I was by that time,' acknowledged Tearlaich with a wink.
'Anyway,' he continued, 'in this fellow comes. "You get
out!" he orders, only his language was a lot worse than that
and when I didn't offer to get out he started screaming at
me : "Bugger off, you." "Take it easy," I told him. "I'm
doin' nobody any harm here and I'll be away at first light."
But no, he wasn't going to have me stay and he went off
out of the kitchen swearin' to bring down the owner to turn
me out. Well, I knew the owner had no reason to like me seeing he was a Campbell and me a MacDonald so I got out.'
He chortled. 'All the same, I got my own back on that
foreigner fellow, I can tell you.'

'How?' I asked.

'Well, d'you see there was this big pan of porridge at
the side of the stove all ready for warming up for the
guests' breakfasts and the other side of the stove there was a
big baking dish full of raw eggs all taken from their shells
and set ready to go straight into the oven. I lifted the tray of

eggs and tipped half of them into the pan of porridge and
stirred it all up so that it looked O.K. Then I buggered off
like I was told to.'

'It must have been damty queer porridge they got for
their breakfasts,' said Angy.

'Did you ever hear what happened?' Behag asked.

'No, I never did. Ach, I knew fine I'd best not go back
that way again for a while so I didn't think about the
waitress any more.'

'Whereabouts was this hotel?' I enquired.

'Well, now,' said Tearlaich, 'it'll be only just about a
mile along the road now. Like I was sayin', I know this
waitress so if she's still there she'll see we get a good
meal.'

'Tearlaich!' I exclaimed. 'Do you mean you're taking us
to the hotel where you spoiled the porridge?' In the mirror
I saw his uncontrite expression. 'Oh, no,' I told him. 'I'm
not going there in your company.'

'Ach, it's all right now,' he soothed. 'I know for a fact
the foreigner's been gone over a year so I don't need to bother
any more.'

'Isn't there anywhere else we can get a meal?' I pleaded.

'Not that I know of,' returned Tearlaich. 'Not for
another ten miles anyway.' He rustled a paper bag. 'Here,
take a mint,' he invited. 'It'll stop you getting indigestion.'

'Tearlaich's a right joker,' enthused Angy when everyone was steadily sucking.

'Indeed if it's jokers we're speaking of then there's the
biggest one of them sitting right beside me at this minute,'
retaliated Tearlaich.

'Angy?' asked Behag.

'Aye. Why only the week before he came back to Bruach

didn't he and his pals kidnap a bride and groom the night before they was to get married.'

'That's not so unusual,' I reminded Tearlaich. I had heard of bawdy escapades sometimes taking place the night before a weddding though I had never been aware of such a happening in Bruach.

'No, but this was one of the best,' Tearlaich continued fervently. 'They got a hold of this lorry and an old lavatory from the builder's yard and they stuck this lavatory on the lorry and tied the bride sitting down on it with a po on her head. Then they drove round and round the place till folks was near sick with laughing.'

'Oh, my,' commented Behag.

'We got the groom, too, don't forget,' Angy reminded him.

'Aye, so they did and seeing they was friendly with one or two of the night nurses up at the hospital they carted him up there, tied him down on the table and gave him an enema.'

'Really !' I was horrified.

'Honest to God, they did,' averred Tearlaich. He turned to Angy. 'I believe the groom wasn't too pleased about it, was he?'

'I should think not,' I told him.

'Aye, well it wasn't so much what we did to him he minded but he was wearin' his weddin' trousers when we got a hold of him an' they got a bit torn.' Angy explained. 'He said we was to get him a new pair but ach! where would we get new trousers till the tinkers come round?'

'You certainly carry your jokes to the limit,' I remarked.

'The limit indeed,' confirmed Tearlaich. 'He's lucky he hasn't been banned from one or two of the pubs on the mainland for some of the tricks he's got up to.'

'Such as . . .' I encouraged.

'Such as,' he began, winding down his window to throw out a cigarette butt. A small wedge of coolness probed down the back of my neck before the window was closed again tightly. 'By God! There's still some rain out there,' he observed superfluously.

'You were going to tell us about another of Angy's tricks,' I reminded him.

'Aye, well there was the moocher, wasn't there, Angy?'

'Oh, him,' muttered Angy with a show of reticence. 'He deserved all he got.'

'What happened to him?' I enquired.

'D'you know what a "moocher" is, for a start?' asked Tearlaich.

'I've always taken it to be a lazy, good-for-nothing sort of fellow,' I answered.

'No, well to us a "moocher" is one of them fellows that if you leave your drink for a minute in the pub he nips in while your back's turned and drains the glass. That's right, isn't it, Angy?'

Angy's smiling face was reflected in the driving mirror. 'So Angy decides to teach him a lesson,' resumed Tearlaich. 'And he goes to the chemist's and buys a box of worm pills.'

'For dogs?' interrupted Angy.

'Aye, for dogs,' agreed Tearlaich. 'Now go on,' he urged Angy. 'Tell her yourself what you did.'

Angy took up the story. 'The instructions on the box said one pill for small dogs, two for medium and three for large dogs.' He smiled. 'Well, I reckoned the moocher was twice as big as a large dog so the next time he was in the pub before I left my pint of beer I slipped six of the pills into it. Sure enough when I got back my glass was empty and the moocher was gone.'

'Oh, here,' remonstrated Behag. 'It's a wonder you didn't poison the man.'

'Poison, hell!' scoffed Angy. 'No, but he was off work for three weeks afterwards with what the doctor said was a bad dose of dysentery,' he added with deep satisfaction.

'Here's the hotel,' proclaimed Tearlaich as a long low building loomed up out of the rain. I pulled 'Joanna' off the road and we went inside. Like most Highland hotels it was clean and cold and a little intimidating. Tearlaich disappeared muttering something about arranging for food and Angy led us unerringly to a small bar where he first rapped, then thumped and eventually yelled for service. His summons brought a tartan-kilted, sporraned and tweed-jacketed man who gave us a greeting that was as cheerless as the day itself and served us our drinks with an air that conveyed that bar service was not his normal occupation and that we were not the class of customer the hotel normally catered for. Once we had our drinks he disappeared again.

'He's a snooty one,' I commented.

'Snooty?' echoed Angy. 'No, it's not that what's wrong with him. It's just he hasn't learned yet how to behave right. He's learned himself to dress like a toff but it'll take him a long time to learn the rest, for when I first knew him his head was that empty his cap used to rattle when he talked.'

'I was thinkin' I'd seen him before,' said Behag.

'An' so you have,' Angy assured her. 'The last time I saw that man he had a broken-down old fish van takin' seconds kippers round the villages. He wasn't wearin' any of his fancy clothes then, he couldn't afford them, an' his hands was that black with engine grease he left thumbprints on every kipper like they say St Peter left on the haddocks.'

Tearlaich came back looking mightily pleased with himself. 'They say we can take our soup right away if we've a mind,' he informed us.

'I've a mind,' I replied.

'An' so have I,' said Angy, tossing down the last of his drink. 'Lead the way, boy,' he instructed and we followed Tearlaich through to the dining room of which we were the sole occupants.

'Did you see your waitress?' asked Behag as we took our seats.

'Aye, I did. But she's cook now, that's why we're gettin' such big helpings.' Tearlaich regarded with approbation the four deep plates of steaming Scotch broth that were being put before us by a young waitress.

'And did she mention the incident of the porridge?' I probed.

'Only that she didn't hear of any complaints about it,' returned Tearlaich lightly as he tied his table napkin round his neck. 'You'll be seeing her yourself in a whiley. She says she's coming to drink a cup of tea with us when we've finished eating.'

'Is she still keen on you, then?' asked Angy.

'Aye, I believe she is,' replied Tearlaich modestly.

As soon as the young waitress had cleared the table the cook appeared with a large tray of tea and biscuits. Greeting us with great cordiality she sat down and Tearlaich made the introductions.

'Angy,' she repeated when she heard his name. 'Now would it be your father that had the half of the boat with my own Uncle Seamus at one time? Him that had the wooden leg?'

'I believe you're right,' agreed Angy. 'I mind my father

speakin' of workin' with somebody that had a wooden leg.'

'I could see the likeness,' the cook complimented herself smugly. 'An', Behag,' she went on, 'Tearlaich was sayin' you married Hector that was Morag McDugan's sister's boy?'

Behag smiled and nodded confirmation.

'An' they were sisters to deaf Ruari, were they not? Him that was workin' for a time over on the mainland along with that fellow that was always threatenin' to commit suicide by stranglin' himself with his own hands an' then only died of the measles.'

The trace of mockery in the cook's voice kindled brief smiles from the two men but appeared to disconcert the gentle Behag who stared mournfully down at her tea. I was accustomed now to the knowledge that wherever Bruachites went they invariably discovered family connexions that had to be enthusiastically researched and confirmed and as always I soon began to feel excluded. My attention wandered to the innumerable stags' heads that made a melancholy frieze around the room; the stuffed wild cat and the various fish in their glass cases. When the second pot of tea had been disposed of I made a move to go and after some hesitation and a good deal of whispering and chaffing between Tearlaich and the cook we were back again in 'Joanna' with the rain still falling relentlessly.

At the hotel where Behag and I had booked for the night we parted company with Angy and Tearlaich. They, again on the principle that they would sooner be uncomfortable than lonely, proposed to call on a relative of Angy's who, they felt sure, would insist on offering them a shakedown for the night.

'See you at the roup,' they called.

'See you at the roup,' we replied, though with such a selection of pubs to visit I doubted if either of them would recollect the ostensible purpose of their trip. 'And if you're not here by three o'clock tomorrow we go without you,' I threatened.

'I believe the bitch would, too,' I overheard Angy murmur to Tearlaich.

'What shall we do with ourselves tonight?' I enquired of Behag. 'The shops are closed but we could go to the pictures.'

'Would you mind if we took a look round the shop windows first,' Behag asked. 'It seems so long since I could look at things that weren't just drawings in a catalogue.'

'Of course,' I told her, and was glad she had suggested it.

To dawdle round town streets in the pouring rain looking in the windows of closed shops does not seem such a crazy thing to do when like Behag and me your eyes have for years lit on no more an enticing display of merchandise than the confusion of biscuits, homespun socks, potmenders and boiled sweets in the grocer's window or the welter of garments in the bundles carried by the tinkers. It was more than three years since either of us had seen a real shop and we were perfectly happy, in our town wear of brogues, burberries and sou'-westers, touring the quiet, dripping streets. When Behag declared she was satisfied we had a meal in the cinema restaurant before taking our seats in the auditorium.

'How long is it since you was at the fillums?' asked Behag.

'Oh, seven years at least,' I replied after a moment's thought.

'It's ten or more since I was there,' said Behag. 'I'm lookin' forward to it more than I can say.'

'I believe I am too,' I confessed.

We settled ourselves in our seats with a box of chocolates I had bought to celebrate the occasion and as the lights dimmed I remembered the excitement that moment always used to bring. But then the music started. Behag and I turned to each other aghast at the volume of the noise. We put our hands over our ears until the cartoons came on and the music was suppressed by other sound effects. The big film began. I believe it had what is generally decribed as a star-studded cast but I found every one of them lifeless and tedious. After the lilting Gaelic voices I had grown so used to they appeared to speak without inflexion and almost without moving their lips. The significant pauses while one character looked deep into another's eyes were so dragged out that I found myself tapping my foot with impatience. I looked at Behag to note her reaction and saw she was fast asleep. After enduring for another half-hour I was cramped and hot and utterly bored and Behag still slept soundly. I prodded her.

'Let's go,' I suggested. 'You're obviously tired and I'm bored and this blessed thing is going to continue for a couple of hours yet.'

She made no objection. 'I saw what happened in the beginning,' she confided as we were walking back to the hotel. 'But I wonder what happens at the end?'

'I don't know or care,' I replied. 'But I do know if I'd had to sit there much longer and watch close-ups of sweaty faces it would have spoiled my appetite for these chocolates and I'm damned if I'm going to let that happen.'

Back in the hotel she said, 'It's funny, I used to like the fillums but now I seem as if can't take to them at all.' She yawned. 'I think that's what sent me to sleep, it all bein' so slow.'

'Slow!' I exclaimed. 'Why, they even sweated in slow motion.' I proffered the box of chocolates. 'I'm always hearing that life is lived at a much faster pace nowadays than it was even ten years ago but from what I've seen to-night I'd say the film producers haven't noticed it.'

In bed with the light out I lay and listened to the noises of the town and thought of life in Bruach and how slow that always seemed and I realised suddenly how quick and how constantly alert one's mind had to be compared with people in town. Admittedly in town one had to keep a good look-out to avoid traffic or bumping into other people but at least that look-out was, or should be, reciprocal. In Bruach the sole responsibility for evading hazards was on oneself and no one else. We had to watch where we walked in case a foot went into a rabbit hole or a bog; we had to spot which clumps of heather would brush out of one's path and which would tangle one's foot and cause a fall; we noted cracks in hill paths that could easily become minor landslides; we watched the sky for signs of weather and the tides if we were going out in a boat, and all the time we had to look out to see which way the cattle were working in their search for grass so that we should not waste time when we went to milk or feed them; to watch them for signs of bloat or mastitis and sheep for signs of maggot or footrot or any of the many other ills which afflict them. We noted any gathering of crows which might indicate a carcase or at best a sick animal to be rescued; we plotted the source of smoke in case it was an incipient heather fire, and we kept an eye alert for moor gates left open, fences collapsed, tilting hay or peat stacks; stones among the grass that would blunt the scythe; the tracks of a rat near a potato store; a hen laying away from the nest; a loose stone in a dyke which if not firmly wedged in again could bring down a whole section of the dyke with the next storm or with the rubbing of an animal.

'Ahhhhhh.' From Behag's bed there came a long musical yawn. 'I'd like fine to know what happened in the end,' she murmured sleepily.

Pianissimo

THE hall where the roup was to be held was more full of people than furniture when Behag and I arrived and as we wandered deviously among the damp onlookers we watched prospective buyers bouncing on beds and settling into chairs like visitors at a ceilidh. I caught the sound of a piano and made my way in the direction from which it came, leaving

Behag to admire a bundle of rugs which she was already coveting. A youth was prodding at the jaundiced keys of an old upright piano and I waited for him to tire of his play before I ventured with similar inexpertise to try them for myself. The notes sounded muffled with damp, several were completely dumb but when I wanted to inspect the inside I found I was prevented from doing so by two arthritic old men who had each appropriated an end of the piano and braced himself against it, with folded arms resting determinedly on the lid. I suspected the shock of being asked to move might prove too much for them and I remained standing nearby hoping they would detach themselves before the auctioneer got round to selling it. It appeared that the old men were not remotely interested in the sale.

'Did you try the liniment I gave you for your rheumatics?' one was enquiring of the other.

'Aye, I tried it.'

'Did you rub it on or did you put some in a basin of water an' soak your feet in it like I told you?'

'I did neither.' The voice sounded a little startled. 'I swallowed it.'

'Oh God!' The ejaculation was followed by a brief lull in the conversation and then the questioner began again. 'An' did even that not help your rheumatics at all?' ·

'It did not. Indeed there's nothin' helps my rheumatics save a good prayer of damnin' every mornin'.' The morose reply was followed by a duet of wheezy chuckles.

As Tearlaich had reported there were at least two pianos in the sale I went on searching for others but finding only one, which was a grand and therefore out of the question, I returned to my position near the upright. The old men were still *in situ* but now two women were trying simultaneously to pick out the tune of 'Kathleen Mavourneen' while an attendant male alternately nodded and belched approval.

'Oh God! Bridie!' declared one of the women in indisputably Irish accents. 'I can feel tears comin' with the sound of it.' She touched her eyes with the tips of her fingers.

'Sure, Teresa, aren't I the same myself?' responded the other fervently and in an even stronger brogue. 'I declare the last time I heard it played was in a pub an' I had to rush off to the lavatory I was that affected.'

'With the tears,' suggested Teresa.

'Just that. Rainin' down they were.'

'Ah, you'd be that touched,' sympathised Teresa while Bridie nodded and murmured something about her 'lovely land' and the attendant male belched consolingly.

At that moment the auctioneer appeared and made his way to the desk and after giving us a brief résumé of how he intended to conduct the sale the bidding began for the larger items of furniture. At this juncture I was only mildly interested in the goods being auctioned but I was thoroughly intrigued by the conversation of the old men which continued despite the penetrating voice of the auctioneer, the hammering and the constantly murmured comments.

'Ach, he was a decent kind of man for all that, with a strong look of a minister about him when he was dressed,' one of the old men told his companion.

'An' did they not get the doctor then?'

'They asked him but he didn't come except to help dig the grave.'

This piece of information was followed by some mumbled comments which I could not catch but then the first old man was speaking again. 'He never left no will. He was a man that enjoyed seein' his relatives quarrel when he was alive an' I daresay he wouldn't want to give up his enjoyment when he was dead.'

'Then the lawyers will get the most of it,' concluded the second old man.

The auctioneer's men approached and I realised the piano was about to go up for sale. Mentally I had set a price over which I must not go but when the time came I continued bidding until I had exceeded it by two pounds and the piano became mine. Admittedly I need only have gone thirty shillings above my limit but at the crucial moment the Irish male behind me belched and the auctioneer went up ten shillings. The old men gave me congratulatory nods but still clung to it and I was glad that it would be the carrier and not myself who would have the job of prising it away from them.

Some of the smaller items were now coming up for sale and I bought a set of copper bottles because I liked their shape and an old copper warming pan which I suspected would have to be useful as well as ornamental. Behind me the two Irish women were commenting on how cheap the last jumble of items in the sale were going. A lot comprising a step-ladder, a zinc bath and a sweeping brush was displayed. The auctioneer managed to push the bidding up from one shilling which was the minimum bid he would accept to two shillings.

'Come on,' he urged, 'we don't intend to give things away.' There came a bid of another sixpence and he knocked them down for that amount.

'Mother of God for half a crown!' gasped one of the Irish women, and a few moments later when three bedroom chairs went for the minimum bid there was an ejaculated 'Jesus Christ for a shilling!' In fact the Jesus Christ bid had been my own and I glanced behind me half smiling at the two women. 'You can't lose anything on that,' one of them assured me.

'Well, did you get your piano?' Tearlaich, Angy and Behag had threaded their way through the crowd to my side. The men's breath was swamped with whisky fumes and their eyes were over bright but they showed no other signs of inebriation.

'I did,' I replied. 'And several other things besides. Did you get your bed, Tearlaich?' He nodded affirmation.

'I got this rug.' Behag unrolled the bundled rug she was carrying. 'Will it go in the car to get home, d'you think?' I doubted it.

'I got a mangle,' said Angy.

'A mangle?' echoed Behag in surprise. 'Why would you be wantin' a mangle?'

'Aye, well you see my wife was thinkin' if she could get a bit built on to the house she might start takin' in bed an' breakfasters. Her mother used to do it at one time an' she tells me some of them leave the sheets that clean if you can put them through a mangle you don't need to wash them before you put them back on the beds again.'

At twelve there was a break for lunch so we went to join the queue where we were to pay for our purchases and when that was done we discussed arrangements for getting our goods back to Bruach.

'We'll be best hirin' a lorry,' advised Tearlaich. 'I know a man with a lorry would do it for us and then we wouldn't need to wait on the railway.' It sounded a good idea so after arranging to meet us later for a meal Tearlaich and Angy went off to see the man with the lorry while Behag and I indulged in a modest, and, because it proved to be early closing day, a hurried shopping spree. Behag bought a purse for her small daughter, a milk sieve for Morag and a box of cartridges for Hector as well as a frilly blouse for herself and a variety of cakes and 'teabread'. I bought fruit and vegetables and, after a certain amount of hesitation, succumbed at last to permitting myself the luxury of a new alarm clock. We managed to snatch a quick cup of tea before the small café we chose slammed its doors and with an hour to go before we were to meet the two men we sought refuge from the unceasing rain in a nearby church.

'Oh, it's lovely to be off my feet for a while,' sighed Behag. 'I feel as if I'm wearin' sandstone shoes.'

'Slip them off,' I encouraged.

'Will I?' She looked doubtful. 'What will the minister say if he comes in an' sees me?'

'Town ministers are used to it,' I assured her, 'and anyway you'll hear anyone coming.'

She slipped off her shoes and leaned back in the pew, her eyes closed and a contented smile touching her mouth. I wandered round renewing contact with carved wood and chiselled stone, refreshing my memory of skilled craftsmanship, and contrasting it with the utilitarian artefacts of Bruach with their total lack of ornamentation.

'These kind of churches must cost a terrible lot of money,' Behag said when I too went to sit down.

'Yes, but they're beautiful, aren't they?' I replied.

'Morag doesn't like them,' she told me. 'She says she doesn't get the same feelin' of religion in them as in our own.'

We collected 'Joanna' and drove to the restaurant. 'Now this is the way of it,' Tearlaich explained as we were having our pre-departure meal. 'This fellow says he'll collect the stuff first thing in the mornin' as soon as the sale room's open an' he'll take it across the ferry in his own lorry an' have it at Bruach by tomorrow evenin'.'

'It doesn't sound possible,' I said.

'Aye, it's possible right enough. So long as there's no hitch on the way,' replied Tearlaich.

'There's sure to be a hitch,' Angy put in. 'The road to Bruach's as full of hitches as a herrin' net's full of holes.'

'That's because we have to rely on botchers, half the time,' retorted Tearlaich. 'No, you can take it from me there'll be no hitches this time. This fellow's a professional.'

'Is he going to charge a lot for it?'

Tearlaich told us how much and after dividing the cost among us we agreed that though it seemed a lot we must accept that such speedy delivery naturally cost more than goods coming by train, ferry and carrier. We expressed ourselves content with our bargain.

'Here's to Bruach, with beds, mangles, pianos and rugs,' proclaimed Tearlaich gustily as we set off in 'Joanna'. 'An' I believe the rain's lifting at last.'

'An' not before it's time,' said Angy.

'I've been wet inside an' outside for the past twenty-four hours,' confided Tearlaich, producing a half-bottle of whisky. 'I'm no' wantin' to dry out yet.' He put the bottle to his mouth. 'Are you sure you won't take a wee drop yourself?' he asked Behag and me for the second time. We both shook our heads.

'An' did everybody enjoy the roup, then?' he enquired.

'I enjoyed it fine,' replied Behag. 'It was as good as a ceilidh.'

'I enjoyed it too,' I told him. 'The people around me kept me pretty well entertained and the auctioneer was quite amusing too.'

'That auctioneer!' burst out Angy. 'I couldn't get over

him. God! the way he could keep on speakin' without takin' a breath an' sayin' the same thing over and over again like a bloody corncake. You'd think he'd wear a hole in his tongue.'

'I can tell you why he can do that,' Tearlaich volunteered.

'Did you know him then?' queried Angy.

'I didn't know him but my uncle worked for this auctioneer's father at one time and I mind my uncle saying how the old man used to breed parrots. He said he used to feed the young birds on a porridge made of maize and oatmeal and they turned out such good talkers he started feeding his children on the same stuff. There's not a one of them that's stopped talking since.'

'Is that true?' asked Behag.

'True as I'm here,' affirmed Tearlaich. 'I know because a fellow was with me during the war and he'd married one of the auctioneer's sisters. He said if he hadn't been called up he would have volunteered because he needed to get away from home for some peace and quiet.'

We took our time on the journey home, calling in to take a strupach once again with Tearlaich's friendly cook and by the time we reached the ferry the rain had ceased and a full moon spread light over the dark water. I flashed 'Joanna's' headlights to indicate we wished to cross.

'It's slow enough comin',' complained Angy after we had waited nearly half an hour. He got out of the car and wandered down the pier. A moment or two later he was back and talking to us through the window. 'I'm seein' a great pile of stuff here waitin' to go across on the ferry,' he informed us in a puzzled voice. 'They're part covered with a tarpaulin but they're pretty wet all the same.'

'It's queer they should be here this time of night,' said Tearlaich. 'What sort of things are they?'

'There's a mattress,' began Angy with commendably restrained glee. 'An' some chairs with a rug on them an' somethin' else pretty big.'

'And that could be a piano?' I questioned with mounting dismay.

'It could well be,' admitted Angy.

'Oh God! I'd best go and see what went wrong,' muttered Tearlaich, struggling out of the car and hurrying down the pier. Behag and I followed.

'That's the way of it,' he confirmed when he and Angy had made a more thorough inspection. 'There's a big crate and one or two other things that's not ours but the rest is what we bought ourselves.' He scratched his head. 'That man swore to me . . .'

I cut him short. 'Does that mean it will have to stay there out in the open all night?' I demanded.

'Not if I can help it,' responded Tearlaich. The ferry was now nosing into the pier. 'I'll go and see what they have to say.' He threw the words over his shoulder as he went to meet it. Behag and I went back to the car and waited while Tearlaich, Angy and the two ferrymen lifted the tarpaulin. There seemed to be explanations interspersed with protests, arguments and gestures but eventually the tarpaulin was thrown off and the four men, helped now by two youths who had suddenly appeared out of the darkness, carried the goods down the pier and loaded them on the ferry. At last I was able to drive 'Joanna' aboard.

'There was a message from the lorry man,' Tearlaich disclosed. 'Seemingly just after we'd booked him for our lot he had another customer wanting something delivered here urgent tonight so he rushed off to the sale room, loaded up our stuff and brought the whole lot together to save himself another journey. He couldn't get across the ferry because the tide was out so he had to leave it here.'

'I knew there'd be a hitch,' exulted Angy. 'All the same,' he added, 'it's funny he got past without us seein' him.'

'Unless it was while we was takin' our tea,' suggested Behag and we decided that is when it must have been.

'What's going to happen to the stuff when we get it across?' I asked.

'It can stay in the waiting room,' Tearlaich replied. 'It's all right, I've arranged all that.'

It was much too nice a night to waste it on anger or recrimination even if there had been anyone to be angry with. The surrounding hill peaks were washed with moonlight and tiny drifts of tinselled cloud sailed across the sky. It was so calm that one could see the wash of the ferry like a white arc across the water. Behag and I got out of the car.

'I'll tell you what we should do,' said Tearlaich. 'We should get Miss Peckwitt to give us a tune on her piano.'

'Not here,' I demurred but I knew, and I suspected Tearlaich guessed, how quickly I should comply. I was longing to finger those piano keys.

'Come on!' he urged and calling to Angy bade him drag up the long wooden crate which had come along with our own goods to provide me with a seat.

I played first 'Mairi's Wedding' and Tearlach and Angy started to sing with gusty enthusiasm. When I changed to a reel they pulled Behag into a 'Dashing White Sergeant' and the two youths set each other before leaping into their versions of a Highland Fling. It was a wonderful experience, playing the piano on the open water while the dancers swirled in the moonlight and I enjoyed it so much that I did not know the ferry had cocked a snoot at the island pier and had made three wide circles so as not to

berth until the dancers paused for breath. I stopped playing and got back into 'Joanna' ready to drive her ashore.

'I could have listened all night,' approved one of the
ferrymen as I passed him. 'I fairly enjoyed that.' Parking
'Joanna' I went to stand beside Behag and watch the unloading of the goods. There came the sound of an engine
approaching and a dusty van drove halfway down the pier.
Three men alighted from it.

'Is it the corpse you're wantin'?' one of the ferrymen
called to them.

'Aye, that's what we're here for,' they confirmed.

'What a time to come for a corpse,' I murmured to Behag. 'I suppose that means the ferry will have to go over and
collect it for them?'

'I suppose so,' she assented.

Tearlaich came to stand beside us and I repeated my
question to him. He looked distinctly uncomfortable. 'Well,
y'see, Miss Peckwitt, it's like this.' He rubbed a self-conscious
hand over his chin and with horrid suspicion I followed his
glance to where the long wooden crate waited on the otherwise empty ferry.

'Tearlaich!' I almost choked. 'You surely didn't . . .?'

'I reckon I'd best go and give them a hand,' he said and
hurried to join Angy and the three men from the van. I
watched, horrified, as they lifted my erstwhile piano stool,
carried it off the ferry, past us and up the pier where, not
ungently, they loaded it into the waiting van. 'Oh God!' I
whimpered and turned to Behag, intent on denouncing
both Tearlaich and Angy but seeing her anxious expression I went silently back to the car. She slipped in beside
me and I believe had I been able to decide at that moment whether I was more angry than shocked I should
have driven off and left the two men to find their own way

back to Bruach. As it was I waited until they were in their seats.

'Did you know that was a coffin you got me to sit on?' I taxed them.

'Surely we did,' admitted Tearlaich. 'But it wouldn't have given way. It was in a good strong box.'

'You shouldn't have let her do it,' Behag rebuked them. 'Women doesn't take to corpses the same as men. You've upset her.'

'She's easy upset then,' Tearlaich returned impenitently, but he subsided temporarily and we drove for perhaps two miles before he spoke again. 'I'll have a bit of money to give back to you for the lorry,' he said in an attempt at appeasement. 'Seein' we shared the load with a corpse it's goin' to work out a good bit cheaper for us.'

'Oh, shut up about corpses!' I snapped at him.

I heard the sound of a cork being pulled from a bottle. 'I thought you'd be pleased to hear it,' he defended himself.

The carrier delivered my piano and chairs in the late afternoon of the following day, the unpredecentedly quick delivery, so the carrier informed me, being due to the complaints of prospective passengers that they could not get into the ferry waiting room.

'I'll have to go and ask for some help to unload it,' I observed.

'Ach, there's plenty on the way,' he replied. 'They're expectin' you to have a good ceilidh tonight so they'll get finished before they come down.'

'What about you?' I asked.

'Me? I'm waitin' on the ceilidh too.' He took a quick strupach before going to 'look up the lads,' leaving the piano on the lorry parked in front of the cottage. It was about nine and quite dark before anyone arrived to unload and when I went outside with a lantern it seemed to me as if every able-bodied man, woman and child in the village had come to help, impede, encourage or advise. However, the piano defied all attempts to manœuvre it into my cottage.

'You'll need to higher this door or move one of the stairs,' Erchy reported.

'Then it will just have to go into the barn,' I said sadly, thinking how cold I and my piano were going to be together.

My decision was greeted by something like a cheer. 'All the better,' they assured me. 'We can have a better ceilidh in there than in the cottage.'

'I'm afraid the mice will be making their own ceilidh house in it,' I told them.

'An' there's plenty of room for them too inside it, I'm thinkin',' replied Erchy insensitively.

Once it was in position in the barn about six pairs of hands were punching at the keys and an equal number of feet trying to thump the pedals.

'Give us a tune,' they demanded and to save my piano from complete destruction I agreed immediately. Erchy brought a chair over from the house. 'Seein' you'll be here for the rest of the night you may as well be comfortable,' he told me. I realised the ceilidh had begun. The roadman brought along his melodeon; the postman brought his mouth-organ. The young people danced and the elderly watched and gossiped. The barn grew warm and the piano seemed to respond to the exuberance of the dancers, for after an hour's playing I detected no dumb notes and the keys were yielding to the touch of my fingers.

'It's a lovely noise your piano's makin',' someone complimented me enthusiastically at one juncture and when I left the barn to go and supervise the making of tea Hector came in to tell me he thought he'd as soon listen to the piano as to the bagpipes which was praise indeed. By half past four many of the older folk had left save for a few who were still bunched together savouring their tea and gossiping; the young were still cavorting around the barn. I finished playing and slewed round in my chair. Behag was coming towards me with yet another cup of tea. She looked at me quizzically. 'You're tired,' she accused as if she had detected a secret.

The Bruachites considered it discourteous to admit to feeling tired whilst they were in company and managed to give the impression of being fresh and alert until they quite literally keeled over with exhaustion. I was well aware of my own infringement of protocol when I agreed ruefully that I was very tired indeed. It had been a long and heavy day following directly upon the excitement of the journey and I was aching for my bed.

Behag turned to Janet. 'I'm thinkin' it's time we was away to our beds. Miss Peckwitt says she's tired.'

'Oh yes, indeed,' agreed Janet with instant sympathy. She raised her voice. 'Come away home now, everybody. We're keepin' Miss Peckwitt from her bed.'

The dancers turned to me with looks of consternation. 'She cannot be tired,' Tearlaich denied. 'She's done nothing but sit and play all evening.'

'I am,' I insisted.

'Go to your bed then!' commanded Erchy with a cheeky glint in his eye. 'We'll carry on by ourselves. We still have the melodeon.'

'Here, no indeed,' said Janet, shocked by his rudeness.

'One more dance, then!' shouted the postman, tucking

his mouth-organ into his pocket and pulling me into the centre of the dance floor.

'Last dance!' called Erchy authoritatively. 'Eightsome reel, an' keep it goin' till you drop!' he instructed the road-man. The melodeon played on until at last the roadman sat back, his arms dropping at his sides, his head shaking a tired refusal to commands to 'carry on'.

There was a procession to the cottage to retrieve coats and gumboots and then everyone returned to join hands for 'Auld Lang Syne'. I never knew until then that 'Auld Lang Syne' had so many verses but at last it was over and, un-hooking the lantern from the rafter, I followed my friends outside.

'Good night!' I called again and again in response to their receding farewells and, thankful to see the very last guest depart, I secured the gate against trespassing cattle. My mind was already so obsessed with the desire for sleep that there was difficulty in convincing myself of the chores I must attend to before I could give in. I banked up the fire; filled the kettle; wound the alarm clock; put out the kitchen lamp. It was only eight steps now to my bedroom where I could drop my clothes, turn out the lamp and tumble into the blessed sanctuary of my bed.

As I opened the bedroom door I discovered that the last of my guests had not gone. Indeed the last of my guests was wrapped in my eiderdown fast asleep on my bed. I was so cross at being thwarted that the tears came into my eyes.

'Get out of my bed!' I snapped.

The muffled voice of Tearlaich came from the bundle. 'Ach, I was tired.'

'I'm tired too,' I replied, 'and I want to go to bed.'

'So do I, my darlin'.' The response was cheerful. 'I've been wantin' to all evening. Come and cuddle beside me.'

He lifted the eiderdown invitingly and revealed lying beside him a bottle of whisky pushed into one of his boots. The other boot was still on his foot. I had heard of champagne being drunk out of a lady's slipper but whisky out of a boot seemed too preposterous even for Tearlaich. He started muttering in Gaelic and though I could not decide what he was saying his tone sounded distinctly seductive. I gave him a push.

'Everyone else is away home to their beds and you must go too,' I shouted into his ear. 'Your mother will wonder what on earth's happened to you.' It wasn't true, of course. Hospitality in Bruach was such that mothers did not have to wonder where their sons spent the night.

'I'm hellish drunk,' admitted Tearlaich, rolling over.

'I know you are and you'll be downright ashamed of yourself tomorrow. You won't dare to look me in the face for a week.' That would certainly be true. I put down the alarm clock and went downstairs to make him a cup of black coffee and while I was about it I opened the door to listen for signs that some of his friends might still be within hailing distance. There was only a soft sweep of wind and a scattering of stars throwing a faint shimmer over the sea. I cupped my hands to my mouth and yelled as loudly as I could hoping that somewhere some of my erstwhile guests would hear me and come to my aid. No response broke the silence of the night.

I took the coffee upstairs and persuaded Tearlaich to sit up. Shaking his head and squinting through his tousled hair like a bemused calf he took up the cup and after drinking about half of it started to ramble jerkily about love and how good it would be for me but as his eyes were screwed tight shut the whole time it was plain he had no idea whom he was addressing. The cup was tilting dangerously and to save my eiderdown I took it from him whereupon he grabbed the whisky bottle, drained it and settled down to sleep again.

I gave up, resolving to leave him there and make up the bed in the spare room for myself but as I was taking the blankets from the chest I heard voices outside and the kitchen door was flung open. Someone was bumping about in the dark. I was halfway down the stairs when Erchy's voice called :

'Have you seen that bugger Tearlaich? We've lost him.'

'He's upstairs in my bed,' I called testily. 'And I hope you'll be able to drag him out of it. He's a damn nuisance.'

I lit the way upstairs and Erchy, assisted by the roadman, pulled the protesting Tearlaich off the bed and put on his boot. Leaving me with the empty whisky bottle as a memento they hauled him down the stairs and outside.

'That's no' a nice thing to do at all, man,' Erchy chided as they struggled to get him through the gate.

The reproof sobered Tearlaich momentarily. 'What wasn't?' he asked stupidly.

'To take a woman's bed an' not let her into it,' retorted Erchy.

'I would have let her into it,' objected Tearlaich defensively. 'I'd have made it cosy for her.'

'Ach, if folks behave like that Miss Peckwitt will be packing her bags an' goin' back to where she came from,' Erchy told him.

Tearlaich's dragging feet dug into the ground, halting his supporters. He struggled round to face me.

'You'll not go back to that backwards place, Miss Peckwitt?' he pleaded apologetically.

'To what backwards place?' I asked, smiling despite myself.

'England,' replied Tearlaich.

I laughed outright then. 'Oh, no,' I assured him. 'I'm not thinking of doing that for a long time.'

'I wouldn't . . .' began Tearlaich but Erchy cut in with 'Ach, come on, man! I'm wantin' my bed.' He and the roadman shouldered Tearlaich between them and as their footsteps merged into a rhythm Tearlaich broke into a song. I went back indoors, intent again on the prospect of bed and the few hours' sleep I hoped would chase some of the weariness from my limbs. As my hand was on the bedroom door my new alarm clock, set for half past seven, made me jump with its raucous ringing.

It was time to start another day.

If you would like a complete list of Arrow books please send a postcard to P.O. Box 29, Douglas, Isle of Man, Great Britain.

The Ponytail Girls

Lost On
Monster Mountain

Bonnie Compton Hanson

Dedication

To every girl who loves Jesus and wants her life to count for Him.

THE PONYTAIL GIRLS/LOST ON MONSTER MOUNTAIN
©2005 by Legacy Press, fifth printing
ISBN 1-58411-031-7
Legacy reorder# LP48043

Legacy Press
P.O. Box 261129
San Diego, CA 92196

Illustrator: Aline Heiser

Scriptures are from the *Holy Bible: New International Version* (North American Edition), ©1973, 1978, 1984 by the International Bible Society. Used by permission of Zondervan Bible Publishers.

Printed in the United States of America

Contents

~ Introduction ~

Welcome to the Ponytail Girls! Whether you wear a ponytail or not you can share in the adventures of Sam Pearson and her friends, the PTs (that's short for Ponytails!). Just like you, the PTs love sports and shopping and fun with their friends at school.

The PTs also want to live in a way that is pleasing to God. So when they have problems and conflicts, they look to God and His Word, the Bible. They might also seek help from their parents, their pastor or their Sunday school class teacher, just like you do.

Each chapter in this book presents a new problem for your PTs to solve. Then there is a Bible story to help explain the Christian value that the PTs learned. A Bible memory verse is included for you to practice and share.

There may be words in this book that are new to you, especially some Bible names and Spanish words. Look them up in the Glossary on page 201, then use the syllables to sound out the words.

In addition to the stories, in each chapter you will find questions to answer and fun quizzes, puzzles and other activities. Also, at the end of each chapter starting with Chapter 1, you will get a clue that leads to the finished Valentine Heart Puzzle. Don't forget to fill in the puzzle so you can see the secret message!

The fun doesn't end with the stories. At the end of the book, there are more Ponytail Girls activities. If you didn't start your own Ponytail Girls club after you read the first book, there is information on how to do so, along with membership cards.

The first Ponytail Girls book, *Meet the Ponytails*, began just after school started in the fall. In *The Impossible Christmas Present*, you followed the PTs through the tragedies and triumphs of their holiday season. This third Ponytails book begins just after Christmas. The next two books continue on through the school year and into the summer. So as soon as you finish this book, Sam and her friends want to share more Ponytail Girls adventures with you. Now turn to page 11 to meet the PTs!

Meet Your Ponytail Girls!

· WHO ARE THEY? ·

T he PTs are girls your age who enjoy school, church, shopping and being with their friends and family. They also love meeting new friends. Friends just like you! You will like being a part of their lives.

The Ponytail Girls all attend Madison Middle School in the small town of Circleville. They're all also members of Miss Kotter's Sunday school class at nearby Faith Church on Sunday mornings. On Sunday evenings, they attend the special Zone 56 group for guys and girls in fifth and sixth grade. Their pastor is Rev. J. T. McConahan, and their youth leader is Pastor Andrew Garretti, whom they call "Pastor Andy."

Sam and Sara grew up in Circleville. Le's and LaToya's families moved into their neighborhood last year. When Sam and Sara met them at school, they invited them to church. Then Maria moved in next door to Sam and became a PT, followed by Jenna and Sonya, who joined the club at Christmas. Now it would be hard for all seven to imagine not being Ponytail Girls.

How did the PTs get their club name? Well, as you can see from their pictures, they all wear a ponytail of one kind or another. So that's what their other friends and families started calling them just for fun. Then one day LaToya shortened it to "PTs." Now that's what they all call themselves!

The PTs' club meetings are held whenever they can all get together. The girls have a secret motto: PT4JC, which means "Ponytails for Jesus Christ." But most of the time they don't want to keep secrets. They want to share with everyone the Good News about their best friend, Jesus.

So have fun sharing in your PTs' adventures. Laugh with them in their silly times, think and pray with them through their problems. And learn with them that the answers to all problems can be found right in God's Word. Keep your Bible and a sharpened pencil handy. Sam and the others are waiting for you!

GET TO KNOW THE PTS

Sam Pearson *has a long blond ponytail, sparkling blue eyes and a dream: she wants to play professional basketball. She also likes to design clothes. Sam's name is "Samantha," but her friends and family just call her "Sam" for short. Sam's little brother, Petie, is 7. Joe, her dad, is great at fixing things, like cars and bikes. Her mom, Jean, bakes scrumptious cakes and pies and works at the Paws and Pooches Animal Shelter. Sneezit is the family dog.*

LaToya Thomas' *black curls are ponytailed high above her ears. That way she doesn't miss a thing going on! LaToya's into gymnastics and playing the guitar. Her big sister, Tina, is in college, training to be a nurse. Her mom is a school teacher; her dad works nights at a supermarket. Also living with the Thomases is LaToya's beloved, wheelchair-bound grandmother, Granny B.*

13

Le Tran *parts her glossy black hair to one side, holding it back with one small ponytail. She loves sewing, soccer and playing the violin. Her mother, Viola, a concert pianist, often plays duets with her. Her father, Daniel, died in an accident. Mrs. Tran is a Buddhist from Vietnam, but Mr. Tran became a Christian before he died. Le's mother is a new Christian.*

• Le Tran •

Sara Fields *lives down the street from Sam. She keeps her fiery, red hair from flying away by tying it into a ponytail flat against each side of her head. Sara has freckles, glasses and a great sense of humor. She loves to sing. She also loves softball, ice skating and cheerleading. Sara has a big brother, Tony, and a big dog, Tank. Both her parents are artists.*

• Sara Fields •

When **Maria Moreno** *moved in next door to Sam in September, she became the fifth PT. Maria pulls part of her long, brown hair into one topknot ponytail at the back; the rest hangs loose. She is tall, the way basketball-lover Sam would like to be! But Maria's into science, not basketball. At home, she*

helps her mother take care of her 6-year-old twin brothers, Juan and Ricardo, and a little sister, Lolita. The Morenos all speak Spanish as well as English.

Miss Kitty Kotter, *the girls' Sunday school teacher, is not a PT, but she is an important part of their lives both in and out of church. Miss Kotter works as a computer engineer. She also loves to go on hikes. Miss Kotter calls the Bible her "how-to book" because, she says, it tells "how to" live. Miss Kitty volunteers at the Circleville Rescue Mission.*

Jenna Jenkins *is tall and wears her rich auburn ponytail high on her head, like a crown. Jenna loves ballet, her little sister Katie and the adorable new twins, Noel and Holly, who were born at Christmas time. Jenna's mom makes delicious cookies. Jenna's dad is an accountant.*

• Jenna Jenkins •

Sonya Silverhorse *is disabled and uses a wheelchair. She has a sweet smile. Her bouncy cocker spaniel's name is Cocky. Sonya wears her coal-black ponytail long and braided in honor of her Cherokee background. She and her dad are new in town. He is Mr. Moreno's and Mr. Pearson's new boss. Her mother died in the accident that disabled Sonya.*

• Sonya Silverhorse •

Get ready for fun with the PTs!

Chapter 1

Hello, Good Buy!

When the phone rang the day after Christmas, Sam Pearson was busy putting away her Christmas presents. She could hardly find room for everything in her dresser and closet.

"Hi!" Sara Fields said at the other end. Sara was a member of Sam's club, the Ponytail Girls, which they called the "PTs" for short. "Did you see this morning's paper? All the stores are having after-

Christmas sales. Mom and I are going down to the mall this afternoon. There's this sweater I'm dying to get. Want to come along?"

"Thanks, but I'm going shopping with my mom and Petie this morning. Mom wants to find some things on sale for Jenna's baby sisters and for the animal shelter. Petie and I got some money from our other grandparents for Christmas. So Petie's looking for stuff for his new bike. And I'm looking for another new sweater."

Later that morning, Mrs. Pearson and Sam dragged Petie away from his new video game to head out for shopping. Mr. Pearson had gone with Mr. Moreno and Mr. Silverhorse to look over their new car repair shop. Sneezit, the family's tiny poodle, begged piteously to go shopping, too, but without success. "See you later, Sneezit," Petie called as he ran out to the car.

What a gorgeous day! The sky was blue, the ground was white, the bare trees were brown and all the houses on the Pearsons' street were still bright with Christmas decorations. It was easy to figure out where the mall was — every car seemed to be headed that way!

"We have to stay together," Mrs. Pearson said. "It's too easy to get lost in this crowd. Understand?"

First, they took off for a sports store to find bike accessories for Petie. Then as they passed a toy store, Petie cried, "Look, Mom! They have that game on sale that I've been asking for!"

Mrs. Pearson sighed. "Honestly, Petie, I don't

know why we bother getting you anything for Christmas. We should just wait until afterward and let you pick out your own presents!" But of course she didn't mean it.

At the Four-Legged Friends store, where Sam's Aunt Caitlin worked, they found some collars and leashes for the animal shelter where Mrs. Pearson was employed. They also bought a cute, little sweater for Sneezit. "No, fair!" Sam pretended to grumble. "I'm the one who wants a sweater!'

And then she looked in the With-It! store window. "That's it!" she cried as she ran to the window. "It's perfect!" The "it" was a gorgeous blue and white button-up sweater with matching scarf and hat. And it was marked down 75 percent! Sam counted her Christmas money carefully. Yes, even setting aside some to give to church, she had exactly enough.

As the sales clerk removed the sweater from the display window, she remarked, "You're very lucky, you know. I've sold five this morning already, and this is the very last one we have."

The next morning, Sam had a hard time deciding what to wear to church. The blue velvet dress her grandmother gave her for Christmas? Her red plaid jumper? What she really wanted to wear, of course, was her new sweater. But she decided to wait to wear it that evening to the Zone 56 youth group instead. She knew everyone would love it as much as she did.

Sara was already waiting when Sam arrived in

their Sunday school class. "Wait'll you see the new sweater I found yesterday!" Sam cried. "I'm so excited! Did you find the sweater you wanted, too?"

Sara sighed. "No, I had to get another one instead. I mean, the one I bought is cute enough. It's green with little poodles all over it. But yesterday Brittany called everyone on the cheerleading squad and told us to all buy some matching set she saw at the With-It! Store. It was a blue and white button-up with a hat and scarf. We were all going to wear them together to Winter Camp."

Suddenly, Sam felt very strange. "Uh...like the one in the store window?"

"Yes! Wasn't it adorable? Well, the other girls got theirs. They wanted the sales clerk to save the last one for me, but she said she couldn't. And by the time I got there, it was gone."

That morning in class Miss Kitty, their teacher, told about Abigail and how kind and gracious she was to King David, even though it would have been easier for her not to be. "Sometimes we think with our heads," Miss Kotter explained, "and sometimes with our hearts. It's best to do both at the same time, especially if you first ask God to guide you."
Then she handed everyone a big heart.

Maria looked at hers. "It has lines all over it," she remarked. "Is that for 'heart surgery'?"

Their teacher laughed. "No, it's a puzzle. Remember our Secret Birthday Circle and our Christmas Advent Calendar? This is a Valentine Heart Puzzle to remind you that your heart should be full of love for others just as God's heart is full of love for you. Each week I'll give you clues. By the time Valentine's Day is here, your puzzle should be complete and ready to share with someone."

By the time Sunday school class was over, Sam had already figured out what she needed to do to show God's love to someone. A "someone" named Sara Fields, that is! When she explained her idea to Sara, she almost cried with delight and appreciation.

That's why that evening Sam wore a new green sweater with poodles on it to Zone 56 and why Sara wore a blue and white one with a matching hat and scarf. And why both of them wore smiles as big as all outdoors!

· Good News ·
from God's Word

This is the story that helped Sam make her happy decision to share.

Abigail's Graciousness

FROM 1 SAMUEL 25

King Saul was very jealous of the young shepherd David. In fact, the king was so jealous, he

wanted to kill David. So David ran away and hid in
the mountains. A lot of his friends went along to help
him. But it was hard to find enough food for everyone.

Not too far away lived a very wealthy rancher.
Nabal had 1,000 goats and 3,000 sheep! David, of
course, loved sheep. So his men protected the animals
and their shepherds from robbers in the area.

Then sheep-shearing time arrived. That meant
lots of work needed to be done. But also parties with
lots to eat! "Maybe Nabal will share some of his food
with us because of all we have done for him," David
decided. So he sent some of his followers to see Nabal.

Nabal was not only rich, he was stingy. Instead
of offering the men some food, he pretended he'd
never even heard of David! Then he insulted the men
and sent them away.

Nabal was pleased with himself for being so
mean and saving all that money. Then he got ready to

put on a big banquet for himself.

But his wife Abigail was horrified. Right away, she rounded up 200 loaves of bread and piles of other food. After loading all the food on donkeys, she and her servants hurried off to David's hideout.

David was hungry, hurt and angry. Abigail gave him the food and apologized for her husband's bad manners. David thanked her. Then she hurried back home.

When she got there, her husband was in the middle of his big banquet, and he was very drunk. So she couldn't tell him what she had done until the next day. Then he was so shocked that he became paralyzed and soon died.

God didn't forget the gracious things Abigail had done for David. David didn't either. In fact, after Nabal died, he married her!

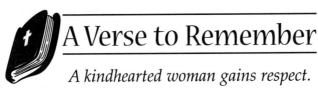

A Verse to Remember

A kindhearted woman gains respect.

— **Proverbs 11:16**

Spot a Bargain

Sam was looking for bargains at the after-Christmas sales. Do you know a bargain when you see one? In each of the examples below, circle the price that is better.

1. Cans of beans

    39 cents each   2 for $1

2. Notebook paper

    3 packs for $1   5 packs for $2

3. T-shirt

    $5.99 each   2 for $10

4. Jeans

    $14 each   2 for $29.95

5. Sweater

    1/2 off   55% off

Check your answers on page 203.

Baby Talk

Did you ever feel the way Sam did when she went to the mall, thinking about nothing but what she was going to get for herself? That's the way little babies think: "me, me, me, me, me!" Unfortunately, some people never grow up. They always put themselves first. Circle the words below that express the way God wants YOU to be:

SHARING   HELPING   GIVING

GRABBING   YELLING   BRAGGING

HUGGING   SHOVING   POUTING

CHEATING   TEACHING   LOVING

Check your answers on page 203.

You Gotta Have Heart

The Valentine Heart Puzzle that Miss Kitty gave to the PTs is on the next page. Each chapter of this book will give you a Secret Letter to add to one of the spaces in the puzzle. When the heart puzzle is complete, you will discover a Valentine message! For today, add Secret Letter "G" for "graciousness" to space 1 of the puzzle.

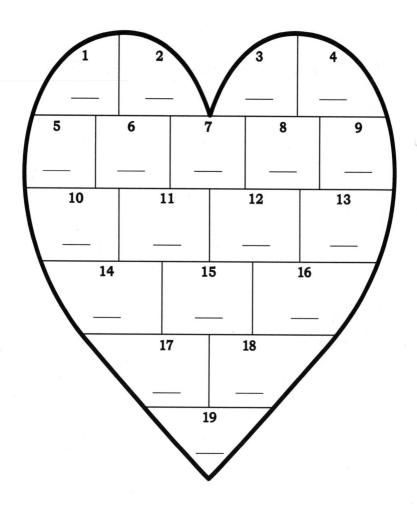

Chapter 2

New Year, New You

That night at the Zone 56 meeting, Pastor Andy discussed the New Year's service at Faith Church, which would be the following night. "There will be refreshments for everyone afterward," he said. "How do we want to help?"

The Zone 56 members decided they would pour the fruit punch and put away the chairs after the fellowship time ended.

After announcements, Pastor Andy discussed New Year's resolutions.

"Every New Year's Eve millions of people make resolutions," he said. "They want to live new lives, different lives, better lives. They want to stop arguing or to get better grades or to come to church more often. They want to start exercising or lose weight or get along better with others.

"All these people really intend to do better. They really want these resolutions to work. But think about it. If these resolutions really worked, why would people have to make new ones all over again the next New Year's Eve?"

Kevin raised his hand. "Because people forget them?"

"Or can't do better by themselves without God's help?" added Jenna Jenkins, one of the PTs.

Pastor Andy nodded. "You're both right. The only way we can really get control of our lives and do better is to ask Jesus to help us. Every single day."

But Sam wasn't listening to that part. As soon as she heard the words "New Year's resolutions" her mind started zooming a zillion miles into space.

That's what I'll do tonight, she told herself. I'll make some resolutions for the New Year. Now that I'm a Christian, it should really be easy to keep them. God would like that.

As soon as she came in from church that night,

Mrs. Pearson asked, "Sam, could you help me in the kitchen for a few minutes?"

But Sam threw off her coat and ran upstairs. "Sorry, Mom," she called back, "but I have to work on something."

Then she sat down at her desk and pulled out some paper and a pen. At the top, she wrote, "My New Year's Resolutions." Then she stopped to think. Really, what could she make resolutions about? She was already doing so many things right.

Then she remembered what her mother just said, and wrote:

Resolution #1: I resolve to help my
mother when she asks.

But instead of jumping back up and going down to help her mother right then, Sam wrote:

Resolution #2

...but she couldn't think of another one.

Just then, Petie came in. He was trying to put new batteries in one of his toys, but they kept falling out. "Sam, could you help me?" he asked. "Please?"

"Later, Petie," she replied, and waved him away. But that gave her another resolution to write down:

I resolve to help my little brother when he asks.

Petie stood there a while hoping she would change her mind. But she didn't, so finally he just left.

The phone rang. It was another PT, Le Tran. "Sam," she began, "Maria and I have been working on our science project. It's due the day after New

Year's. Could we bounce a few ideas off you?"

That did it! All these interruptions! "Sorry; I'm too busy right now," Sam barked, and hung up. But that phone call gave her a great idea for Resolution #3:

I resolve to always be there for my friends when they need me.

Sam's dad came in from the garage. "Sam," he called, "get right down here and put your bicycle up on the rack where it belongs. I almost ran over it."

"Sorry, Dad!" she called. But instead of going downstairs, she wrote:

Resolution #4
Put all my things away.

Well, four resolutions, that's enough, she thought. But there was still room on the paper. *Maybe I should write resolutions for other people, too. People too "blind" to realize they really should do better.*

So for her mother, Sam wrote:

Be more organized, so you don't have to ask other people to help you with your chores.

For her dad:

Spend money on your children and take them fun places.

For Petie:

Keep your room clean and don't bug your sister when she's busy.

Sam was on a roll. So she made resolutions for all her PTs, and for Miss Kitty, too. She copied them all onto note cards, placed them in envelopes and addressed them. She'd give everyone their "presents" at the New Year's Eve service at church to help them start their New Year off right!

By the time she went to bed, Sam was pretty proud of herself. "Thank You, God," she prayed, "for helping me show everyone else the faults they need to correct."

The next day, Sam looked through her closet. What could she wear for the first day back to school after Christmas vacation?

"Sam," her mom called, "I'm running down to work for a while to feed the animals. Could you fill the Christmas tree stand with water while I'm gone? Oh, and please vacuum the living room, too."

Sam groaned. But then she remembered her Resolution #1. So she headed down to the living room, feeling very proud of herself.

Petie was still trying to put new batteries in his toys. So this time Sam helped him. That was Resolution #2. Why, her halo was practically shining!

After vacuuming the living room floor, Sam went out to the garage and put her bike away. Resolution #3. Then she called Le back from the night before. Le wasn't home, but Sam left a message, anyway, offering to help. So that counted for Resolution #4. Wow, did she feel good about that!

In fact, that evening at the New Year's Eve service at church, Sam felt so good about herself she practically glowed. Stuck in her Bible were all the cards she planned to give her friends and family so they could improve themselves during the coming year.

Then Pastor McConahan began talking about how no one was righteous, "no, not one." He told about the Pharisee who thanked God that he was so perfect. And then about the publican who realized that he wasn't perfect at all, but needed God's forgiveness and help to do better.

Then her pastor told of young King Hezekiah and his mother, Abi. Hezekiah wanted to be a good king and do everything right for God. He instructed his people to stop worshipping idols. He even stood up to the King of Assyria. How good he felt about that! Then God let the Assyrians capture the neighboring kingdom of Samaria. Hezekiah was scared! Instead of asking God to help him, he tried to bribe the Assyrians with gold. But they still demanded complete surrender. Only then did Hezekiah admit he had done wrong and asked God for help.

After the service, Sam threw all her cards into the trash can. Then she asked God to forgive her for being so self-righteous. And the next day she made a big batch of cookies for her family and friends. Now that was starting the year off right!

· Good News ·
from God's Word

Can you figure out why this Bible story helped Sam see what she was doing wrong?

Queen Abi Helps a Young King

FROM 2 KINGS 16:1-18:8

When her young son Hezekiah became king of Judah, Queen Abi had high hopes for him and for their country. She even gave him a name that meant "the Lord is strength." She thought he might be able to unite the countries of Judah and Samaria again, they way they once were under David and Solomon, and they could live in a nation for God.

Although his father, King Ahaz, had been wicked, Hezekiah knew how to serve God, and he had an earnest desire to do right. He also had good ministers, such as the prophet Isaiah, to help him.

First, he ordered all the places of idol worship to be torn down. He even got rid of the bronze snake Moses had made long ago because people were worshipping that as an idol, too! They were being as wicked as the Samaritans in turning away from God.

Hezekiah followed all of God's commands. And the Lord helped him do well in all that he did. He even rebelled successfully against the great, cruel Assyrian Empire. Then God let Assyria capture Samaria. Instead of asking God to help His people, Hezekiah got scared. He tried to buy off the Assyrians using gold he robbed from God's own temple. Of course, that didn't work. The enemy had 185,000 soldiers ready to invade Jerusalem.

"Your God can't save you now," they laughed. The king was more frightened than ever. He was frightened enough to do what he should have done in the first place: ask God to forgive him for doing things his own way. He asked Him to save his people.

God did. That very night, He struck dead every Assyrian soldier. Jerusalem was saved.

Hezekiah was thankful for his wonderful God!

A Verse to Remember

*If we confess our sins, he is faithful
and just and will forgive us our sins.*

— *1 John 1:9*

What About You?

It's always easier to see what others do wrong than to recognize and admit what we do wrong ourselves. What is a bad habit or shortcoming with which you have a problem? Write it here with today's date. Then ask God to help you change.

_____

_____

_____

Life of the Party

Your friends or group at church might want to get together for a New Year's Eve party, too. You can include refreshments, games and other types of activities. Of course, parties are fun any time of year, but a party that is safe, fun and honors God takes careful preparation. Look on the next page for questions to ask yourself when you are planning a party.

1. For what occasion, if any, am I having this party?

2. Whom will I invite?

3. Where will it be held?

4. What will the date and time be?

5. From whom do I need to get permission?

6. How long will the party last?

7. Who, if anyone, will be helping me host the party?

8. Am I (or my family) paying for everything? If not, who will help?

9. What will we eat?

10. Who will help prepare it?

11. What activities will we do?

12. How will I let everyone know?

13. What do I need to do to prepare the place where the party will be held?

14. What adults will be there?

15. Do we need transportation? If so, who can drive?

16. Mark the date on a calendar and get ready for fun!

The Valentine Heart Puzzle

Add Secret Letter "A" for "asking for forgiveness" to space 12 of the puzzle on page 26.

Chapter 3

Really, Really Bugged

There was lots of news buzzing around school the day after Christmas vacation. Everyone wanted to tell about their presents and trips, of course. Plus there was a new girl at school. And she wasn't just any new girl — she was Sonya Silverhorse, the newest PT member, with her sparkling smile and black braided ponytail. Sonya was nervous about getting her wheelchair around Madison Middle School, but many kids stopped to help her, including all of the PTs.

But the biggest buzz at school was about Winter Camp.

"It will be held the last week in January," explained Le and Maria's homeroom teacher. "The camp holds 200 students. We'll share the campsite with a group from Washington Middle School in Midland. Everyone will get a flyer to take home to your parents today explaining more about what you need to take and how long you'll be gone. Any questions?"

"Where is the camp, Miss Temple?" Le asked.

"About 50 miles from here, near Monder Mountain." Chuckling, she added, "Monder Mountain isn't really a mountain...it's more of a very high hill. But it will feel like a mountain when you start hiking up it."

Ric Romero yanked at his green and purple bangs, a change from the green and red he had during the Christmas season. "Don't you mean 'Monster' Mountain?" he sneered.

Le shook her head and rolled her eyes. *That Ric! Why did he always have to act like a jerk?* she thought.

But their teacher chuckled. "Well, some people call it that, Ric. But, believe me, it's just a beautiful park out in the peaceful countryside. You'll love it."

"Isn't January a cold time to go camping?" Maria

asked. "I mean, how will we keep warm in our cabins?"

"Good question, Maria. All the cabins are heated. Plus they have wood stoves in them. The walls are well-insulated. And they even have indoor bathrooms. So you won't turn into icicles when you shower!"

Sonya felt strange speaking out on her very first day at a new school. But she felt she had to. "Do the cabins have, uh, ramps? You know, for wheelchairs?"

Ric snickered. "You planning to do wheelies, maybe?"

Their teacher frowned. "That's enough, Ric, unless you want another detention." Then she turned to Sonya, "Yes, they do, Sonya. It'll all be explained in the flyers you'll receive today. So be sure to stop by here to pick one up before you go home."

But Sonya felt so bad, she couldn't even look up.

"I wish I could go home right now," she sighed to Maria and Le as they headed for science class. "That guy Ric made me feel stupid."

"Aw, don't worry about him," Maria said. "He's just a loser with an attitude. You'll love our science teacher, Mrs. Eldridge."

"Right," Le added. "She's helping Maria and me get ready for the county science fair. I can't wait until she sees what we've been doing on it over Christmas!"

But when they walked into science class, the teacher behind Mrs. Eldridge's desk didn't look like Mrs. Eldridge at all. In fact, "she" was a "he"!

"Everyone, please take your seats at once!" he said the minute the bell rang. "My name is Mr. Andover. Mrs. Eldridge became quite ill over Christmas and won't be back for a few weeks. So I'll be your teacher until then. And I want you to know that I don't allow any goofing off in my classroom."

Holding up their textbook, he said, "Turn to page 134 and read to page 140. Be prepared to answer questions on what you read. Meanwhile, sign the attendance sheet as it goes around. And do it all quietly."

Maria felt strange. What about the science fair project she and Le had been working on? Maybe she should ask. So she raised her hand.

Mr. Andover frowned. "What part of my instructions didn't you understand, young lady?" he barked at Maria.

"Uh, nothing, I..."

"Then no questions until you've completed your assignment."

Maria's heart dropped inside. How were she and Le ever going to work with a teacher like that?

After class, the two girls cautiously approached their new teacher's desk. Le carried a large folder. "Mr. Andover," she began, "Maria and I got a blue ribbon at the Madison Science Fair last fall for our project on insects."

"Yes," Maria added quickly, "and Mrs. Eldridge wanted us to do more experiments on it over Christmas so we can enter the county science fair. So we wanted to report our results." And she handed over the folder.

Mr. Andover flipped through it. "I see," he said. "This is fine as far as it goes. But it doesn't go far enough. I want you to go back and recheck all the insect sites you first reported on. See whether you can find any of those insects there after all these weeks of snow. If you do, figure out or guess why they have survived. Also, note whether each kind of insect is harmful or helpful — and why or why not. I'll expect your new report by Wednesday at the latest. Dismissed."

And without another glance at them, he walked away.

Sonya, who had waited for them just outside the door, was shocked. "I heard what he said. What a horrible man!" she cried as soon as they reached the hallway.

"Do you think he treats everyone that way?" Maria asked. "Or just me and Le because we're Hispanic and Vietnamese?"

"That must be it," Sonya decided. "Because everyone else knows you two are really smart. He treated you like dirt!"

They were still complaining about Mr. Andover as  they returned to their homeroom to pick up their Winter Camp flyers. "What's the matter, girls?" Miss Temple asked.

When they explained, she smiled knowingly. "Girls," she said, "were you ever scared to death to try something new? This is Mr. Andover's very first teaching job. He's worried that he won't do a good job — that you kids will turn his classroom into a zoo. Under that gruff voice is a very nice man. Remember that old saying, 'Don't judge a person unless you've walked in his shoes'? Why don't you give him a chance?"

"Besides," Miss Temple added with a smile, "those were pretty good suggestions he made. I think he's really on your side, after all. In fact, I think he wants you to win!"

· Good News · from God's Word

Here's a Bible story about learning not to "judge a book by its cover."

A Shulammite Girl's Joy

FROM THE SONG OF SOLOMON

Did you ever feel people don't accept you because of how you look? Or the way you talk? Or how tall or short you are? Or what country your parents or grandparents are from?

One whole book in the Bible tells of a girl who could have been very discouraged about how she looked. When she looked into mirrors — which in those days were made of metal — she didn't look like the other girls. In that culture, girls wanted very pale complexions, as if they stayed inside all day long.

We don't know this girl's name. She's called a Shulammite. We're not even sure what that means —

whether she was from a certain small town or if it simply means that Solomon liked her. But we do know she was very dark-skinned and very beautiful. And very busy. She had to work outside in the fields and vineyards. So she didn't have time to sit around and worry about how she did or didn't look.

But even out there in the country someone discovered her — someone who didn't care about her skin color. In fact, he thought she looked wonderful just the way she was. That person was King Solomon himself! Indeed, either he or one of his music leaders wrote the whole Song of Solomon to praise her and Solomon's love for her.

The rich, noble women of Jerusalem were surprised that the king fell in love with such a "nobody" — someone who did not have the most popular appearance. But looks can be deceiving. The real girl inside her was a wonderful person to know and love, just as the real person inside you is, no matter what your outside looks like! Aren't you glad?

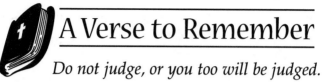

A Verse to Remember

Do not judge, or you too will be judged.
— *Matthew 7:1*

Turn Over the Label

It's so easy to judge people the first time we meet them. We give them labels, too: mean, lazy, stuck-up, jock, geek, funny, pretty, nerd, cool, popular, loser.

But maybe there's another side to the story. Maybe that "stuck-up" girl is just shy. Maybe the "funny" guy is trying to cover up a deep hurt inside. Maybe the "jock" enjoys sports but really wants to be a scientist. Maybe the "clothes horse" would rather have her parents really love her than just give her lots of clothes. Maybe the "geek" feels so lonely he's considering suicide.

Ask God to help you see people the way He sees them: with eyes of love. Write a name below of someone whom you need to show God's love.

This person needs to know God's love:

_____

Mother Goose-Bumps

What is the best way to think of the following nursery rhyme and fairy tale characters? Find a friend to help you choose answers. Make up more yourself. Have fun!

1. Little Miss Muffet, who ran from a spider:

   a. She was just a scaredy-cat.

   b. She was smart. She might have gotten bit!

2. Little Boy Blue, who slept instead of doing his chores:

   a. He was smart to get his rest.

   b. He was lazy and irresponsible.

3. Little Jack Horner, who sat in a corner:

   a. He was using poor manners.

   b. He was a bragger.

   c. He was both!

4. Old King Cole:

   a. He was a merry old soul.
   b. He was bossy.

continued on next page…

5. Jack, who jumped over a candlestick:

   a. He was a nimble athlete.

   b. He was doing something dangerous.

6. Goldilocks, who visited the three bears:

   a. She had very bad manners.

   b. She was not kind to animals.

   c. She was both!

7. Jack, who climbed the beanstalk:

   a. He was a poor farmer.

   b. He was a clever trickster.

The Valentine Heart Puzzle

Add Secret Letter "N" for "not judging" to space 13 of the puzzle on page 26.

Chapter 4

Wheelie Dealies

At breakfast the next morning, Sonya's dad beamed as brightly as the sun streaming in the kitchen window. "You know, kid," Mr. Silverhorse said, "God had an especially good plan when He led us here. Moving to Circleville and helping Mr. Moreno and Mr. Pearson open up a new SuperService shop here are two of the best decisions I've ever made."

Then he smiled. "Besides marrying your mother,

having you, and becoming a Christian, of course."

He poured some steaming hot coffee into a Thermos to take to work. "So what do you think of your new school?"

Sonya reached for some oatmeal. "It's okay. I like most of the teachers, except for Mr. Andover. And I'm really excited about Winter Camp. But there's one kid who doesn't like me. His name is Ric Romero, and he's always making fun of my wheelchair. He makes me so mad! I just wish I could get even with him!"

Her dad patted her arm. "Remember what your mom always said: 'Don't get even, get better.' People who are mean are usually hurting inside. Maybe Ric just needs a friend. Why don't you pray about it?" Then he kissed her good-bye on the top of her head and left for work.

Sonya came out her front door just as Sam and Maria were walking by. She wheeled down the ramp to the sidewalk. But the part of the sidewalk that had been cleared of snow was so narrow, they had to move in a single-file line.

"I love all this snow," Sam exclaimed. "I hope we have lots at Winter Camp."

Maria laughed. "Puh-leeze! I sure hope we have wider paths there. When the snowplows cleared the streets, they piled so much up on each side you can practically ski down the snow piles! I don't know how Le and I are going to check for insects under all of this. And I'm still ticked at Mr. Andover for asking us to!"

Just then Sara ran out of her house to join them, still pulling on her backpack. "Hi, girls!" she called. Then she teased, "Hey, Sonya, sure you like our school enough to come back a second day?"

Sonya laughed. "Well, if you guys can take it, I guess I can, too. Sticking together — that's what PTs do, isn't it?"

As they neared the school, the narrow sidewalks began filling with students. Some kids had to stomp over the deep snow to get by. Suddenly, a bicycle on the sidewalk whizzed up behind the girls. All of them scrambled to get out of the way. But there was nowhere for Sonya's wheelchair to go. The impact with the bike tipped her right over into a big snow bank!

But the biker didn't stop to help her up. Instead, he turned around and grinned.

"Oops!" he yelled. "There you go, doing wheelies again! Wait'll we get to Monster Mountain!" And he raced on, roaring with mean laughter.

"That mean Ric Romero!" Sam and the other PTs said as they put down their bookbags to assist Sonya.

Other students rushed over to help Sonya, too, including Josh and Kevin from their church. "That jerk!" Josh muttered. "You ought to go right to the principal and get him expelled. We'll all be your witnesses."

Sonya was covered with snow, but not hurt otherwise. "Maybe so," she sighed. "On the other hand, maybe God has another way. Promise to pray with me about it today, okay?"

In social studies class, Mr. Talley discussed

great discoveries by famous explorers, such as Christopher Columbus and Leif Eriksson. "I want you all to think about how such great discoveries have changed your own life," he explained. "For instance, maybe your great-grandparents came to America from Italy. If Columbus hadn't come first, would they have immigrated here? Does anyone have any ideas about this they'd like to share?"

"Yeah," Josh joked. "If America hadn't been discovered, I probably wouldn't be in this social studies class. At least, not studying American history!"

After the laughter died down, Sam added, "And maybe people would still think the world was flat, instead of round."

Maria noted that her parents came from Mexico. "If Europeans hadn't come to America, my background would be only Indian, instead of both Indian and European."

Sonya giggled. "Even if Columbus hadn't come to America, I'd be here, because my ancestors are Cherokee Indians. That's why I have a different kind of last name. And the Indians were here first of all."

Suddenly she felt that God wanted her to say more. "But I've made some discoveries of my own, too, Mr. Talley…even if I'm not a famous explorer. For instance, even though I'm new here, I've discovered some good friends here at Circleville and a new church.

"And," she added, grinning at Ric, "I've discovered that some of the students here are really good at bike racing and doing 'wheelies.' I'd love to discover how to be their friend, too. And maybe discover how to do real 'wheelies' — without ending up in a snow bank."

Mr. Talley looked puzzled. But the kids who had seen what Ric had done that morning started snickering and clapping.

Ric blushed scarlet to the edge of his green and purple bangs. But after class he muttered, "sorry" to Sonya, then rushed away.

Josh patted Sonya on the back. "You really got even with him!" he said.

Sonya smiled. "Thanks, Josh. But what I really wanted to do was to get better. And to help Ric get better, too!"

· Good News ·
from God's Word

People are not always easy to get along with, but God wants us to love them anyway. Here is a story about some Bible people who kept on living for God even when a lot of people thought they were crazy.

Isaiah's Wife's Faith

FROM ISAIAH 6:1-8:4

Isaiah was a minister for God. He wrote down God's Word for all of God's people to read. But he didn't have a nice church to pastor, with lots of people who loved him. Instead, he lived in Jerusalem and preached about God to the kings there and to anyone else who would listen. Many people wouldn't. They wanted to worship idols and live their own sinful ways instead. They thought God's way was too old-fashioned and dull.

God loved His people. He wanted them to come back to Him. One day, He gave Isaiah a great vision, probably while he was worshipping in the temple. In the vision, God asked whom to send to tell His people His message. "Here I am," Isaiah said. "Send me."

But being God's prophet wasn't easy. Some people listened, but others hated Isaiah. He needed a friend to be with him, so God gave him a wife. His wife wasn't just any young woman, but someone who loved and spoke from God's Word, too — a prophetess.

Together, Isaiah and his wife depended on

God for guidance on how to deliver His message. They helped people know about the great troubles that awaited them if they didn't turn to God. They even gave their sons long names that described the trouble ahead.

But God also gave them messages of hope. One message said that after a long time of captivity some of God's people would come back to Israel. The other was that one day God would send His Son, Jesus, to be their Savior.

Even though life was hard for all of Isaiah's family, they were so glad that they could help tell the world about God's love for His people and for everyone.

A Verse to Remember

If any of you lacks wisdom,
he should ask God.

— James 1:5

What About You?

Did you ever get so angry at someone that you wanted to give that person "a piece of your mind"? Or so worried about something you weren't sure what to do? Maybe you have a problem like that! If so, write it below with today's date.

I am angry at _____

because _____

Today's date: _____

It's so easy to say or do something first and then be sorry about it later. God wants to help you with all your problems. Insert your name in this chapter's Scripture: "If _____ lacks wisdom, _____ should ask God." Ask Him right now to help you. Keep praying about it. When you do find an answer, write it here with the date. Then tell God, "Thank You!"

Answer: _____

Today's date: _____

The Valentine Heart Puzzle

Add Secret Letter "D" for "dependent on God" to space 17 of the puzzle on page 26.

Chapter 5

Snow Day!
Hooray!

Maria and Le had never worked so hard. "We've finally done everything Mr. Andover asked for," Maria said with a tired sigh as Le printed the last page from her computer. "I sure hope he's satisfied. I guess we'll know tomorrow when we turn it all in."

Le nodded grimly. "If he doesn't okay things this time, we'll know for sure he really is just prejudiced against us. I can't wait until Mrs. Eldridge is well and back teaching again. She's the one I want to have at the county science fair with us, not that old meanie."

Mrs. Tran sat in the living room watching the evening news. But she could still hear Le. "Shame on you, Le!" she scolded. "You know Christians are supposed to be loving to others. And talk lovingly about them, too."

Le blushed. Her mom was just a new Christian and here was Le setting a bad example! "I'm sorry, Mom," she apologized. "It's just that it's all so discouraging. But we're done with all our homework and projects."

"*Si*," Maria agreed as she put on her parka and scarf. "I need to get home and help my little brothers. They're having a special art day at school tomorrow."

"Maybe not," Mrs. Tran replied as they walked into the living room. She pointed to the TV. "Look at this weather report."

The weatherman was pointing to a huge map of the United States. "A big storm's heading our way," he said, "with 10 to 12 inches of new snow expected overnight. If that happens, the County Superintendent says area schools will be closed. There's no way all the county roads can be cleared in time for the buses to get through."

Maria and Le hit high fives. "Yeah!" they shouted.

Mrs. Tran frowned. "But you girls don't ride school buses; you walk to school."

"Yes, Mrs. Tran," Maria explained, "but about

half the kids at Madison come from farther away and ride the bus. It wouldn't be fair for us to get to attend classes when they couldn't."

"Or for us to have to," Le giggled. "Besides, if the snow's that deep, the teachers' cars wouldn't be able to get through. Not until most of the streets and sidewalks are plowed."

By the time Maria read a bedtime story to Ricardo, Juan and Lolita that night, the storm had already hit. Sure enough, the next morning there was a radio announcement that all schools in the county would be closed.

"Snow day! Hooray!" her twin brothers shouted.

They scrambled to the window and scraped frost off the glass. Rushing into the kitchen, still in their pajamas, they pleaded, "Mama, can we go play in the snow? Please? Please?"

"Boys!" Mrs. Moreno cried. "It's still storming outside!"

Mr. Moreno and Sam's father braved the wind to shovel as much off their front walks as they could. "If anyone calls needing help with their cars today," Maria's dad told her mom, "tell them SuperService Automotive will be open. I'll be operating the tow truck myself." Then they headed off on foot to the auto shop.

Maria thanked God once more for her father's new job. She listened to the weather on the radio as she helped her mother in the kitchen. "The storm should subside by midmorning," the d.j. reported. By

9:00 that morning, the snow had indeed stopped. In fact, at 10:00 the sun came out.

Sam called Maria. "Want to come outside? Petie wants to go sledding. And Mom and I are going to shovel out the driveway. She's worried about the animals at the shelter and wants to drive down there if she can."

"You're on! I'll bring Ricardo and Juan, too!"

Shoveling, sledding, sliding, snowballing! What fun everyone had — especially Sneezit, although most of the snow was over his head. They finally got both of their driveways cleared, too, just in time for the snow plows to push a huge pile right across them!

"Never mind," Mrs. Pearson said. "I'll walk down to the shelter after lunch instead of driving. Why don't you girls stop by Mrs. Greenleaf's to see if she and Mrs. Ryan need anything?"

The two older women were fine, and thrilled to have company. By the time Sam and Maria returned home, it was lunchtime. Sam's mom had the news on. "Here is an appeal from the Circleville Rescue Mission," the announcer said.

"As all of you know," a young woman said, "it really snowed last night!"

"It's Miss Kotter!" Sam said with surprise. "She must have had a snow day at her work too, so she went to the mission to help out."

"That's fun for kids with their sleds," her Sunday

school teacher continued on the radio. "But terrible for the homeless who have no place to go and for those whose homes may be without heat. So please pass the word that we are open for those who need a warm place to stay. If someone needs transportation here, we'll try to provide it. And if any of the rest of you who are warm and dry can help us, we can use all the donations of blankets, food and medical supplies that we can get."

"Mom!" Sam cried. "Do we have anything we can donate?"

"I'll look before I leave for the animal shelter. Why don't you check with your other PTs, too? I'll see if your Uncle Todd can come by with his SUV and take whatever you collect to the Rescue Mission."

Right away, Sam started calling everyone she knew. Meanwhile, Maria and Sara went around the neighborhood asking if anyone else could help. Petie carried the donations on his sled. Sonya, Jenna and Le worked at Sam's house, folding the items and putting them into bags. Granny B. and LaToya made cookies, cornbread and a big pot of soup. Mrs. Moreno donated a box full of homemade tortillas.

Miss Kitty and the other Mission workers were happy to see the PTs arrive loaded down with supplies and food. So were the cold, hungry people waiting in the shelter for food.

And so were the exhausted PTs.

· Good News · from God's Word

When you see a homeless person, you might think that he or she is lazy or that the person should go get a job. But that person may have had a serious illness or another problem that is too big for him or her to overcome alone. Instead of dismissing such people, God wants us to try to understand them and to be sympathetic and help them. In this story, Job's family was sympathetic, but his friends weren't.

Job's Daughters Comfort Him

FROM JOB 1, 2 AND 42

Job greatly loved the Lord, and God blessed him in return. He gave him a loving wife and wonderful family: seven boys and three girls. Job also had almost too many animals to count — 7,000 sheep, 3,000 camels, 1,000 oxen, and 500 donkeys! So, of course, he had many, many servants to help take care of them.

When Job's children grew up and married, they stayed close to him and to each other. The sons took turns each week holding feasts for the entire family. Afterward, Job gave God sacrifices for them and prayed for his children.

But then Satan decided to challenge Job. He made terrible things happen to him. First, his donkeys, camels and oxen were stolen. Then his sheep were killed. A tornado destroyed the house where all of his children were visiting, and almost all of his servants were killed, also.

Job was so sad! But he worshipped God anyway and trusted Him. Satan was really angry! So he made Job sick with a disease that covered his body with huge painful boils.

Three of Job's friends rushed to see him. "You must have done something bad to cause all these troubles," they said. Of course, they were wrong.

But Job kept on trusting God, and one day God healed him. Job became wealthy again. God even gave him and his wife seven more boys and three more girls to welcome into their home. The girls' names were Jemimah, Keziah and Keren-Happuch. They were so loving and beautiful that they became famous throughout the land.

In those days, sons inherited everything. But Job appreciated his three daughters so much that he gave them all inheritances, too!

A Verse to Remember

Whatever you did for one of the least of these brothers of mine, you did for me.

— **Matthew 25:40**

Million-Dollar Deeds

Wouldn't it be wonderful to have a million dollars with which to help people? Well, God knows that you don't have a million dollars. But He wants to help you do good with what you do have. Do you have a younger brother or sister or friend who needs help with homework? Or with in-line skating lessons? An elderly neighbor or grandmother who could use a hand with her housework? Or in writing a letter? Or in planting a garden? A neighbor who would love to have someone watch her toddler while she takes a long, restful bath?

Think of something kind you could do to help someone. Write it below with today's date.

What I can do to help someone:

_____

Today's date: _____

Now go find out what it will take to do that good deed. Then write down the date you actually do it, and what you learned from it.

continued on next page...

What I learned: _____

_____

Today's Date: _____

Flake and Take

Many good deeds are simple to do, but they still mean a lot to the recipient. Here is one idea:

First, make a snowflake. You can do this by cutting a small, white paper doily into a snowflake shape. Or, cut a 4" square from a sheet of white paper. Fold the square three times, then cut little snips from the folded sides. Open the paper — and presto: a snowflake. Next, fold a piece of colored paper, gift wrap or wallpaper (about 8" x 11") in two twice to make a greeting card shape. Glue your snowflake on the front. Inside, write:

> Each snowflake is special, just like you.
> Thank you for being my friend.

And then at the bottom, write:

> "A friend loves at all times." — Proverbs 17:17

Give or mail your card to a special friend!

The Valentine Heart Puzzle

Add Secret Letter "S" for "sympathetic" to space 8 of the puzzle on page 26.

Chapter 6

Math Makes Me Sick!

On the way to school the next morning, Maria, Le and LaToya were all very nervous.

"What if Mr. Andover doesn't like our changes?" Le moaned. "Or, even worse, he likes them and wants us to do a lot more work?"

LaToya sighed. "At least all the work you're

64

doing is for science, which you like. I'm all worried over math. We have a big test tomorrow, and I hate tests. I hate math, too. I've tried to talk to my big sister about it, but she just looks at me like I'm from a different planet. I mean, she was born loving math and science both."

Sonya wheeled up behind them. "At least math is something you can study for," she remarked. "I'm afraid of Ric Romero. I know I embarrassed him in class. What if he tries for revenge? I'm worried about Winter Camp coming up, too. Will I have to stay inside by myself while the rest of you are out in the snow having fun?"

"Well," Maria said, "my mama always says, 'People stand the tallest when they're down on their knees.' Sounds as though we need a lot of PT prayer time today!"

Inside the school, the PTs found an empty classroom for a quick prayer together. And that prayer really helped! Mr. Andover declared Maria and Le's research "superb."

"Now," he said, "you can add this material to your display. I'm really excited. I know you're going to impress the judges. Thanks for doing your best!"

Afterward, Maria giggled to Le, "I won't even have to put on my snow boots to walk home this afternoon! I'm already walking on air!"

Sonya had a good day, too. The kids in her

social studies class were all very friendly, except for Ric. But at least he didn't say anything mean about "wheelies." In fact, when Mr. Talley asked everyone to team up with a partner for a project to do during Winter Camp, much to Sonya's surprise Ric asked if he could work with her!

But it wasn't a good day for LaToya. "Your test Friday will cover pages 125 through 150," Miss Derrin announced. "We've already gone over this material thoroughly. I know you're all excited about Winter Camp coming up next week. But this test comes first, so take time to review everything. You'll do fine."

LaToya felt like crying. After class she told her teacher, "Miss Derrin, I know we went over all those pages, but I didn't understand anything. How can reviewing help?"

Her teacher patted LaToya's shoulder. "Promise me you'll discipline yourself to study hard tonight. And I promise you you'll be surprised at how well you do."

When LaToya got home, the first thing she did was pull out her math book from her book bag. Her sister, Tina, was surprised. "Hitting the books already?"

LaToya sighed. "Big math test tomorrow. I just know I'm going to flunk no matter how much I study. But of course a genius like you wouldn't understand about that."

She made a peanut butter sandwich and took it with her math book into the living room. Flopping on the floor, she turned on a cartoon channel and opened her book.

Her big sister walked in. "Wait a minute, kid. How can you study with the TV blaring like that?"

Just then the phone rang. It was Pastor McConahan. "LaToya," he said, "could you and your Granny B. sing a duet for our worship service on Sunday morning? You can play your guitar, too, of course. And if Sara wants to join you, that would be great."

LaToya gulped. "Well, uh, okay," she mumbled. But as soon as she hung up, she was more anxious than ever. "It's not fair! How can I study for the test, pack for Winter Camp and practice for church all at the same time?" she said to no one in particular.

Tina grabbed the TV remote. Click! Suddenly the room was very quiet. "That's how," her big sister said. "By being self-disciplined. Not only is singing for God's glory important — everything we do every day of the week should be for Him. Wasn't your Bible verse last week 'Whatever you do, do it all for the glory of God'? Wouldn't that include studying as well as singing? As for the packing, do it Saturday after your test is over but before you get busy with church stuff on Sunday."

LaToya didn't say anything for a minute. Then she got up from the living room floor and went into the kitchen. She spread her books out on the table.

"Look, I have a suggestion," Tina said, following her. "How about if I set the kitchen timer for an hour? When it rings, you can get up, pour yourself some juice and go talk to Granny B. about a song for Sunday. Call Sara about singing, too, then get right back to studying until dinnertime. That will help you to become disciplined, the way God wants you to be."

LaToya groaned and grumped. What a bossy
big sister! But after a while the math
pages began to make sense. She wrote
down things she didn't understand,
and tried doing hard problems over
again. When the timer rang, she talked
to Granny B. Then she called Sara.

"I've already done my homework for tonight,"
Sara said. "How about if I come over and help you
study for that test?"

"Would you really?"

"Hey, what are friends for?"

With Sara sitting beside her, LaToya was
tempted to talk about school and what to pack for
Winter Camp and what fun it would be. But she
remembered Tina's warning about being self-disciplined.
So instead, she sat right there until she had reviewed
the entire section. And this time she understood
almost everything.

"I'm proud of you, kid," her big sister said. "Have
you decided yet what you're going to sing Sunday?"

Granny B. wheeled in just then. "You know,"
she said, "I've been thinking about that Bible verse
you learned last week. How about us singing 'To God
Be the Glory'?"

The girls looked at each other. "Great idea,
Granny B.!" And they each gave her a big hug.

· Good News · from God's Word

Self-discipline isn't easy. But this Bible story shows how important it was to one mother long ago.

Jochebed's Self-Discipline

FROM EXODUS 1:1-2:10

Jochebed loved God very much. She had a little home and a loving family. They all lived in the beautiful country of Egypt. But they also had a very big problem. They were all slaves.

Being a slave is a terrible thing. Other people can keep you out of school if they want. They can make you marry, or not let you marry. They can make you work as hard as you can all day. They can beat you or kill you.

Jochebed and her husband, Amram, never stopped working. The powerful Pharaoh, the king of Egypt, wanted them to build more and more palaces, monuments, statues, temples and tombs.

But the masters did not have power over Jochebed's heart and soul. She truly believed in God. She wanted to live the way God wanted her to by obeying all His commands.

Jochebed had a little girl named Miriam. Next she had a little boy named Aaron. Then one day the Pharaoh did something terrible. He ordered that from that time forward all new baby boys must be killed.

Jochebed and Amram had another baby, and it was a boy. They knew it was wrong to kill babies. So Jochebed hid her new baby until he was three months old. By then he made too much noise when he cried or gurgled. She couldn't hide him any more.

But Jochebed had great faith in God that He would help her save her little baby. Secretly, she made a basket watertight. Then she put her baby inside and put a lid on it. "We must take it down to the Nile River," she told Miriam.

It broke Jochebed's heart to put her precious baby in the water. She left Miriam to watch the baby as he floated along because Jochebed had to get back to work or she might be killed, too. God gave her the self-discipline to do all she had to do.

That little baby was saved. He was found by a royal princess, who then paid Jochebed to be his babysitter. He grew up to be the mighty Moses.

A Verse to Remember

Whatever you do, do it all
for the glory of God.

—1 Corinthians 10:31

What About You?

What's hard for you to do? Apologizing? Practicing an instrument you play? Trying not to brag? Not whining when you don't get your own way? Not being jealous of a brother or sister? Controlling your temper? Whatever it is, write it down below. Then pray for God to help you do right even when you don't want to.

_____

_____

_____

_____

The Valentine Heart Puzzle

Add Secret Letter "D" for "disciplined" to space 14 of the puzzle on page 26.

I've Got Your Number!

This code has only numbers in it. See if you can figure out the secret message. Check your answers on page 203.

Secret Code

% = 7	0 = 8	1 = 9	A = 10	B =11
C =12	D = 13	E = 14	F = 15	G = 16
H = 17	I = 18	J = 19	K = 20	L = 21
M = 22	N = 23	O = 24	P = 25	Q = 26
R = 27	S = 28	T = 29	U = 30	V = 31
W = 32	X = 33	Y = 34	Z = 35	

Secret Message

$\overline{11}\ \overline{14}\quad \overline{9}\ \overline{8}\ \overline{8}\ \overline{7}$

$\overline{15}\ \overline{24}\ \overline{27}\quad \overline{16}\ \overline{24}\ \overline{13}$.

Chapter 7

Packed and Sacked

That Friday morning in homeroom, Miss Temple had an announcement to make. "I'm glad that you all turned in your signed permission slips for Winter Camp. As you pack this weekend, remember to check the list we sent home for things you'll need. It'll be too late to pack an extra set of long johns once our buses take off Sunday afternoon. Unless you have them dropped down by helicopter, of course!"

The kids laughed at such a silly idea. But the weather had suddenly turned so much warmer that the whole idea of long underwear seemed just as silly. Even that early in the morning, the icicles and snow outside the classroom windows were already melting. What if the snow was all gone by the time they reached Monder Mountain?

But warm as it was, LaToya was freezing. That is, freezing up at the thought of her math test coming up later that day. Sara gave her a hug. "Don't worry. You'll do fine!"

And she did! In fact, she had one of the best days ever at school! Even Miss Derrin praised her. Before they went home that afternoon, Principal Anderson made another announcement. "Listen up, campers. There has been a slight change in plans. Because of the sudden warming trend, rain is forecast for Sunday, with possible ice on the roads later that afternoon. So our drivers have decided to leave at 1 p.m. instead of 2. Which means you'll need to be here with your bags packed and ready to go no later than 12:45. If you don't get here before we leave, you'll have to get to camp on your own."

"I'm so excited!" LaToya said after school. "That means we'll get there before dark. I hear the area around Monster Mountain is really pretty."

But Sara looked worried. "LaToya, don't you remember? You and I will be singing at church Sunday morning. Morning worship never lets out before 12:30. How in the world can we get home from church, eat lunch, pack up and be back at school — all in just 15 minutes?"

Just then Ric Romero rode up behind them. "Well, that's a no-brainer," he remarked. "Stay home from church the way I do!" Grinning, he sped off, his bike wheels again spraying them with snow.

"Well!" LaToya said. "At least he didn't knock Sonya down this time!"

Sonya laughed. "And he did smile. That's an improvement, too."

"Look," Sara decided, "what if we do this: put our packed bags in our cars before we leave for church and take sack lunches along? Then we can change clothes at church and eat on the bus."

During Sunday school class that week, the PTs had a hard time settling down. Everyone was far too excited about leaving for Winter Camp right after church.

"You'll get homesick," Miss Kotter said. "That's normal. And maybe you won't like all your cabin mates or the camp food. But do take your Bibles with you and spend some time each day in Bible study and prayer. And always dare to do right."

Sam raised her hand. "How do we know what's right all the time, Miss Kotter? For instance, most of the campers said they were skipping church today so they wouldn't miss the bus. Is that okay? What if we're late? That wouldn't be a good Christian witness, would it?"

"If you don't know the right thing to do, ask God," their teacher replied. "Trust Him to help you. Just as Joanna did." Then she told them the Bible story of a brave woman who dared to do what was right.

At the end of Sunday school class, Sam was still tempted to skip church. But she thought of that day's Bible verse: "Do what is right and good in the Lord's sight." So she didn't skip church. And was she glad! Sara, LaToya and Granny B.'s music was so wonderful, everyone gave them a standing ovation.

Then Pastor McConahan asked the kids from the church who were going to camp to come forward. He prayed for them all to have a great week. He also asked for God to help them do right all week, too, so they could be good Christian witnesses to the non-Christian kids there.

By the time the kids from Faith Church reached the school parking lot, everyone else had already boarded the buses. Sonya got on a special wheelchair bus; so did her dad, as one of the camp's volunteer helpers.

When the PTs climbed onto the bus clutching their lunch bags, Brittany sneered. "Is that what you babies carry your pacifiers in for when you get homesick?" Several other kids snickered, too.

Sara started to snap back a remark. Then she noticed that Brittany's face was flushed as if she'd been crying, and there were dark circles under her eyes. *What happened to her?* she wondered.

So instead, Sara smiled. "How did you guess, Brit? We brought enough pacifiers for everyone. Genuine designer labels." Now the kids laughed with her, not at her.

After she found a seat, Sam waved out the windows to her family waiting by the bus. So many people! But she noticed that Brittany wasn't waving, and Sam didn't see Brittany's parents in the crowd. In fact, the only time she had "seen" Brittany's parents was in a picture a few years ago on "Tell About Your Family" day.

Soon the buses roared out of the Madison  parking lot. Everyone waved and yelled to their families until they were out of sight. Then Sam reached into her lunch bag and took a bite. It was only a peanut butter and jelly sandwich and a bag of chips. But knowing she'd trusted God and done right by going to church made it taste as good as a sizzling pepperoni pizza!

· Good News · from God's Word

This is the Bible story Miss Kotter told before the girls left for camp.

Joanna's Courageous Stand

FROM LUKE 8:1-3; 23:55–24:10

As Jesus traveled around the country teaching and healing, many, many people came to see Him. They listened to His words. They asked to be healed. And they went home rejoicing!

Many of these people were poor villagers. But Jesus' fame spread. Soon, even the wealthy people had heard of this amazing teacher and were gathering along with the poor to see Him.

When Joanna first learned about Jesus, she wasn't sure if she should believe or not. After all, she was married to a very important man. Her husband, Chuzas, was the ruler over King Herod's household. He took care of all the palace's day-to-day business. It wasn't an easy job because Herod was a very cruel man. Herod was the same person who had had John the Baptist killed!

But Joanna also had a problem: she was very ill. We don't know what kind of illness it was, but she became desperate. Finally, she asked Jesus to heal her. And He did!

Joanna was so grateful that she wanted to do something to help Jesus. Since she was so wealthy, she joined with Mary Magdalene and other women to travel around with Him, helping pay for food for Him and His disciples to eat.

Joanna's actions took humility. After all, she was used to servants doing this kind of work at her house. It took courage, too, for everyone knew who her husband was, and how important he was. She didn't want him to get fired or killed or be killed herself.

But she stayed true to Jesus, even when He was captured, brought before that same Herod and killed. She even went with the other women to Jesus' tomb that first Easter morning and then to tell His disciples the glad news: "He arose!"

Joanna was thankful that God had given her the courage to do right.

A Verse to Remember

*Do what is right and good
in the Lord's sight.*

— **Deuteronomy 6:18**

Right On!

Just for fun, match the blanks on the left with the best answer from the rhyming words on the right. Check your answers on page 203.

1. This skirt's too   A. sight.

2. Turn on the   B. height.

3. Try to do   C. fight.

4. Try with all your   D. bright.

5. What a beautiful   E. tight.

6. Don't get in a   F. right.

7. Measure the right   G. light.

8. That light is too   H. might.

The Valentine Heart Puzzle

Add Secret Letter "D" for "daring to do right" to space 3 of the puzzle on page 26.

Secret to Success

Look at the letters inside the church shape. Going from left to right on each row, copy the letters from top to bottom in the following spaces. What is the secret of success in your Christian life? Check your answer on page 203.

__ __ __ __   __ __   __ __

__ __ __ __ __ . __ __ __

__ __ __ __ __ __ __

__ __ __ __ __ __ __ .

__ __ __

__ __ __ __ __

__ __ __

__ __ __ __

__ __ __ __ __ .

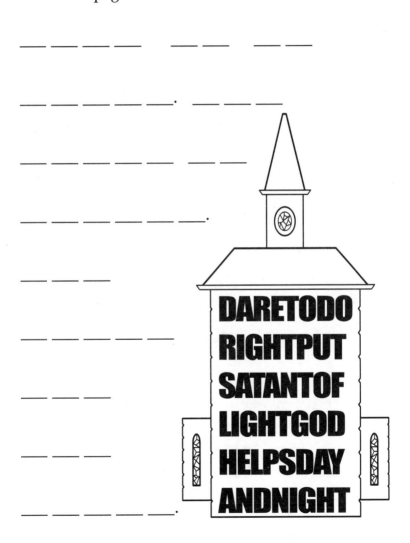

DARETODO
RIGHTPUT
SATANTOF
LIGHTGOD
HELPSDAY
ANDNIGHT

Chapter 8

Cabin Fever

The Madison bus caravan was zooming along through the open countryside toward Winter Camp. Snow-covered fields stretched as far as the eye could see.

Inside Sam's bus, though, space was at a premium. Students, backpacks, bags, books and sleeping bags were piled everywhere, with Mr. Talley, Miss Temple and the bus driver, Mr. Dollar, barely squeezed in between.

"Isn't it beautiful outside?" Sam exclaimed, nodding toward a window.

Sara laughed. "Sure, if you prefer gloomy old clouds instead of sunshine."

Soon snowflakes began falling from those clouds. Then raindrops. Then buckets of rain.

"I can't believe this!" Brittany grumped as she looked out at the rain. Then she began griping about everything else, including "this stinking dump of a bus."

"And when we get to camp," she complained to Lauren, her friend from the cheerleading squad, "we can't even choose our own cabin mates." She looked around. "Can you imagine getting stuck with some of these losers?"

Jenna rolled her eyes. "Anyone stuck in a cabin with her will be the loser!" she whispered to Sara. "I don't know how you cheerleaders put up with her."

Sara shrugged. "Sometimes she's okay. I just keep praying about it."

After a while the road became more winding and hilly. Tall pine trees bordered the road. "Are we there yet?" Josh squeaked in a silly, little-boy voice as he hid behind the back of a seat.

Mr. Talley laughed. "Sounds like the perfect time to sing some old camp songs. Anyone have a favorite?"

"Row, Row, Row Your Boat!" a girl called out.

"Ugh!" everyone exclaimed at the same time.

"How about something with more of a bang to it?" asked Ric Romero as he "banged" the head of the guy in front of him with a fist.

But just when Mr. Talley started to admonish Ric for hitting, there was a real BANG! Their bus had blown a tire!

The bus driver fought desperately to keep the bus from tipping over as he swerved all over the rain-slick road. Finally, the bus shuddered to a stop, still upright.

Everyone sat in stunned silence. Then they let out a big, relieved "Oh!"

Except for Brittany. "Great!" she grumped. "Stuck out here in the sticks with a busted tire and nothing to do. This trip just gets better and better!"

Mr. Talley and Mr. Dollar bundled up in their slickers. "Well, I can think of plenty for you to do, young lady," Mr. Talley scolded Brittany. "First off, you can thank God we weren't all killed. And then pray that we can get the tire changed in this storm and not be stuck out here for hours."

Josh volunteered to help them. Surprisingly, so did Ric! Then, after calling ahead to the camp and to the highway patrol on a cell phone, all four headed out into the blinding rain.

As the short winter day drew near a close, the dark clouds became even darker. *If only Dad were here!* Sam thought. *He'd get us going again in no time.*

She tried to wipe the condensation off her window. *Oh, no! It was turning to ice!* Even worse, the freezing rain had turned to sleet, which meant the road would soon be covered with ice, too.

Sam and Sara held hands and prayed quietly together for everyone's safety and protection, including the guys working on the bus in the storm. So did LaToya and Jenna.

A gloomy feeling settled over the people on the bus. Everyone was worried. Then suddenly Miss Temple disappeared behind the bus driver's seat. Over the top of the seat popped two "puppets" — looking suspiciously like their teacher's mittens!

"Hello!" one squeaked. "Let's play 20 Questions."

"Are you kidding?" the other one asked. "No one on this bus can count that high!"

"How stupid!" Brittany protested. But everyone else hooted her down and had a great time. They even sang along with the puppets when they started in on all the old camp songs they had learned years before.

"I hear a siren!" Sara suddenly shouted.

Maria scraped ice off her window. "And I see red lights! It's the highway patrol!"

As the kids cheered, the officers pulled over and helped finish changing the tire. They had even brought along an urn of hot chocolate and boxes of doughnuts for everyone. After the bus was repaired and everyone had enjoyed their snack, the highway patrolmen escorted the bus all the way to camp on the now dangerously-slick highway.

By the time the bus reached camp, the sleet had stopped. But the parking lot was still a mess — full of snow, ice, slush and big, freezing puddles. When Sam's busload dragged in with their bags, the kids from the other buses had already eaten dinner. They were sitting around the tables in the combination assembly room/cafeteria, singing and enjoying the fireplace.

"Singing!" moaned LaToya. "That's the last thing on earth I want to do!" But after a sandwich, a huge bowl of steaming vegetable soup, a glass of milk and a cookie, that's exactly what she did, too!

Then it was time to head for their cabins. "All right, everyone!" announced Mr. Carter, the camp director. "Cabin assignments are posted on the bulletin board. There is also a map to the cabins, which are in a circle around this cafeteria. Your paths are lighted. Each cabin will have kids from both Madison and Washington schools, plus at least one teacher.

"Bunks are assigned on a first-come, first-served basis, except for those students with special needs. Keep your bunk area neat. Take turns with the showers. Lights out at 10 promptly. And everyone up at 7!"

Ric groaned. "Seven? Ugh! I thought camp was like a vacation. People sleep in on vacations."

The camp director smiled. "Not vacations so great that you don't want to miss a minute of them, young man! Breakfast is from 7:30 to 8 back here. Everyone will take turns with KP duty — helping with the table cleanup and dishes. That list is on the bulletin board, too. Then promptly at 8:30, everyone should show up here again for morning assembly. Any questions?"

"What if we get sick or have an emergency during the night?" a girl asked.

"Each cabin has a phone," answered Mr. Carter. "There is also an intercom system that is connected to the main office."

"Okay, any other questions?" he asked. "If not, check out the cabin lists, grab your bags and let our great adventure begin!"

Sonya's dad helped her reach her cabin. Each of the other PTs headed for their own. Sam and Jenna discovered they were in the same cabin, along with Miss Temple, three girls from Washington, and four others from Madison.

Sam and Jenna gave each other a hug.

But then Jenna looked at the list again. "Oh, no! What luck!" she groaned as she read through the list. "How did we get in the same cabin as that horrible Brittany? Why did God do this to us?"

Sam laughed. "Well, God says we should love everyone, Jenna. Now He's really giving us an opportunity to do it!

"Race you inside. And dibs on the top bunk!"

· Good News ·
from God's Word

No matter what your problems are — critical classmates, running out of time, or something much worse — God can help us trust Him to get us through it, just as He helped this Bible woman long ago.

Acsah's Loving Request

FROM JUDGES 1:12-15

Caleb was a great hero to the Israelites. Everyone knew him as brave, loyal and completely true to God. He was one of the men Joshua trusted to send to Jericho and check out the land for him before the rest of the people entered. Even at 85, Caleb was a brave and honorable warrior for God.

Acsah was Caleb's daughter. He was very

proud of her. Caleb was so thrilled when Acsah married a fine young man named Othniel that he gave them both lots of land in the Negev as a wedding gift. This land wasn't too far from the land Caleb owned, so his daughter and son-in-law would be able to visit him often.

After Acsah and her new husband moved to their new home, though, they discovered a problem. Although they had plenty of land for their sheep, they didn't have much water for them. Her father's land, though, had plenty of wells. If he shared them, there would still be plenty of water for his animals and hers both. Of course, she didn't want to look selfish or make it look as though she didn't appreciate her father's generous wedding gift. She didn't want to hurt his feelings or make him angry.

Worrying and hoping, though, weren't going to solve anything.

"We need to go directly to father and ask him about it," she told her husband. "I'm sure he'll help us out when he realizes our problem."

So off she rode to see Caleb. After he greeted and kissed her, he asked, "What can I do for you?"

Then God helped her have the courage to ask her father for some springs to water her land.

Was he angry? Not at all! "I'll give you two good springs," he said. "Then your flocks and crops will never go thirsty or dry."

God helped Acsah to say the right words. God will help you find right and loving words to say, too, even in the most difficult situations.

A Verse to Remember

Love your enemies and pray
for those who persecute you.

— *Matthew 5:44*

What About You?

Is there someone who always picks on you — a teacher, classmate, brother, sister, teammate? If so, write his or her name here:

_____

What do you usually do when you're picked on?

_____

_____

What do you think God wants you to do?

_____

_____

Maybe you don't know what to do. You may need advice from a parent, coach, counselor, pastor or other trusted adult to help you. Be sure to ask. God doesn't want you to be hurt. On the other hand, sometimes ignoring the person who is picking on you or joking back as Sara did will stop the problem. Pray about it!

Bible KP Duty

KP stands for "kitchen patrol" — meaning you have chore duty to help in the kitchen or around the house. Find the best answers below to answer the KP questions. Check your answers on page 203.

1. Who served a meal for three angels? _____
2. Who wanted to eat the stew his brother cooked? _____
3. Who did a super job of sweeping her house? _____
4. Who was served a meal by an angel? _____
5. Who cooked some meat especially for Saul? _____
6. Which sisters prepared a great meal for Jesus? _____
7. Who set out plates and bowls in the tabernacle? _____
8. Who cooked her last food to serve Elijah? _____

A. Samuel's cook (1 Samuel 9:22-24)
B. Mary and Martha (Luke 10:38-42)
C. A poor widow (1 Kings 17:7-16)
D. Priests and Levites (Numbers 4:1-7)
E. Abraham (Genesis 18:2-8; 19:1)
F. Esau (Genesis 25:29-30)

G. Elijah (1 Kings 19:3-8)
H. The woman who lost a silver coin (Luke 15:8-9)

The Valentine Heart Puzzle

Add Secret Letter "E" for "even-tempered" to space 7 of the puzzle on page 26.

Chapter 9

It's All Downhill from Here

Brittany grabbed the best bunk and jumped in the shower without asking first if anyone else needed the bathroom. But the others in Sam's cabin were eager to share and help each other. The room was already cozy-warm. They quickly rolled their sleeping bags out on the bunk mattresses and slipped

into their PJs. "Five minutes until lights out!" warned
a voice over the intercom.

Snuggling down in their sleeping bags, Sam
and Jenna pulled out their Bibles. "Look at that!"
Brittany sneered as she dried her hair. "This is camp,
girls, not Sunday school."

But Sam noticed that one of the girls from
Washington was reading her Bible, too. So was Miss
Temple. After the lights were off, Sam prayed silently
and drifted off in an exhausted sleep.

Suddenly in the middle of the night, she woke
up. Something strange was going on! At first she
couldn't figure out what. Then her eyes adjusted to
the darkness. Someone was talking on a phone. Was
it Miss Temple with an emergency?

No, it was Brittany with a cell phone, inside

her sleeping bag. "Please,
Mom!" she whispered. "I
know it's the middle of the
night. But I've been trying
to reach you for hours.
Please, please, don't fly off
to New York tomorrow.
And please, please, don't
hang up on..."

But apparently Brittany's mother did just that.
Sam could hear the dial tone. Then Brittany's frantic
sobbing under the covers.

But just as Sam sat up to go comfort her,
Brittany jumped up and ran into the bathroom. The
faucet ran for a long time, covering the sound of her

sobs. Finally she turned off the water and climbed back into bed. After a while, both she and Sam drifted off to sleep.

The next morning the intercom blared out cheerily, "Good morning, everyone! Time to get up!" Miss Temple flashed on the cabin lights. All the girls groaned. But then the smell of bacon and hot cinnamon rolls drifted over from the dining hall. The hungry campers jumped up, showered, dressed and rushed out into the snow.

All except for Brittany. "I'm not feeling well," she whimpered to Miss Temple. "I don't want to eat anything."

The teacher felt her forehead. "Then you just rest, sweetie. I'll check back on you after breakfast."

On the way to the dining hall, Sam caught up with Miss Temple and quietly filled her in on what had happened during the night. "I didn't want to eavesdrop," Sam explained, "but something's wrong. I'm worried about Brittany."

"Thanks, Sam. You did the right thing to tell me. I'll see if I can find out what's going on."

When Brittany finally arrived at the dining hall, breakfast was over, KP duty was done and the other students were sitting at the tables with their notebooks open. "You kids will meet for all your regular classes this week," the camp director explained, "but classes will be shorter and some will be combined.

"We'll divide into eight groups of 25 each for class time. Teachers from both schools will team-teach you. As you can see, this hall is equipped with sliding walls to divide off into classrooms. We call these sections: Hawk, Wolf, Coyote, Cougar, Owl, Bear, Eagle and Badger. Just stay seated. As we close the sliding walls around your tables, you'll discover which group you're going to be in this week! We stop at 11:30 for lunch and KP. Then this afternoon everyone has PE together out in the snow!"

That's when Sam discovered that she was a "Hawk." That morning the students learned about the history of Monder Mountain and its many native plants and animals. They also had short classes on how snowflakes and ice crystals are produced, and on wintertime outdoor safety. Plus a challenge from a Washington teacher: "We want each of you to give a report at the end of camp on what you learned here. So start thinking about it."

Sam and Maria drew KP duty at noon. So did Brittany. But instead of helping, Brittany disappeared, mumbling something about a phone call.

By noontime the sun was out in full force, shining on a snowy hill full of sleds, inner tubes and snowboards — anything at all to slide on! Down below, ice glistened on the lake. Half the kids stayed on the hillside, while the others went down to ice skate.

Miss Temple was in charge of the sledding group. "All right, kids, we're going to have some races. First comes the Bumper Thumper. That's four inner tubes tied together for each team of four. We have enough for 10 teams. Any volunteers?"

Sam, Jenna and Kevin quickly teamed up. Since this was a sit-down race, Sonya was allowed to join them. Ric Romero, Brittany and two Washington guys were together on another team. Brittany kept laughing loudly, but her eyes were still red and puffy from crying so much. At the end of the first try, Ric's team came in first, and Sam's second, eliminating the others. The two winning teams pulled their inner tubes back to the top.

"And now," Miss Temple declared, "here's our final competition for Bumper Thumper champion! Okay, teams, are you ready?" She gave both teams a push and sent them flying.

"All right, gang!" Jenna shouted. "It's all downhill from here!"

Brittany reached over and gave Sam's group a deliberate shove. Sam and the others fell off and went flying head over heels. But the shove also upset Brittany's team's balance and they went flying, too! Over and over down the steep hill tumbled inner tubes and kids, as everyone screamed. Finally they all slid out onto the ice, scattering the skaters who were there.

Just then, the ice broke. And two kids fell into the freezing water — Ric and Sonya!

"Help!" Sonya screamed. "I can't swim!"

"I've got you!" Ric yelled. "I'll hold you up!"

Sonya's dad and some of the other men and boys rushed down the hill. They crept out onto the ice on their stomachs with a rope and one of the inner tubes. Kevin moved the closest to the hole with the tube. Mr. Silverhorse held onto his feet as he reached it out to the struggling pair.

Ric caught it with one hand and held onto Sonya with the other as they were both pulled to safety. Everyone cheered as the leaders threw blankets over them and rushed them back to the assembly hall.

Later, in warm, dry clothes, Ric and Sonya sipped hot chocolate along with the other campers. "Thanks, Ric," Sonya said. "Thanks to you too, Kevin."

Ric grinned. "I guess we both did some pretty good 'wheelies' today, didn't we, partner?"

· Good News ·
from God's Word

Sam's friends discovered that "Monster Mountain" was a great place to enjoy God's gifts of nature. Here's a Bible story about the very first woman to enjoy the great outdoors.

Eve's Joy in God's Gifts

FROM GENESIS 1:26-2:25

Eve wasn't the first person in the whole world. But she was the second. And what an amazing world it was! She and her husband, Adam, lived in a very special place called the Garden of Eden. It was full of every kind of plant and animal imaginable. Everything was for their enjoyment and care.

The garden where Eve lived might not be your idea of paradise. After all, she had no house, no closet, no stove, no clothes. She never bought new shoes. She didn't have any shoes! Money hadn't even been invented yet.

There were no schools, malls or amusement parks. No movies, video games or computers. No cars, freeways or skyscrapers. No cell phones or drive-thru or pizza parlors. No CDs or tennis rackets or jeans. And no zoo. But then, Eve didn't need one of those. The Garden of Eden was full of all kinds of animals.

What made Eve's home most wonderful wasn't just the friendly animals. Or the marvelous fruit trees, flowers and other plants. Or the perfect weather.

What made it special was love — Adam and Eve's love for each other, and their love for the wonderful world God had made and all that was in it. But most of all, they had love for their heavenly Father. It was a perfect place.

A Verse to Remember

Think of a beautiful white winter scene, such as what the kids found at Winter Camp. Where does the snow in it come from? How can it pile up several inches high? Or even several feet? Yes, people operate "snowmaking" machines for ski slopes. But the "snow" they create is not as much fun as the real thing. In the Scripture below, God reminds us of the amazing miracle of a "winter wonderland" only He can create.

Have you entered the storehouses of the snow?

— Job 38:22

What About You?

Look out a window or take a walk outside. Make a list of everything in nature that you see (trees, sun, ants, flowers, etc.) and write them here:

God's Wonders Near Me

_____

_____

_____

Now, write other wonders you enjoy that are someplace else, such as the ocean, mountains or Grand Canyon.

continued on next page…

God's Wonders Far Away

_____

_____

_____

Last of all, thank God for the wonderful world He has given you to enjoy!

Snow Way

Like puns? Try writing or saying the word "snow" (in place of "no") in each of these blanks. Some of the phrases are familiar song or movie titles.

1. "_____-body Knows the Trouble I've Seen"

2. Why study? It's _____ use!

3. " _____ Admittance! Stay Out! This Means You!"

4. "The First _____-el the Angel Did Say"

5. Do I like candy? That's a _____-brainer!

6. He's so smart, he won the _____-bel Prize.

7. If you ask me, she's up to _____ good!

8. "The Hunchback of _____-tre Dame"

9. _____-mads travel around the desert.

10. "I'm Just a Gal Who Can't Say _____"

The Valentine Heart Puzzle

Add Secret Letter "L" for "learning about God's great gifts" to space 4 of the puzzle on page 26.

Chapter 10

It's Snow Use

By the next day, Ric, Kevin and Sonya all had the sniffles. So did Mr. Talley and their bus driver. But they were all still raring to go. Especially since that afternoon would be the snow-a-thon. And that evening, a fun talent show.

"Have you figured out yet what you're going to do tonight for the talent show?" Jenna asked.

"No," Sam replied. "But I'll probably think of something. What about you?"

Jenna nodded. "The minute I read about the talent show in the flier we got at school, I started planning. I'm going to do the dance I did for my ballet recital. I even brought my costume and music tape along."

Sam thought a minute. "I don't know, Jenna. I mean, you're great at ballet. But do you think that will go over well with this group? You're so funny. What about doing one of your silly routines instead?"

"But I really have my heart set on this, Sam. I even pulled my costume out and hung it up on my bunk to get the wrinkles out. I'm sure everything will be just fine."

All morning, Brittany was quiet. She kept slipping out of class to "go to the rest room." But not because she was sick — she was making phone calls. One time when Jenna went into the restroom, she heard Brittany's voice from the next stall: "Please, Dad, don't do this to me! I'll never forgive you! I've called your office, your pager, your lawyer — you never answer. Mom won't call back, either. And neither will your stupid girlfriend or Mom's boyfriend. I'll give you both 24 hours. And then you're going to be sorry!"

Brittany was yelling and cursing when she hung up. Then she began sobbing. But when Jenna asked if she could help, she just cursed Jenna and told her to get out and mind her own business!

As soon as Jenna could, she told Miss Temple.

Her teacher looked worried. "Thank you, Jenna. I've been trying to contact her parents, too. But they're both out of town. Sara and the other cheerleaders think her parents are getting a divorce. Anyway, keep praying for Brittany, and I will too."

First up that afternoon was a snow fort contest based on the class teams. Points were awarded for size, style and usefulness of the forts, and the number of snowballs made and thrown. Each team also had an adult sponsor.

"Okay, Hawks," Mr. Carter said to Sam's group, the team he was sponsoring. "We've got to get organized. What's our plan?"

Their plan was teamwork. One group started making snowballs. "Remember, no ice balls," Mr. Carter warned. Another group picked out the site for their fort and drew a circle in the snow for its base. Then while some helped drag, push or carry snow over to the fort site, others packed it into place until the walls were solid, thick and as high as possible.

The other teams, of course, were busy with their own forts. As all of this was going on, there was plenty of snowball-throwing at each other. Just for practice, of course!

Then each team was paired with another for a rousing snowball fight — but with a catch. Everyone had to keep one hand behind his or her back at all times!

After Mr. Carter blew his whistle, the snowballs stopped whizzing. Instead, each team turned the snow in their forts into a sculpture. The Hawks turned theirs into a huge Snoopy on top of his doghouse. The Eagles turned theirs into a model of Monster Mountain. The winning Coyotes turned theirs into a cheeseburger — complete with fries!

What a blast! By the time everyone was finished, it was time for dinner.

Jenna was hungry and especially grateful for her steaming hot plate of spaghetti and meatballs. "Luckily we didn't pull KP duty tonight," she said between bites. "That gives me plenty of time to get dressed for the talent show."

Sam nodded. "And for me to think up something! But not before I get a piece of that chocolate cake."

As soon as they finished their dessert, the two girls raced back outside, along with most of the campers. But inside their cabin, Jenna let out a scream.

"My costume! My tape player! Everything is gone!"

"Oh, no!" the other girls cried.

All except Brittany. She had disappeared, too!

· Good News·
from God's Word

Being organized is important if you want to get something done. Even making snow sculptures requires planning and teamwork. Here's a Bible story about a woman who was very organized.

A Godly Woman's Life

FROM PROVERBS 31:10-31

Did you ever read the book of Proverbs in your Bible? Proverbs are wise sayings. For instance, "Waste not, want not" is a proverb. Another proverb is "The early bird gets the worm." You've probably heard lots of them in your life.

Well, the book of Proverbs in the Bible is not just a collection of wise sayings. The words in this book are special ones that God helped people to write. That's why they are in the Bible! Most of Proverbs was written or collected by wise King Solomon. But not the last two chapters. Chapter 30 was written by the prophet Agur. Chapter 31 was authored by a woman, the mother of King Lemuel. We don't know about her or the name of the woman she describes.

But the woman she praises is a marvelous person, indeed. She is a hard worker. She cares for her husband and children. She helps her employees. She works in many areas, such as real estate, the garment industry and crafts. She dresses attractively, and likes to sew and shop. She is kind to everyone, including the poor. She has good advice to share. Everyone loves to be around her. Best of all, she loves and praises God.

A woman like that is not a super-woman. She is an organized one, who asks God to help her meet all her responsibilities. In short, she is a grown-up version of Ponytail Girls just like you — just like the woman God wants you to be someday. And will help you to be, if you ask Him!

A Verse to Remember

Everything should be done in a fitting and orderly way.

— 1 Corinthians 14:40

What About You?

What do you want to be when you grow up? Maybe you have lots of ideas — doctor, teacher, counselor, astronaut, musician. Maybe you don't know. Maybe you think women can only be mothers. Being a mother is a wonderful, God-given gift. But think about the woman in Proverbs 31. God helped her to be a mother AND to do other things, too. Just as your own mother probably does.

Think of your own special abilities and talents. Write here what you think God is directing you to do with them when you grow up.

_____

_____

_____

_____

_____

_____

_____

_____

Let It Snow!

Want to play in the snow in the summertime? Soap flakes or detergent make fun play snow. Or use small cotton balls or miniature marshmallows to make snow forts and snowballs. Larger marshmallows make great snowmen. You can stick them together with toothpicks or something sweet and sticky like marshmallow cream.

Or, use an ice cream scoop and vanilla ice cream. Raisins or bits of candied cherries make faces and buttons; stick pretzels make arms. Yum! Just be sure to clean up afterward.

The Valentine Heart Puzzle

Add Secret Letter "O" for "organized" to space 10 of the puzzle on page 26.

Clocking In

Pick a day, any day. Starting with the 7 a.m. section, and going clockwise, write on the clock what you normally do for each hour. Be honest. Afterward, think if you are making the best use of your time. Is there anything you'd like to change? Note the clock on the next page is for the hours from seven in the morning to seven at night.

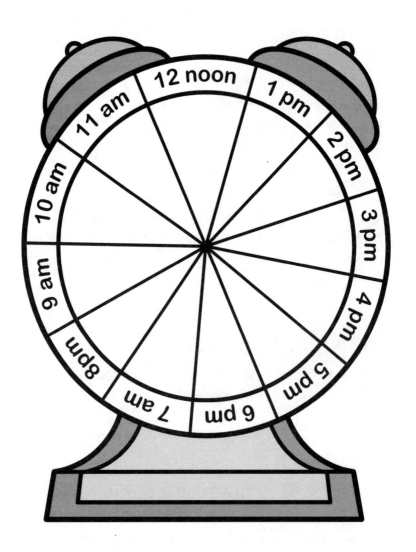

Chapter 11

From Show
to Snow

Jenna couldn't believe it. "My tutu! My tape player! My special tape! Everything's gone!" And she burst into tears.

The other girls tried to comfort her. "Maybe it's still in your bag. Or someone took it by mistake. Maybe it will still show up."

What Sam really thought, though, was: *I bet Brittany's behind this!* But she couldn't ask her because Brittany had stayed behind in the dining hall to make yet another call on her cell phone.

Sam hugged her sobbing friend. "Look, Jenna, even if we report this immediately, we don't have time to find your things before tonight's talent show. It'll probably show up tomorrow and you can do it tomorrow night. Okay? Remember that time when you did a take-off on Goldilocks for Zone 56? Well, I have an idea. I mean if you're open to suggestions..."

After she explained it to Jenna and their cabin mates, there were high-fives all around. Then they quickly got to work.

Later, when they trudged in to the main hall, scraping snow off their boots, it was packed with campers — in an assortment of last-minute costumes.

What a fun night! First Mr. Carter led them in some silly camp songs. Then LaToya and Sara sang "You Are My Sunshine"; LaToya played her guitar while Sara waved a flashlight around in people's faces.

Maria and Le pretended to be Central American women grinding corn to make tortillas for dinner. Finally Le said, "Forget this. Let's just go to Taco Bell." Sam and Sonya did a duet on "A Bicycle Built for Two" while Sonya sat in her wheelchair, with Sam behind her in a chair. They both pretended to hold onto "handlebars."

The guys in Kevin's cabin produced a garage band, only they called it a "garbage" band. They played a wide assortment of "instruments," such as pan lids, spoons and plastic milk bottles they borrowed from the camp cooks. Even can openers and rolled-up newspapers!

One team from each school held a mock debate on which school was better and why. Arguments included reasons like "Washington has prettier trash cans" or "The water in the Madison drinking fountains is wetter."

But what really brought down the house was Jenna's "Goldilocks and the Three Bayer Aspirins" skit, including Sam and some other cabin mates — especially when Goldilocks' troubles in the Bayers' too-hot, too-cold, just-right house gave her a terrible headache. Forcing her, of course, to swallow the Three Bayers to get rid of it!

Last of all for the night, Brittany donned a monster mask she'd brought from home. Then she sang "Climb Up Sunshine Mountain" in a very silly voice. Only she used the word "Monster" in place of "Sunshine." The audience yelled and clapped in appreciation. But Sam felt a shiver go up her back. Everyone would indeed climb "Monster" Mountain the very next day. She'd been looking forward to that adventure for weeks. Why did she suddenly feel that something terrible was going to happen there?

Back in their cabin after the show, Miss Temple helped everyone look one more time for Jenna's missing belongings. Even Brittany took a second to glance through her bags.

"I'm reporting this to the camp director," their teacher finally announced. "Maybe a teacher or camper in another cabin happened to see Jenna's things."

After the lights were out, Sam reached over to pat Jenna's arm in the dark. "Dear God," she prayed silently, "please help these lost things be found. And Brittany, too — she seems so lost herself, even if she is mean. She needs to find You and see how much You love her. Please help us tomorrow so our hike turns out all right."

The next morning after a delicious breakfast of sausage and pancakes, the campers met for classes on hiking safety, especially when out in the snow. And especially when hiking on "Monster" Mountain.

"You know, Shorty," Ric said to Sonya during a lesson break, "we have that report to do for next week. What if we do it on hiking dangers?"

Sonya giggled, partly from Ric being so friendly, but mostly from the idea of a disabled person being an expert on hiking! "Ric, I can't hike! I'm not even doing wheelies, in case you hadn't noticed!"

He laughed, too. "No, but we can study the rules Miss Temple gave us and write them up. Maybe make them into a handbook with sketches. What do you say, partner? Is it a deal?"

And even though Sonya didn't like Ric's ugly, dyed hair or the ring on the side of his nose, she suddenly liked the guy inside. They high-fived.

"Okay, partner, it's a deal."

Then everyone put their lunches inside their

backpacks along with ropes, mirrors, pickaxes, matches, tents, blankets and energy bars. Even though the day was rapidly warming up, all the campers had to wear heavy jackets, leggings, boots, mittens, hoods and scarves because it would be colder as they hiked higher. Then the team leaders looked them all over.

"I thought we were taking a fun hike, not climbing Mt. Everest!" complained one kid.

"Well, we do hope it's a fun hike for everyone," replied the camp director. "But that bright sunshine above you could change to a howling storm in half an hour's time or less. We all have to be organized and prepared for the worst, just in case. Everyone pick a partner if you haven't already done so. And let's get rolling!"

Sam picked Jenna. Maria and Le teamed up, as did Sara and LaToya. Sonya, of course, couldn't go; she stayed in the main hall for an afternoon of board games. Brittany picked Jennifer, one of her fellow cheerleaders. Soon all the hikers started off, two by two, up the snowy trail.

"Isn't this fun?" Miss Temple laughed. "Two by two, just like Noah's ark."

"Yeah," sneered Brittany, "just like the ark…before the Flood came and everyone was killed!"

And suddenly, even in her warm parka, Sam shivered.

· Good News · from God's Word

When Jenna's costumes and tape disappeared, she was open to suggestions on something else to do for the Talent Show. Here's a Bible story about someone else who learned to keep an open mind and heart for God's answers when problems came her way.

Huldah's Answer from God

FROM 2 KINGS 22; 2 CHRONICLES 34

When Prince Josiah was just a little boy — only 8 years old — his father was killed and Josiah became king. Being a king may sound like a wonderful idea, but not having your father killed. Even worse, he knew that his father and grandfather were both very evil men. The nation of Judah hadn't had a good king since his great-grandfather, Hezekiah.

Josiah decided to be like his great-grandfather. He had good counselors to help him. By the time he was 16, he was really seeking to do God's will. By the time he was 20, he was getting rid of all the idol worship he could find. Then he and the priests began collecting offerings to repair God's temple in Jerusalem. With all of the idol worship, God's house had been neglected.

What a mess the temple was! It had to be cleaned from top to bottom. But in the midst of all that mess the workers found something precious: a copy of God's Word!

They rushed with it to the king. People hadn't read from God's Word for a long time. The priests read it to Josiah. He learned about all of God's laws that he and the other people had broken, and how their nation would be punished for disobeying God.

"Oh, no!" the king cried. "What should we do now?"

So he sent the priests off to find out what God wanted them to do.

They didn't go to the temple, though. They didn't ask other priests. They asked a woman named Huldah. Everyone knew that she loved and worshipped God with all her heart.

Huldah could have lied and said, "Oh, nothing's wrong. Go home and be happy." After all, the king and his men had the power to put her in jail or even kill her.

Instead, she asked God what she should say. And God said yes, the land would be punished for all its evil, but because Josiah and his people were trying to do right, there would be peace as long as he was alive.

So for many years Josiah, his godly men and this godly woman helped God's people stay true to Him.

A Verse to Remember

A wise man listens to advice.

— Proverbs 12:15

What About You?

When you have a big decision to make, it's usually best to talk it over with someone you can trust, such as a friend, a teacher, a pastor, parent or grandparent. Some girls, unfortunately, aren't sure whom they can turn to. Others refuse advice from everyone. They think they are so smart, they don't need it! Unfortunately, they're usually wrong. Write below the names of people you can turn to for good advice. Don't forget God!

_____

_____

_____

_____

_____

Acting Up

Acting can be fun for just about everyone, even those who think they have no talent for it. On pages 192-195 of this book you'll find "Miriam to the Rescue," a play that you and your PT friends can read together. Or stage it as a play for your Sunday school class, youth group, children's church or other group. It's based on the Bible story in Chapter 4 of this book. You may be surprised to discover God has given you a talent you didn't even know you had!

The Valentine Heart Puzzle

Add Secret Letter "O" for "open to suggestions" to space 16 of the puzzle on page 26.

Searching for Talent

The word search on the following page contains some of the talents, interests and abilities girls have or can learn to develop. See which ones apply to you. Think about which ones you would like to develop.

Words can go forward, backward, up, down and diagonal. (Letters may belong to more than one word!) The answer key is on page 203.

Word List

acting	building	child care
computers	cooking	crafts
dance	fashion	games
gardening	hair	horses
law	mechanics	nursing

nursing	painting
pet care	science
selling	singing
speaking	sports
teaching	writing

```
E E S P O R T S P E A K I N G G X S
R R C A C T I N G N I G N I S A X C
A A O I S X U O C O M P U T E R S I
C C O N E R L I X S T F A R C D H N
D T K T S X A H X G A M E S N E A A
L E I I R X W S C I E N C E A N I H
I P N N O T E A C H I N G X D I R C
H G G G H X X F X B U I L D I N G E
C X G N I L L E S W R I T I N G X M
```

Chapter 12

Go Take a Hike

Unlike the stomped-down snow around the camp, the snow on the mountain trail made crisp crunching sounds under the campers' feet. It also hid rocks, logs and other obstacles under its smooth, white surface. Everyone had to be careful where they stepped, especially the trailblazers up at the front of the crowd.

The campers started out in an open field, with just a few bare trees here and there. Now and then a rabbit hopped by. Soon, though, the trees became more numerous. Then the trail went right through a thick forest. It got more zig-zaggy, narrow and steep with a lot of towering pine trees.

"Isn't this fun?" Sam said. "Smell the fresh air. I'm glad we brought our lunches along, because I'm really working up an appetite."

Jenna laughed. "Me, too. Umm! These trees smell just like Christmas trees. Remember when your dad worked at the Christmas tree lot? And we decorated Whispering Pines with all those extra boughs?"

Suddenly Sam felt very homesick. "Oh, Jenna, I sure wish Petie were here right now. He loves to go hiking. Even better, I wish we could take Monster Mountain home to him. Maybe put it in our backyard."

Jenna laughed. Then she sighed. "I miss my parents, too, and little Katie and the twins. They are so adorable! Every night I help Mom feed them and give them their baths. And they're just starting to smile. I hope they don't forget me!"

"I miss everyone!" Sam decided. "Miss Kotter, too. Wonder if they miss us?"

Jenna grinned. "Well, one thing's for sure that I don't miss: all my homework!"

Just then they noticed Maria and Le behind them and waited for them to catch up. "I'll be glad to get out of these trees," Le said. "I want to look down and see how far we've come up."

"Hey!" Maria cried. "Do I hear singing?" She certainly did. Someone at the head of the climbers was singing, "Climb, Climb Up Sunshine Mountain" the way Brittany had done it the night before by substituting "Monster" for "Sunshine." Soon all the hikers were singing along. Then someone started "On Top of Old Smokey," again using "Monster" instead of "Smoky."

Finally, the trail broke through the trees as the hikers neared the top of the hill. At that point, they could look out over the whole countryside, including the camp buildings below.

Mr. Carter, the camp director, pointed out the areas they could see, including a stream that started from a spring on that hill. "Look for it on the right side of the trail on your way back down," he explained. "Right above the tree line. When the snow thaws in a couple of months there'll be a nice waterfall there." The he laughed as he looked around at the hikers. "Okay, I can hear your stomachs growling. I can take a hint. Chow time!"

On a flat space at the top, camp rangers had built picnic tables and benches for hungry hikers just like Sam's crowd. There was plenty of room for everyone if they pushed off the snow and sat very close together. As a cold wind suddenly picked up, the close quarters were also a great way to stay warm.

"Hi!" said a girl beside Sam, as she pulled out her lunch. "I'm Ginger. I'm from Washington. I loved your Goldilocks skit last night."

"Thanks," Sam replied. "That was fun. Are

you doing something for the show tonight?"

Ginger giggled. "A funny skit about our principal. And he's here, too! Good thing he has a great sense of humor!" Then after another bite, she said, "Do you mind if I ask you guys something? I mean, I saw you two pray before you started eating. Do you always do that? Is it magic or something? Or do you have to do it because of your religion?"

Jenna smiled. "No magic, just good manners. We're telling God thank You for helping us get something to eat. Even," she pointed at her sandwich, "for bologna."

Sam took a big bite. "And these sandwiches are not a lot of 'baloney.' They're de-lish!"

Brittany leaned over to Ginger, "Actually, they just do it to prove how totally un-cool they are. Losers!" Then she turned her back on them.

Soon Mr. Carter called, "Okay, gang, time to start heading back. We'll go back in the same order we came up. Everyone stow your trash back in your own backpack — they'll be your 'litter' boxes. That way we'll keep our park beautiful and clean for everyone, including our animal friends." Then standing up, he said, "Let's see who's first to discover the spring on our way down."

"First dibs on swimming in it!" Ric joked.

But Sam wasn't in a joking mood. "That Brittany!" she simmered to Jenna. "Honestly, one of these days someone's going to choke her. And I'm afraid it's going to be me!" Then sighing she added, "I sure wish God would show me how to lead her to Christ and change her completely so she's not such a jerk."

Suddenly she was ashamed of herself. "I mean, change her so she can know God's love like we do."

A few minutes after they started down the hill, someone called out, "Hey, there's the spring!"

Sam leaned over, straining to see. "Where?" So did the crowd behind her. Pushing and shoving, they yelled, "Let me see!"

Suddenly, some of them started sliding downhill on the slick snow and rocks, pushing those in front of them, including Sam. She struggled to regain her footing by reaching out to Jenna to steady herself.

But when Sam grabbed her, they both lost their step.

The next minute, they were flying over the edge of the trail — right out into thin air!

· Good News ·
from God's Word

Sam wanted God's guidance to help Brittany know Him. In this Bible story, five young women also need God's help with a problem.

Mahlah and Her Sisters Seek Help

FROM NUMBERS 27:1-11

God had told Moses to lead his people out of Egypt to their new home in Canaan, where Abraham and Isaac used to live. The fastest way for them to travel there would have been to go along the coast around the Mediterranean Sea. There were good roads there. Even if they could only move slowly because of all the children and animals, they might have arrived in Canaan in just a few days.

But if they went that way, the Egyptian soldiers would have captured them and brought them back to be slaves again. So instead, God had Moses lead the people around the long way through the Sinai desert. Even then, it shouldn't have taken too long. Instead, it took 40 years because so many people sinned and turned against God.

At last they were ready to go into their new land. God told Moses to count all the people again. Then they would be ready to divide up their new lands to make room for every family.

The way Moses planned to divide the land was to give some to each male head of a family — that is, to a father or husband or brother. But five sisters had a problem. Their names were Mahlah, Noah, Hoglah, Milcah and Tirzah. Their father was dead and they had no brothers. But they were God's people, too. Didn't their family deserve a home in the new land?

So all five went to the tabernacle together. They asked to speak before Moses, the priest, the leaders and everyone else there.

"What about us?" they asked. "Doesn't God want us to have a place to live in the new land in our father's name?"

Moses and the leaders didn't know the answer. But they knew God did. So Moses prayed and asked God about it. And God said, "Those women are right. You must certainly give them property there along with everyone else." And then He made that a new law for His people.

All of this happened because five sisters, Moses and the leaders sought God's will about a problem. He will help you with your problems, too.

A Verse to Remember

Asking God to fill you with the knowledge of his will.

— Colossians 1:9

What About You?

How do you know what God wants you to do and be? Some answers are very simple and can be found in the Bible. For instance, you know God wants you to be honest, loving, helpful, joyful, thoughtful, and prayerful — just like a PT. For other matters in your life — such as whether to join the soccer team, how to study for a math test or how to help a friend when she has a problem — pray and ask God. He can help you find the answer, just as He helped those five sisters in the Bible story.

A problem I need to find an answer for right now:

_____

_____

Where I will get the answer:

_____

The Valentine Heart Puzzle

Add Secret Letter "S" for "seeking God's will" to space 15 of the puzzle on page 26.

God's Answers

Here's a secret message from the Bible to help you find the answers to your problems. Use the code to translate it, then check your answers on page 204 or in your Bible.

Secret Code

A = "   B = %   C = ‹   D = ›   E = fi   F = fl

G = ‡   H = f   I = Δ   J = (K = &   L = *

M = !   N = ...   O = @   P = ®   Q = ©   R = ™

S = £   T = ^   U = Ø   V = Æ   W = ≠   X = ¨

Y = #   Z = ˝

The secret message that God wants you to know:

‾ ‾ ‾   ‾ ‾ ‾
" £ &   " ... ›

‾ ‾   ‾ ‾ ‾ ‾
Δ ^   ≠ Δ * *

‾ ‾   ‾ ‾ ‾ ‾
% fi   ‡ Δ Æ fi ...

‾ ‾   ‾ ‾ ‾
^ @   # @ Ø

— Matthew 7:7

Chapter 13

The Monster Attacks

Sam and Jenna sailed through the air, head over heels. Then suddenly they landed — hard! Right on top of some huge rocks! Fortunately, the snow was deep enough to soften their fall.

Sam's head was spinning. Her ears were buzzing so hard she thought she was going to pass out. She heard, "Hold on, girls! We're coming!" But the voices seemed to be miles away.

When she could finally open her eyes, Sam carefully sat up and checked herself for injuries. Nothing worse than a sore knee and ankle. Above her, she saw a chain of rescuers working their way down the slope above her, all carefully holding onto ropes. But where was Jenna?

Then she saw her friend farther down the hillside. Jenna sat up, too, and shook off the snow. "I hope you all took pictures," she yelled up. "Because I really don't want to try that again!"

After the girls were checked for injuries, they were hauled back up and gratefully hugged.

"All right," Mr. Carter announced, "you see how dangerous it can be when someone forgets our safety rules? Thank God Sam and Jenna weren't hurt badly. But they fell because some of you crowded too close and pushed them. Everyone grab your buddy and fall into line. Two by two only. And no more bunching up! We're going to call roll and check it against our buddy hiking list to make sure no one is missing."

As the names were called, each buddy team answered. Finally, the camp director announced, "All present and accounted for. The trail gets slippery from here on for a while. Be careful about sliding and pushing into the hikers in front of you. You've already seen how quickly accidents can happen." Then they started back down again.

Although Brittany had been near the front of the line and Sam in the middle, Sam soon passed her up. She had pulled her camera out of her backpack.

"Where's your buddy?" Sam asked.

Brittany shrugged. "She's taking pictures at the front of the line. I'm taking the ones back here. That's our joint project for the week: a photo essay of 'Monster Mountain.' "

Jenna frowned. "Buddies are supposed to stay together, you know."

Brittany stared. "Well, excuse me! Since when are you my babysitter?"

About an hour later the hikers finally streamed back into camp. By then the sun had already set and the sky was darkening quickly. But a wonderful welcome awaited them in the dining hall, courtesy of the students who'd stayed behind in camp. Chili dogs, chicken noodle soup, cold milk and hot apple pie!

"Oh, smells great!" the camp director said. "Hikers, sign in on the hiking roster so we know everyone made it back. Then grab your tray and get in line."

Sam could hardly wait to tackle her food. "I could eat a horse! Doesn't this smell yummy?" she said to Le.

The PTs all found a table together, held hands and prayed.

Just then one of the teachers said something to Mr. Carter and showed him the check-in list. He frowned, then walked to the microphone. "One of you didn't sign in. Brittany Boorsma, are you in the hall?"

No answer.

Miss Temple jumped up. "Maybe she went to the cabin. I'll go check."

But a few minutes later she returned. "She's not there. Her backpack's not, either. Jennifer, you were her buddy. When did you see her last?"

Jennifer turned as pale as her cup of milk. "We stayed together all the time, Miss Temple. I mean, until we split up to take pictures near the end. You know, for our camp project. I...I..."

She burst into tears. "Oh, no! Maybe she's-- she's lost!"

Sam's heart dropped to the bottom of her snow boots. The sky had become pitch-black. But the moon was coming out. Maybe Brittany could see her way back by moonlight, especially since the camp lights were so bright. Unless, that is, she had fallen the way Sam and Jenna had fallen, and now lay somewhere helpless, maybe freezing to death.

Immediately, Mr. Carter and the other staff leaders called the sheriff and highway patrol. Then they bundled up and headed back outside, taking the camp dog along to help. Sam could hear them calling "Brittany!" through a megaphone, the same kind of megaphone Brittany used as a cheerleader. Finally, their voices and flashlights faded away among the trees.

Although another talent show had been scheduled for that evening, no one had the heart to go ahead with it. Instead, they divided the hall. One side was for those who wanted to watch a movie. The other side, by the fireplace, was set up for reading

and quiet games, and for a Bible study for those who
wanted to participate.

Miss Temple led the Bible
study. Ginger and some of the
other Washington students
participated, along with the Zone
56 kids from Sam's church.
They discussed Phoebe and
how she helped other people
come to know God.

"Brittany's been sad, too," Sam said.
"Something seems very wrong with her family. She
keeps calling and calling them on her cell phone. But
they don't seem to answer."

"Maybe that's why she's late," Sara offered.
"Maybe she finally reached them on the phone."

"Maybe," Kevin sighed. "Or maybe she didn't
and just gave up. Maybe she's lost — and doesn't
want to be found!"

Then the whole group bowed their heads and
prayed that the beautiful, broken-hearted cheerleader
would be found. Before it was too late.

· Good News · from God's Word

This is the Bible story the camp kids studied together.

Phoebe's Loving Help

FROM ROMANS 16:1-2

Travel in the time of the Apostle Paul wasn't easy. Some soldiers rode on horses. Their generals rode in chariots. Most people, though, went from place to place on land by riding donkeys, riding in ox carts or simply walking. To cross large bodies of water, they rode in boats. We know that even the Sea of Galilee could have dangerous storms. Those in the Mediterranean Sea could be even worse. Besides being dangerous, the trips were very uncomfortable and they took a long time.

But that's the way Paul went from place to place to tell about Jesus, and the way many other Christians traveled to new homes — especially when they were persecuted for believing in Christ. It was also the only way mail could get from place to place.

When Paul visited new lands and helped the people there learn about Christ, they became his friends. He wanted to keep in touch with his friends, just the way you do with yours. But he couldn't pick up a phone or send mail or e-mail. He had to give his letters to people he could trust to make the long journey for him — people like Phoebe, for instance. When the Gospel message first came to the small Greek harbor town where Phoebe lived, she was thrilled. As soon as she became a believer, she began helping other Christians. She may even have had a church meeting in her own home. And she helped Paul financially.

When Paul wrote a letter to the Christians in Rome, someone needed to take it to them. Phoebe volunteered. It would have been much easier for her to stay home safe and sound, of course. But she did it out of love for Paul and for the new Christians in this faraway land whom she had never even met.

Today, that letter is in our New Testament as the book called "Romans." When you read it, you can be blessed not just by what Paul says, but by the actions of a kind friend of his from long ago.

A Verse to Remember

*And this is his command: to believe in
the name of his Son, Jesus Christ,
and to love one another as he commanded us.*

— 1 John 3:23

What About You?

We all love to be loved. God wants us to love others in return. But it's hard to love people like Brittany who aren't very nice. Can you think of someone you know like that? If so, write his or her name here:

_____

Pray for that person that God will help him or her to change, and that He will show you how to love mean people with His perfect love.

The Valentine Heart Puzzle

Add Secret Letter "I" for "involved in helping others" to space 19 of the puzzle on page 26.

An A-MAZE-ing Trail

On the next page, see if you can get Sam safely through all the winding trails and down Monster Mountain to camp. Then go find Jenna and get her safely down the mountain, too! The solution is on page 204.

Chapter 14

Whiteout!

Nobody really wanted to hit their bunks that night. Not with Brittany lost somewhere out in the snow and another big storm on the way.

Rescue teams — who were specially trained for tracking in the snow — were mobilizing from all over. There would be a large force of them by morning, including a helicopter. Even some of the campers' families would be there the next day to help with the search, as well as Pastor McConahan, Miss Kotter and a school crisis counselor, all coming in Uncle

Todd's truck with more food supplies.

If they didn't all get snowed in.

Even if they all arrived and searched long and hard, would they find Brittany? And even if they did, what are the chances they'd find her alive?

That night, with the camp director out on the trail, there was a different voice on the intercom at lights-out time: Miss Temple. She could barely keep from crying.

"Campers," she began, "I know all of you are worried. Please try to get to bed anyway and get a good night's sleep. We'll be needing all of you to be strong and able to help tomorrow."

Sam prayed for Brittany that night — over and over again because she could hardly sleep. She was wide awake at midnight when she heard the searchers come back to camp. So was Miss Temple. She had gone to bed fully-dressed, ready to jump up at a moment's notice. So she leaped off her bunk, threw on her boots and coat and ran through the snow up to the main building.

But after a while she came back. Alone. Brittany had not been found.

Around 3 in the morning, the expected storm struck. The wind howled fiercely! It shook the little cabin so hard Sam was sure the door would blow in. By the next morning, the winds and snow had stopped. But the air was freezing, inside the cabin and out. The winds had knocked down the power lines to the camp. There was no heat and no lights. And no path up to the cafeteria, until the campers dug one out.

"All right, girls!" Miss Temple called. "Everyone up. You know why our cabin is equipped with firewood and a wood-burning stove, as well as an old-fashioned tea kettle and metal wash basin, several snow shovels and a battery-powered lantern! This is real camping. Let's all get to work. I'll give you instructions on everything. And no whining!"

By the time they got a fire going, poured heated water in the basin and got dressed, Sam's

 cabinmates were ready for a good, hot breakfast. And some good news about Brittany. But first they had to shovel their way out.

"This is the 21st century!" one of the girls mumbled. "Not the 19th!"

But outside, the snowy hillside was alive with laughing, shoveling campers. By working hard together — with a little fun of snowballing on the side — they managed to clear the paths from each cabin, including Sonya's, and then clear the path up to the main building.

Breakfast never tasted better!

"Campers," Mr. Carter said, "I'm proud of you all. After breakfast I need help shoveling off an area for the helicopter to land and for all the rescuers' cars."

That day the middle-schoolers worked side by side with the adults, shoveling, cooking, sweeping, cleaning and welcoming all the visitors that poured into the campground behind the snow plow. Nobody had to be asked twice to do anything.

By that time, the battery-powered radios around camp were full of the chilling news of one of the campers' disappearance. Soon, some reporters arrived, along with all the rescue teams and other helpers.

Sam and the others longed to join the rescuers as they outfitted and moved out to search. But they were ordered to stay at camp so that they wouldn't be lost as well.

By noon Uncle Todd arrived with Miss Kotter and the others. They brought some cell phones with them so the campers could call home to their worried parents. Sam was glad to reassure her family that she was okay.

But try as they might, no one could reach Brittany's parents.

Soon Sam and Jenna were busy helping their Sunday school teacher ladle out bowls of hot soup for the workers. "This is just like working at the rescue mission," Miss Kotter said. Behind them, a small radio was tuned to a local radio station.

Suddenly an announcer broke in:

We interrupt to bring you this important news from the Monder Mountain rescue site. Rescuers still have no sign of the missing girl. But a backpack has just been found. And it has her name on the outside!

· Good News · from God's Word

As the campers learned, obedience is not only good, it might mean the difference between life and death in an emergency. This Bible story tells about someone who needed to obey God — but chose not to.

Drusilla's Decision
FROM ACTS 24:22-27

Paul had spent many years traveling from town to town and country to country, telling people about Jesus. What a blessing he was to all those new Christians! What a joy it was for them to have new lives in Christ!

Not everyone was happy with Paul. The leaders had crucified Jesus just to get Him out of their way. They didn't want to hear about Jesus being God's Son.

"We've got to get rid of Paul, too!" they decided.

So they waited until Paul came back from his latest trip and he went to the temple to worship. They grabbed him and had him arrested. Then everyone found out that Paul was a Roman citizen and would have to be brought to trial.

Paul was sent to the governor of Judea, Felix, a wicked ruler. He knew a lot about Christianity, and was curious to know more. His wife, Drusilla, thought it would be fun to hear this famous Paul, too, so they called for him to come and talk to them.

Paul didn't care that they were important people. He spoke to them plainly about the punishment of sin being death. And how God sent His Son Jesus to be our Savior. Only through him could there be salvation, he explained.

That made Felix nervous. In fact, it made him downright afraid, for he knew he had done some terrible things in his lifetime! So had Drusilla. She'd married one king at 15. Then at 16 she'd left him and married Felix. And she knew better — she was a Jew.

She'd learned all of God's commandments, and broken a lot of them.

"Repent of your sins," Paul told them. "Turn to Jesus today, before it's too late."

"That's enough for now!" Felix cried to Paul. "You can go now. I'll hear more later when it's convenient for me."

But as far as we know, it was never convenient for either Felix or Drusilla to obey God. They never turned away from their sins and followed Christ.

A Verse to Remember

To obey is better than sacrifice.

— 1 Samuel 15:22

Following Orders

See if you can unscramble the words below. Each one describes something or someone to obey. If you can't figure them out, look up the Scriptures in an NIV Bible. The answers are on page 204.

1. God's SMDOCMAN (Deuteronomy 11:13)

__ __ __ __ __ __ __

2. MIH (Joshua 24:24)   __ __ __

3. The DROL OYUR GDO (Jeremiah 26:13)

__ __ __ __   __ __ __ __   __ __ __

4. OYRU ENSTARP (Ephesians 6:1)

__ __ __ __   __ __ __ __ __ __ __

5. RUYO SREDALE (Hebrews 13:17)

__ __ __ __   __ __ __ __ __ __

6. God's WAL (Isaiah 42:24)   __ __ __

7. The SWRDO of the Lord (2 Chronicles 11:4)

__ __ __ __ __

8. The LGSPOE (1 Peter 4:17) __ __ __ __ __ __

145

Praying Hands

What You Need

- 8½" x 11" paper, white or colored
- pencils, crayons or markers

What to Do

1. Fold a sheet of paper in half so it becomes 8½" x 5½".

2. Trace your open right hand on the front of the folded sheet.

3. Turn over the sheet and trace your open left hand on the back.

4. At the top of the front write or print: "I will pray and obey."

5. Write your name on the front at the bottom.

6. Inside, write prayer notes and requests. You may also color the hands if you want to.

7. Keep your Praying Hands inside your Bible.

The Valentine Heart Puzzle

Add Secret Letter "O" for "obedient to God" to space 2 of the puzzle on page 26.

Chapter 15

Breaking News

The whole camp was abuzz with the news. Not only had Brittany's backpack been found, but it had been brought to the camp for positive identification.

The TV reporters interviewed Sam in the cafeteria as she and the rest of the Hawks group made sandwiches for lunch. "Young lady," one said, "what would you say to your friend Brittany right now if she could hear you?"

Sam gulped. Brittany had never been her friend.

Not by a long shot! Brittany made it hard for anyone to like or love her. Yet Sam knew that God loved Brittany and he wanted her to love Brittany, too.

With that in mind, Sam could say the words and really mean them: "Brittany, wherever you are, we love you. And we're all praying for you. Please come home soon."

Investigators and five bloodhounds were also on the scene in case foul play was involved. "Miss Temple," one of the investigators asked the teacher, "did the young lady who is missing want to be a dancer?"

And then he pulled out something amazing: a tape, followed by a tape player and a very fluffy dance costume. Jenna's!

"Well, that's one mystery solved," Miss Temple sighed. "Where was this backpack found?"

"Down the hill from the spring. Apparently it fell from the slope above."

Miss Temple jumped up. "Yes! Just the way Jenna and Sam did! It's so steep right there. I bet that's where you'll find Brittany."

"Yes, ma'am," the investigator replied, "that's exactly where we're focusing our search. We're just hoping that we find her while it's still light. Even if the girl's still alive now, I don't think she can take one more night out in this subzero weather.

"If she wants to be found that is," he added grimly. And he showed the teacher a carefully-folded note. "This was in the backpack, too."

With trembling hands, Miss Temple unfolded the sheet of lined notebook paper. It read:

My Winter Camp Project
by Brittany Boorsma
Since no one loves me, I have borrowed this from Jenna for
my Dance of Death. Sorry for the inconvenience, Jenna.

"Oh, no!" Miss Temple gasped.

But just then Josh came running into the hall. "They've found her! I think they've found her!" he shouted.

Josh and some of the other boys had been helping clear the campground of trees that had fallen in the windstorm. "I was up on the roof getting rid of broken branches that had fallen there and I could see all the way up Monster Mountain. There are three helicopters circling the spring. And a whole lot of barking dogs and yelling people!"

One of the helicopters was piloted by a news crew. "They've found her!" a newscaster shouted live over the cafeteria radio. "They've found Brittany Boorsma, the missing girl. We don't know her condition yet, but they're life-flighting her to the trauma center at Circleville Hospital."

"Yeah!" all the kids cheered. "Praise the Lord!" added Sam and her PTs. Miss Temple was crying. "Thank You, God!" she sobbed.

Then the kids cheered again — but this time it was because the electricity suddenly came back on. No more doing everything the hard, old-fashioned way. "Even if I did sort of enjoy it," Maria remarked.

"I love the smell of burning wood. And it was a good feeling to know we could get by if we had to. Hmmm…I think that's what I'll write my Winter Camp paper on."

Soon the rescuers began coming into camp — tired, cold and hungry, but smiling.

"Oh, thank you!" Le cried. "You're all heroes."

Mr. Carter chuckled. "The real heroes are outside barking their heads off for lunch. All eight of them!"

"Tell us about it!" the campers shouted.

"Not now, kids. Let's have lunch first. We're starved! Come on, get in line. Pastor McConahan, would you lead us in prayer before we eat?"

Sam had never been happier to say, "Amen."

· Good News · from God's Word

Brittany felt that no one loved her. Here's someone who found a wonderful way to show her love.

Mary Magdalene's Labor of Love

FROM MATTHEW 27:55-28:10

Jesus had so much to do. Many people crowded around Him as He went from place to place. They wanted to hear His Words about God's love. Some wanted to be healed. It was thrilling to have God's Son right there in their own villages!

Jesus and His disciples were glad to help. But

as they traveled, they needed places to stay and they needed to eat. Yet they had no money to buy food because they were spending all their time in the ministry instead of working at regular jobs.

That's where Mary Magdalene and several other women stepped in. They traveled from place to place with Jesus, making sure He had a place to stay and enough to eat. They paid for everything themselves and were glad to do it. This was their friend, their Savior, the Son of God! How they loved Him!

The women even followed Jesus to Jerusalem for the wonderful Palm Sunday parade. They were nearby when He was captured. And they were right there when He died on a cruel cross and was buried quickly, without loving care and sweet-smelling spices.

The women were sad about his burial. They wanted to show how much they loved Jesus. So first thing in the morning — before the sun was even up — they hurried to the tomb with the spices they had bought to honor Jesus.

But, guess what? The tomb was empty!

"Jesus arose!" said a shining angel. "He arose from the dead! Go quickly and tell His disciples."

So the women ran off to tell them. On the way, Jesus met them and greeted them. They realized that He loved them as much or more than they even loved Him.

A Verse to Remember

Love one another, for love comes from God.

— 1 John 4:7

Stop, in the Name of Love!

Sometimes we think we're being loving when we're not – we're just being lazy or selfish or thoughtless. For the following statements, decide whether the actions are loving or not and check the appropriate column. The answers are on page 204.

The answers are on page 204.

Loving   Not Loving

1. We give our Mom a kiss or two,
   Then leave her with the work to do.

   _____   _____

<u>Loving</u>   <u>Not Loving</u>

2. We're glad Dad is a loving friend —
   Not just 'cause he gives cash to spend.

                      ——   ——

3. We tell Grandma just what to get —
   No thanks, though, for our last gifts yet.

                      ——   ——

4. Though we'd rather watch TV,
   We do chores with a smile — for free.

                      ——   ——

5. Gladly of the Lord we speak
   Just Sundays — not the rest of the week.

                      ——   ——

The Valentine Heart Puzzle

Add Secret Letter "O" for "openhearted" to space 18 of the puzzle on page 26.

Open Your Heart

What You Need

- 8½" x 11" paper, white or colored

- pencil, crayons or markers

- scissors

What to Do

1. Fold the paper in half lengthwise.

2. Draw a heart shape on the paper, keeping a paper "hinge" on the left side. You can use the Valentine Heart Puzzle on page 26 as a pattern.

3. Cut out the doubled heart but be careful not to cut the hinge.

4. On the front, write or print: "Look into my heart and see…"

5. Inside, write "a special note for you from me. I love you!"

6. Sign and decorate your heart and give it to someone special. Anyone can become special if you show them love!

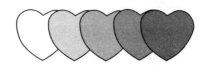

Chapter 16

A Downer That's an Upper

Of course, everyone wanted to learn how Brittany had been found.

"Well, as I was saying," the camp director began when they finally finished lunch, "our heroes today were our four-legged friends. Old Bowzer, our

155

camp dog, helped search for Brittany from the first moment we went out. Then the five bloodhounds came. All six of those dogs gave it every ounce of effort they could, even with all the trees down from the storm and snow up over their heads."

Josh interrupted. "But I thought you said there were eight dogs."

Mr. Talley laughed. "Ah, but that's part of the surprise. Keep listening."

Mr. Carter continued. "You see, as soon as we found Brittany's backpack, we took the dogs up toward the spring. Immediately, Bowzer started whining and wagging his tail. He kept pawing at some big trees that had been knocked down in the storm.

"But when we started to move the trees, we heard growling. Was it a bear? Bowzer? Our bloodhounds? No, it came from inside that pile of new-fallen trees."

"That's when we discovered Brittany," Mr. Talley joined in. "Before the storm hit, she had found shelter under a rock overhang by the spring. But apparently she wasn't alone for long. Two stray dogs found her there. And they stayed right there with her, keeping her warm, even after the trees fell and covered the overhang. They helped save her life."

"But what will happen to those poor dogs?" Sam cried.

"I'm not allowed to keep more than one dog here at camp," Mr. Carter replied. "But we'll see if we can get medical attention for these brave animals and find good homes for them."

"Boy, God really did something wonderful,

didn't He, by sending those dogs?" asked Shannon, one of Sam's cabinmates from Washington Middle School. "Now if He just helps poor Brittany get well."

"And not be so unhappy," sighed Sara.

"Miss Temple," Sam said, "do you mind if I make a phone call home? I want to ask Mom if we can take those poor stray dogs to her shelter."

As Winter Camp drew to a close, Sam marveled at how close everyone had become. The PTs had become very close to Miss Temple. And the kids from both schools had gotten to know each other really well, too.

"We need to keep in touch!" insisted Shannon. "It's so good to meet other Christians. Maybe the kids from our church in Midland can invite the kids from your church over. It's really not that far from Circleville to Midland."

"Sounds great," Sam grinned. "I'll ask our youth pastor about it as soon as I get back."

Maria stripped her bunk and rolled up her bedding. "I hear your church has worship services in several languages, Shannon. If we invite Spanish-speaking kids to the get-together, I could help interpret."

"And I could interpret for the Vietnamese ones," added Le.

Just then, Miss Temple got a call on her cell phone. "Wow!" she cried when she hung up. "Girls, here's some wonderful news. Brittany's still in critical condition, but she's conscious. She has frostbite, but the doctors think they can save her fingers and toes. Best news of all: her mom heard about it on TV in

New York and is rushing back to Circleville to be with her."

"Yes!" the girls shouted. *Thank You, thank You, God*, Sam prayed.

Finally, the campers were all packed up and the cabins cleaned out. A lot of the snow had melted, so even Sonya could wheel easily along the path from her cabin up to the parking lot. The big yellow buses waited there. Along with Uncle Todd's SUV, Mrs. Pearson, Aunt Caitlin, Petie and Suzie. And two carriers for the stray dogs. How Sam had missed her family!

After hugs all around, Jenna gave special hugs to the two dogs. "I'm so glad your shelter will be able to take care of them," she said to Mrs. Pearson. "They need families to love them."

When the campers started piling back on their buses, the camp staff said good-bye. "Remember," Mr. Carter said, "once you've been here, you're family. So come back now, you hear?" Then the buses started pulling out of the campground and heading downhill.

Sam found herself sitting next to Ric. He motioned out their window toward snow-covered Monder Mountain. "See, I told you it was a monster, didn't I?" he grinned. Then he turned serious. "Man, I hope Brittany gets okay. That's rough about her family splitting up. Mine's 'been there, done that,' too, you know. Right now I live with my uncle. He's okay when he's not drinking, but he works two jobs, so I'm pretty much on my own."

Kevin leaned over from the seat in front of them. "Hey, Ric, I hear you play the sax."

"Yeah. Why?"

" 'Cause you might like to jam some time with our Zone 56 group. We do some really good music, and we could sure use a sax player. Hey, why don't you come up and sit by me and I'll fill you in."

Sam smiled as they all exchanged seats. Both Ric and Brittany needed families who loved them. Wouldn't it be great if they could both become part of the family of God? After that, they would always know that they were loved, no matter what!

· Good News · from God's Word

We all need families to love us. So did young Joseph, all alone in Egypt. Then God gave him a larger family than he might have imagined!

Asenath's Loving Family

FROM GENESIS 34:1; 37:9-11; 41:26; 48–50

When Joseph was a young boy in the land of Canaan, he was part of a very large family: 12 boys and one girl. He loved his father, Jacob, and his mother, Rachel.

Then some sad things happened. His mother

died. His older brothers became very jealous of him. They sold him as a slave to a caravan going to Egypt. Suddenly, instead of being part of a large family, he was all alone.

As a slave in Egypt, Joseph worked hard to do right. But someone lied about something he didn't do, and he was thrown in jail. He stayed there until one day he was asked to interpret the Pharaoh's dream. God helped Joseph to explain to the Pharaoh that the dream meant that a famine was coming and it would last seven years.

The Pharaoh was so thankful for Joseph's help that he made him second in command of the entire nation. Joseph was directly responsible for teaching the people to save food so they would be able to eat during the famine.

As this important leader, Joseph made many friends. He married a girl named Asenath, the daughter of a head priest. While he helped the Egyptians save the blessings of their fields, God gave him and Asenath blessings of their own: two little boys. Asenath's parents were part of Joseph's new family, too.

Later, Joseph's brothers came down from Canaan to buy some of the food Joseph had stored up. How surprised they were to see their own brother ruling the land! Joseph forgave them for all they had done. Then he invited them all to move to Egypt, too. Now Joseph's family was bigger than ever!

A Verse to Remember

Better a meal of vegetables where there is love than a fattened calf with hatred.

— Proverbs 15:17

Glad or Sad?

Maybe your own family is perfect for you. If so, that's wonderful. But most families, even loving ones, have problems such as sickness, disabilities, being out of work, not having enough money, living in a rough neighborhood, being worried about the future and so on. Some families have such difficult problems that they break up, which makes even more problems!

Write on the next page what you appreciate most about your family. Then write what concerns you about your family.

What I appreciate about my family:

_____

_____

What concerns me about my family:

_____

_____

Share the good things you wrote with your parents. They will be thrilled! Share your concerns, too. If you are not comfortable sharing your concerns with your parents, discuss them with your pastor, Sunday school teacher, grandparent or another adult friend you trust.

The Valentine Heart Puzzle

Add Secret Letter "V" for "valuing a family's love" to space 6 of the puzzle on page 26.

Smiles Across the Miles

What You Need

- white or colored paper
- crayons or markers
- scissors
- glue or tape
- picture of you

What to Do

1. Cut the card pattern from page 164, or trace it on white or colored (yellow's great!) paper.

2. Color and fold the card on the dashed line.

3. Cut out the square part on the front of the card.

4. On the blank inside, write: "See the smile on my face? You put it there! I love you!"

5. Glue or tape a photo (like a school picture) of yourself on the right side of the inside of the card so it shows through the cut out square. Or draw your own picture in that spot.

6. Sign your card and send or give it to someone in your family.

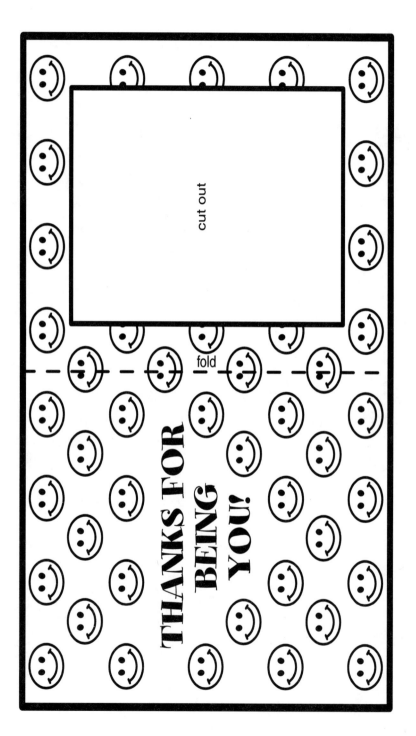

cut out

fold

THANKS FOR BEING YOU!

Chapter 17

Free Indeed!

That Sunday, the middle-schoolers from Faith Church collected enough money to buy a big bouquet of flowers to take to Brittany. She had improved enough to be placed in a regular hospital room. By Sunday afternoon, she could even have visitors. Mrs. Boorsma had stayed by Brittany's side, night and day, ever since she had arrived back in town.

Pastor Andy, Miss Kotter's class and several

other Zone 56 members went to see her. So did Shannon, their new friend from Midland. Not only did they take a beautiful vase full of sunflowers, they also brought pictures — very special snapshots Mrs. Pearson had taken at the animal shelter.

It was difficult for LaToya to reach Brittany in the room because she had so many shiny machines and tubes surrounding her bed. But the sick girl gave a weak smile when she saw the picture. "Look, Mom!" she whispered. "My friends!"

"Yes," her mother murmured as she smoothed Brittany's hair. "These are your classmates from school."

Brittany shook her head. "No, no! In the picture! These were my friends on the mountain. See? Oh, Mom, could we keep them, please?"

Mrs. Boorsma must have been crying, because her makeup was patchy and runny. "Oh, yes, you mean those nice dogs. But, uh, you know…you're in the hospital and…"

"Don't worry," Sam said, "the dogs are fine. The vet's been checking them out and giving them their shots. Mom said they made lots of friends at the animal shelter. So you don't have to make any decisions about them yet."

"Oh, but I already have!" Brittany whispered back. "I've named them both. The fluffy black one's name is Hope. And the other is Sweet Dreams. Only hope and dreams kept me alive out there, you know. And everyone's prayers."

Still clutching the picture, she slipped back into sleep.

Brittany's classmates visited her a lot after that. They told about their Winter Camp reports and helped her write her own. Mr. Carter had found her camera and cell phone under the snow on the trail. The phone was ruined, but the camera's watertight case kept the film dry. So the kids had the pictures developed for her to go with the "Monster Mountain" report she titled "Learning About the Wild."

"And I did learn a lot," Brittany said one day during a visit from a bunch of the Madison girls. "I learned that only friends and family can get us through hard times. I learned I owe a lot of you apologies, too. Especially you, Sara. And the rest of you cheerleaders. I hope you can forgive me for being so awful."

The girls gave her a hug. So did Brittany's mother. "I…I owe some apologies, too," Mrs. Boorsma stammered. "Especially to you, Brittany. My boyfriend and I had a long talk about our lives and made some decisions. He's staying in New York. I'm staying right here in Circleville with you. My daughter comes first."

The next day Brittany had another visitor: her father! He'd been on a skiing trip to France, so it took a long time for him to hear the news. "Then I saw it on CNN and I got here as soon as I could get a flight!" he cried, hugging his daughter over and over.

"That's wonderful!" Sara said when Brittany told her about it. "Maybe your parents can get back together! I'm going to pray about it."

Brittany smiled. "Me, too, Sara."

Soon, Brittany was a lot better. But her frostbitten toes and fingers were still a problem. Her doctors finally decided they would have to amputate three of her toes to prevent the gangrene from getting worse. Sonya visited Brittany and explained how God could help her overcome this new disability, as He had done for Sonya.

By the time Brittany was able to return to school, it was mid-February, almost Presidents Day. "The most cherished rights of Americans are our freedoms," Mr. Talley said. "The right of assembly, free press, worship, free speech and all the rest. Many lives have been lost protecting those precious freedoms we too often take for granted. On Monday I want each of you to report on what freedom means to you."

That Friday, Sara invited Brittany to come to church on Sunday. And she did — to both Sunday school and church. Her mother even came with her. Miss Kotter's class studied the story of Onesimus, a slave who came to know Christ.

"At first he thought he was just a slave to his rich owner," their teacher said. "Then he discovered he was a slave to Satan and sin, too. Satan encouraged him to do wrong things, like steal. Believing in Jesus helped free Onesimus, not just from being a slave, but from doing wrong things as well."

Pastor McConahan had visited Brittany and her mother several times in the hospital. When he learned that Brittany's parents were separated, he invited Mrs. Boorsma to see him about marriage counseling. "I'll come," she said, "even if my husband doesn't."

That Monday, LaToya gave her freedom report about Lincoln freeing the slaves. Le talked about living in America and being free from Communism. Sara spoke about Martin Luther King Day and the freedom marches for civil rights in the 1960s. Kevin shared about his parents helping to register people to vote. Sam gave her report on Roger Williams, the founder of Rhode Island, which was the first state to make freedom of worship a law. Jenna talked about the privilege of being able to attend free, public schools.

Then Brittany got up, still on crutches.

"As all of you know," she began, "when I went to Winter Camp, I was very miserable. My life was awful. My parents gave me lots of stuff, but they weren't around for me. When they applied for a divorce then dropped me off for camp and left town, I felt completely deserted. I thought ending it all would be better than living like that.

"But I didn't want anyone else to be happy, either. That's why I stole Jenna's things. I'm sorry, Jenna. But anyway when I was up on the mountain alone, I pulled your costume from my backpack. I saw a little note pinned inside it. It said, 'If the Son sets you free, you will be free indeed.' I wasn't sure what it meant, but I thought maybe it was about Jesus and God and love.

"Oh!" Jenna burst out. "That was one of my memory verses!"

Brittany nodded. "Well, I did want to be free. I wanted to be free of my anger and broken heart, and be happy like Jenna is. So after I read that, I stuck everything back into the backpack and zipped it up. I decided I wouldn't kill myself, after all. I'd go right back to camp and try again.

"That's when I slipped and went over the hill by the spring. The backpack went flying, too. No matter how hard I tried, I couldn't get back up the hillside by myself. So I crawled under that overhang. That's where those sweet dogs found me. I just know God sent them to me."

She smiled. "And guess what? Mom says we can keep the dogs! We're going to pick them up from the animal shelter tomorrow. And Mom and Dad are going to try marriage counseling to see if they can get together again. I'm free from all that crying and worrying and hopelessness. Free to look ahead to the future.

"And as far as I'm concerned, that's the best freedom of all!"

· Good News · from God's Word

This is the Bible story Brittany heard in Sunday school class.

Apphia's Problem

FROM THE BOOK OF PHILEMON

Apphia lived in the bustling market town of Colosse in what is now the country of Turkey. She had a large home — large enough for a big church to meet there. Apphia was a Christian who loved the Lord.

Living with her in that home were Philemon and Archippus. They were both Christians, too. We don't know if Apphia was married to one of them or if they were her brothers. But Philemon was apparently the head of this quite wealthy family.

In those days, many rich people owned slaves. They didn't stop to think if that was what God wanted them to do. After all, all their wealthy friends had slaves, too — including Philemon's family.

One of their slaves, Onesimus, was very unhappy. He hated being a slave, even though his owners were kind Christians. So one day he decided to run away. He stole money from Philemon to pay for a boat trip to Rome, hundreds of miles away.

"No one will ever find me now," he said. "I'm free!"

But in Rome he met Paul. Paul told him about Jesus. Onesimus believed in Jesus — just as Philemon and Apphia did. But what should he do? Go home and apologize for running away?

"Yes," Paul said. "But don't worry. I'll write a letter for you to take with you that tells the Christians in Colosse that you are a Christian now, too. I will ask them to set you free."

Paul did write such a letter. It is a very short book in the New Testament, called Philemon, after Onesimus' master. Philemon and Apphia did forgive Philemon and welcomed him home — not as a miserable slave, but as a joyful, free man, a fellow believer in Christ.

A Verse to Remember

*If the Son sets you free,
you will be free indeed.*

— John 8:36

Are You a Slave?

You probably don't wear heavy chains around your ankles. And you hopefully don't have a master beating you. But we can be "slaves" just the same. Unscramble the words on the next page. Are you a slave to any of these temptations or bad habits? The answers are on page 204.

1. GNIYL

— — — — —

2. GNISHLIOPFT

— — — — — — — — — — —

3. CHTINEAG

— — — — — — — —

4. EERPELVSONGI

— — — — — — — — — — —

5. FIGONGO FFO

— — — — — — — — — —

6. SINGU DAB SWORD

— — — — — — — — — — — — —

7. NGITKLA BKAC

— — — — — — — — — — —

8. SNBBUNGI ONESMOE

— — — — — — — —

— — — — — — —

9. EDGLU OT VT

— — — — — — — — —

continued on next page...

10. TON LIEVNIBEG GDO

— — —   — — — — — — — — —

— — —

Sometimes "Free" is Costly

We hear about free offers all the time on the radio, TV and in newspapers. But "free" things aren't always really free. Sometimes they're just teasers to make you buy something else that's a whole lot more expensive. Or other times the "postage and handling" on your free offer cost more than the free gift is worth.

There is a gift free to you that's not only worth something — it is priceless. God offers you His love, His joy, His peace, His Good News of salvation through His Son Jesus. It cost Jesus His life. But it will give new life to you. And it truly is free — all you have to do is believe.

If you are ready to make that decision today, talk to your parents, pastor or Sunday school teacher.

The Valentine Heart Puzzle

Add Secret Letter "U" for "unbound from Satan's power" to space 11 of the puzzle on page 26.

Chapter 18

Have a Heart

"*S*tudents," Miss Derrin said in LaToya's math class, "as you know, Friday is Valentine's Day."

"Yeah!" cried the class.

"Yes, a perfect day for…a math test!" Miss Derrin replied with a smile.

"Oh, no!" they all groaned.

"Have a heart!" said a clever girl.

LaToya certainly wasn't looking forward to the

math test. But she was looking forward to the weekend. Brittany had invited over all her friends (and their dogs) on Saturday to meet her new pets, Hope and Sweet Dreams.

And then on Sunday afternoon, LaToya's mom, her Granny B. and her big sister, Tina, were hosting a Valentine's party for all the children who had been at their house for Christmas Camp. All the PTs would be there, too, plus Jenna's baby twin sisters. They were almost two months old, and utterly adorable.

But first, LaToya knew she had to make it through her math test.

She remembered how studying had helped her through her last math test. So she passed up a chance to baby-sit to stay home and study for the test.

When LaToya got to math class the next day, Miss Derrin had filled the whole chalkboard with questions. But it was the strangest math test LaToya had ever seen! It was a mixture of written-out questions, not just number ones. "You have 15 minutes to complete this test," Miss Derrin announced.

LaToya rushed through the test, sweating. It didn't make any sense, but she did her best, anyway.

"Be sure your name is on your paper," said her teacher, "then fold it up and hand it to the person on your right to grade. Then rearrange the answers on that person's paper in the following order: 3, 7, 2, 6, 5, 4, 8, 1. And hand them back." (*See page 181 to try this fun test yourself, and find out the special Valentine answer.*)

In a few minutes the whole room was snickering as they caught on. It was all just a make-believe test!

After that, Miss Derrin passed out candy valentine hearts and a little written valentine to each student.

Saturday dawned bright and sunny. The snow still on the ground melted quickly, so the dogs at Brittany's party were able to play outside together in the back yard.

It was a fun group. There was Sam's tiny poodle, Sneezit; Sonya's golden cocker spaniel, Cocky; Sara's great Dane, Tank; and Brittany's new pets, fluffy black Hope and Sweet Dreams, a German shepherd. "Sweet Dreams" was such a long name, everyone was soon calling her "Sweetie" for short.

Even Scott, the collie the PTs "dogsat" during Christmas Camp, stopped by with his owner to say hi.

Sara and Le had made valentines for all the dogs and their owners. Brittany was so much fun it was hard to imagine her as the bitter, mean cheerleader from just a few months back. She even had a "race" on her crutches with Sonya in her wheelchair. When LaToya invited her to the Valentine Party the next day at her house, Brittany replied, "Oh, wow! Can Mom come, too?" Now that she had her back, Brittany didn't want to spend much time away from her mom.

So the next day Brittany and her mom arrived at LaToya's for the party. Brittany didn't know her own grandmothers, so getting to meet sparkling Granny B. was a great delight. Brittany even helped Granny B. lead the younger children in a few games.

When Sara's good-looking big brother, Tony, came to help with the games, Brittany was so thrilled she hardly knew what to stay. "I just love to watch you play basketball!" she stammered.

Mrs. Boorsma thanked the other women over and over for their help. "And your pastor is such a jewel!" she remarked. "My husband is really hesitant about going to those marriage counseling sessions with me. But I think we both need it if we're going to make a fresh start together. We need to keep from making the same mistakes again."

And of course everyone fussed over tiny Holly and Noel, who giggled and gurgled the whole time. Afterward, the PTs helped LaToya clean up. Then they had a slumber party in her rec room. Brittany was invited, too.

"You know," she confessed that night after they were all in their PJs and sleeping bags, "I've always fought to be popular. But I never had any real friends except the other cheerleaders. Now I feel like I have lots of friends."

LaToya giggled. "Well, you better not invite them all over for a slumber party at the same time. Not even your basement is big enough for that!"

·PTs·

· Good News · from God's Word

Brittany is glad for her friends. Here is a Bible story about two Bible times people who became good friends once they got to know each other.

Rachel's New Friend

FROM GENESIS 28:1-29:18

Jacob had a twin brother, Esau. Esau married two women, as was common in Bible days. However, neither of his wives got along with Jacob's family.

"It's because they don't believe in the one true God," the twins' mother, Rebekah, said to her husband, Isaac. "How can we help Jacob do better and fall in love with someone who is a believer, not a pagan? I know! He can go visit my brother Laban in the city of Haran. Laban can help him meet someone who is true to God."

The journey to Haran was several hundred miles. There were no trains or planes or buses to take him there, of course. Not even a car. Jacob had never been there before, but he could follow a caravan road.

Even though he was a little nervous, he was excited too. After all, this was an adventure!

Jacob was very, very tired by the time he made it to Haran. He was also very, very thirsty. Then he saw a well! There were shepherds there and three flocks of sheep. Then a young woman arrived with more sheep. All the people were thirsty. The sheep were, too.

"Why aren't you drinking?" Jacob asked.

"We can't get the stone off the top of the well," they said.

Jacob pushed the stone off and let everyone drink. Then he met the young woman. She was his own cousin, Rachel! He was so happy to see her, he gave her a big kiss.

Rachel ran home and brought back her father, Jacob's Uncle Laban. Jacob stayed with them for a long time. In fact, he and Rachel got married!

 A Verse to Remember

I have called you friends.

— *John 15:15*

Valentine Math Test

This is the funny test LaToya's class took. See if you can figure it out! Check your answers on page 204.

1. Add both columns of numbers below. Write E in the answer space if both sums are equal or U if they are both unequal.

64	33
15	71
58	15
28	5
39	3
29	42

Totals: _____   _____

Are the totals equal (E) or unequal (U)? _____

2. In this tic-tac-toe game, which wins, the X or the O?

X		O
X	O	
O	X	

Answer: _____

3. The Roman numeral for 1 is:

Answer: _____

continued on next page…

4.   If X + Y = 129
      and X = 63
      then 66 = what?

                              Answer: ___

5. If you multiply 145 by 95, and spell out the answer, what would the last letter of the answer be?

                              Answer: ___

6. The Roman numeral for 5.

                              Answer: ___

7. The twelfth letter of the alphabet.

                              Answer: ___

8. Zero to the tenth power (the number, not the word).

                              Answer: ___

Write out your answers in this order:

3. ___ 7. ___ 2. ___ 6. ___ 5. ___ 4. ___ 8. ___ 1. ___

Check your answers on page 204.

The Valentine Heart Puzzle

Add the Secret Letter "O" for "offering friendship" to space 5 of the puzzle on page 26.

Doggone Cute

Here's a picture of Brittany's two new dogs playing together. Draw collars and sweaters on them.

Chapter 19

Peanut Butter and Jammin'

When Sam and the other Faith Church kids asked Pastor Andy about a get-together with the Midland church group, he was all for it.

"Why didn't I think of that!" he exclaimed. "I went to college with their youth pastor. In fact, Bill and I roomed together one year. We used to call him 'Buffalo Bill' because he was from Buffalo, New York."

A few days later Pastor Andy called Pastor Bill at Grace Church in Midland. After Andy suggested that the two youth groups have a joint meeting, Bill said, "Yeah, Shannon Hendricks from our group has been bugging me about that ever since Winter Camp. Let's do it! Plan on about half an hour's music from your group and half an hour's from ours. Then about 10 minutes for a devotional at the end. Okay?"

"Great! Does the last Saturday in February sound doable on your end?"

"I'm checking the church calendar right now... Yep, let's go for it!"

All of Zone 56 was excited. "Ric, you've got to come, too," Kevin urged him at school that week. "For instruments we've got me on the drums and Scott Schneider on the bass and LaToya on the guitar. Let's see, who else?"

Ric fiddled with his earring. "Doesn't Le play something?"

"Just the violin. But when we do country stuff she's great on the fiddle. And Pastor Andy can play a ukulele. I bet he could do a banjo or something else, too. Let's ask around and see if we're missing someone."

That's when they discovered that Brittany played the electric keyboard. "Not great," she admitted. "I never liked to practice. But I can help out."

Josh played a trumpet, Jenna was learning the flute, and Sonya played the harmonica! Also, several of the kids loved to sing, including all the PTs. Sara was a great soloist. Ric's voice was changing, but he was willing to try.

"Wow!" Pastor Andy exclaimed when he heard them all. "This is great. We have enough of you that some can play on the praise songs, some on the hymns and some on the quiet, more worshipful songs. Who has suggestions for songs?"

The night of the big event, several cars caravaned in driving rain. Mr. Thomas took a night off from work just to take some of the kids. Miss Kotter and Pastor Andy each took a load. And so did Brittany's mom. They all took the wrong turn into Midland and got lost. Then they all got soaked unloading their equipment. Several times during the night it rained so hard that all the lights (and power to the amplifiers and mikes) went off in the Grace Church sanctuary.

They were supposed to have hot dogs afterward. But when the church stove went out with the power, they resorted to peanut butter and jelly sandwiches.

But they had a great time, anyway — even Ric and Brittany. When Sara began singing "Jesus, Draw Me Close," and all the lights went out again, she kept right on singing in the dark. Someone turned on a lantern. Then everyone who knew the words began singing along quietly with her in the flickering light.

Right after that, Pastor Bill quietly explained, "Jesus is always ready to draw us close to Him. He's always right there waiting. We're the ones who hold back, who think we don't need Him. Who think we're doing just fine, thank you. Even when we feel like we're drowning inside. He always loves us. He wants to help us. And He is always able to. All we have to do is ask."

Just then Brittany's hand shot up. Brittany's! "But how? How do we do it?" she asked out loud.

After Pastor Bill explained the Gospel and God's wonderful plan of love and salvation, five kids said they were ready to make decisions for Christ — including Brittany! They came forward and knelt at the altar while both pastors prayed with them. Sam and LaToya also came forward. They each knelt on either side of Brittany. Sam put a gentle arm around Brittany as they all prayed together.

After the prayer, Pastor Andy said, "You are all new people. Oh, things may look the same on the outside. Your clothes and shoes are still wet. Our  church lights are still off. But inside you are a brand-new child of God. He will help you every day to be more and more like Jesus, if you turn to Him."

Brittany smiled and sniffled at the same time. "I already feel like Jesus! 'Cause I love everyone in the whole world!" And she gave Sam and LaToya a big hug. Both at the same time!

·PTS·

· Good News ·
from God's Word

Did you ever wonder where musical instruments come from? Here's a Bible story about it.

Naamah's Musical Brother
from Genesis 4:17-5:24

People have always loved music. Music is all around us in the wonderful world God has made. We can hear the wind blowing, birds singing, ripples tumbling in streams and crickets chirping. Even a baby loves to coo and make happy-sounding noises. The Garden of Eden must have been filled with joyous music.

So people naturally began singing. And humming.

And whistling. And beating on things for rhythm to express love for each other, joy in life and thankfulness to God.

But no one had any musical instruments until a man named Jubal came along. Jubal had two brothers and a sister named Naamah. He also had parents, of course. But his father, Lamech, was not a very nice person, which must have caused a lot of unhappiness in Jubal's family.

It's hard to do your best when there is a lot of unhappiness at home. But Jubal's brothers did their best anyway. One of them became a nomad — he figured out how to travel around with his sheep and live in tents.

Another invented metalworking. He was the very first person to melt and shape iron and bronze. That meant he could make helpful tools, like plows and knives.

But for Jubal, music was the most important activity in life. Jubal loved music so much he wasn't content just to hum and sing and whistle and beat on homemade drums. He invented special musical instruments like the flute and the harp to create even more music. We play modern versions of these flutes and harps today. Maybe music helped Jubal overcome the problems caused by having a father like Lamech.

Naamah must have been glad to hear her brother's music!

A Verse to Remember

*Jesus answered, "I am the way
and the truth and the life."*

— John 14:6

Music, Music, Music!

Listed below are some of the musical instruments mentioned in the Bible. See if you can unscramble their names.

1. prah   ___ ___ ___ ___

2. ttperum   ___ ___ ___ ___ ___ ___ ___

3. nroh   ___ ___ ___ ___

4. rely   ___ ___ ___ ___

5. tembarouin   ___ ___ ___ ___ ___ ___ ___ ___ ___ ___

6. teflu   ___ ___ ___ ___ ___

7. balscym   ___ ___ ___ ___ ___ ___ ___

8. ssbra   ___ ___ ___ ___ ___ gong

9. llebs   ___ ___ ___ ___ ___

Check your answers on page 204.

The Valentine Heart Puzzle

Add Secret Letter "Y" for "you" to space 9 of the puzzle on page 26. Your Valentine Heart Puzzle is complete. Aren't you glad God loves you? Aren't you glad He helps you love others, too? See the completed puzzle on page 204.

Extra Stuff!

The following pages contain bonus Ponytail Girls activities especially for you. In this section you will find information on forming your own Ponytail Girls Club, including membership cards.

At the end of this section, be sure to check out the coupon for a **free scrunchie!**

Miriam to the Rescue

Do you like to be in plays? Maybe you have staged a play with the kids in your neighborhood, with your class at school or with your church friends. Maybe your church stages a play about the first Christmas, the way Faith Church does.

Plays help us look at a story in a fresh way. Because we seem to see everything happening right before our eyes, it seems very real.

Of course, not everything we read and see is real. But the following play tells a story that is very real because it is from the Bible. Because this special type of play doesn't require the performers to memorize a lot of words, you can spend more time thinking about how you want to present it. You can sit around with your friends and read it. Or you can stage it with costumes and props. You can have one person read the narration, or have several take turns.

Practice well so everyone knows just what to do. Ask God to help you, and then thank Him afterward.

Be glad that God didn't think a little girl like Miriam was too young to handle a big job and do it well. God thinks the same way about you, too!

Characters

- Pharaoh
- Miriam
- Miriam's mother
- Pharaoh's daughter, the Princess
- Princess' maidens
- Narrator

Props

- Basket with lid (a picnic basket, for example)
- Homemade costumes, such as sheets, towels, or long

dresses for all the characters to wear. Pharaoh and Pharaoh's daughter should have gauzy, sparkling or otherwise more elegant costumes, such as a crown cut out of cardboard, stapled together, and painted gold. Pharaoh can have a throne (throw a bright towel over a chair) and carry a staff (decorated stick).

- Long, stiff straight "bulrush" leaves, such as those cut from a lily plant, or cut from cardboard and painted.
- Crocodile head. Make one by covering a person's arms with green fabric, then stick on eyes. The "mouth" will open and shut as the arms move. Or draw a crocodile silhouette and attach it to a pole or a length of string.
- River. If you want to show water, you can place a strip of wavy blue plastic or a large piece of blue wallpaper or gift wrap on the floor.
- Doll wrapped in towel or blanket

Setting: Egypt, about 3500 years ago

Script

Narrator: Long ago in Egypt-land, Pharaoh lived in a palace grand.

Pharaoh comes out, sits on throne, his daughter's friends kneel before him.

Narrator: Everyone had to be his slave

Pharaoh frowns and looks very stern.

Narrator: From when they were born until the grave. He had no pity. No, instead, Pharaoh would yell,

Pharaoh: "Off with his head!"

Narrator: The Israelites were his servants, too — even kids like me and you. They had no fun. They had no toys. Then Pharaoh yelled:

Pharaoh yells: "Kill the baby boys!"

Pharaoh stomps off. His daughter's friends pick up the cover off the "throne" and take it out with them.

Miriam and Mother: "Boo hoo!"

Narrator: Cried Miriam and her mother,

They come in carrying baby Moses and pretending to cry. Mother sits in chair and rocks baby.

Narrator: For Miriam had a baby brother.

Mother: "I'll ask God 's help,"

Narrator: her mother cried,

Mother lifts up hand and looks upward as if praying.

Mother: "Then take a basket and put him inside. Oh, if only our baby we could hide!"

Narrator: They put him in, then after a while, they went down to the River Nile.

Put baby in basket, close lid, stand up, walk a little way. Someone can put down the "river" for them, or they can do it, then set the basket on it. They can prop up the "bulrushes," or other kids can crouch down and hold them up by the river. Also, show crocodiles with big, sharp teeth!

Narrator: They put the basket down to float on the water like a boat. There were bulrushes there, and down beneath, crocodiles with big sharp teeth! Said Mother,

Mother: "Dear, as you can see, I must return home speedily.

Mother pretends to speak to Miriam, then she rushes off.

Narrator: Please stay and watch. And I will pray God will take care of you both today."

Miriam "hides" in bulrushes.

Narrator: Then suddenly came someone new — a princess and her maidens, too.

Pharaoh's daughter and her friends come.

Princess: "A basket!"

Narrator: she cried.

Princess: "Oh, let me see! Maybe something's inside for me!"

Princess points to basket. Maidens lift basket; she looks in.

Narrator: Inside was a baby, as cute as could be.

Princess: "A baby!"

Narrator: she cried.

Princess: "I found it! It's mine."

Maidens take out baby; princess holds him.

Narrator: Miriam smiled. Things were working out fine.

Miriam gives a big smile; jumps out.

Miriam: "Can I find you a nurse for your baby?"

Narrator: said she.

Princess: "Oh, please!"

Narrator: said the princess.

Princess: "As quick as can be. Find me a nurse. I'll pay her well."

Narrator: Oh, what a story Miriam had to tell!

Miriam "runs" to get Mother.

Narrator: She quickly got her mother, who was hired on the spot.

Mother comes back, bows to Princess.

Narrator: Were they both thankful? You bet! A whole lot!

Princess hands Mother baby; she hugs him.

Narrator: Miriam was young, but she helped save *her* entire nation — because she was brave. For that baby brother whom she loved so well became Moses, God's leader of all Israel!

Princess, maidens, Miriam, Mother, all smile. Maidens clap.

THE END

The Ponytail Girls Club

Would you like to be a part of a Ponytail Girls Club? You can be a PT yourself, of course. But it's much more fun if one of your friends joins with you. Or even five or six of them! There is no cost. You can read the Ponytail Girls stories together, do the puzzles and other activities, study the Bible stories, and learn the Bible verses.

If your friends each have their own Ponytail Girls books, you can all write in yours at the same time. Arrange a regular meeting time and place, and plan to do special things together, just like the PTs do in the stories, such as shopping, Bible study, homework, or helping others.

Trace or copy the Ponytail Girls membership cards on page 197 and give one to each PT in your group.

Membership Cards

Trace or photocopy these cards. Fill them out, date them, and give one to each member of your Ponytails club. Be sure to put your membership card in your wallet or another special place for safekeeping!

_____

is a member in good standing of
The Ponytail Girls Club.

_____
Signature

_____
Date

_____

is a member in good standing of
The Ponytail Girls Club.

_____
Signature

_____
Date

Bible Verses to Remember and Share

These are the Bible verses the Ponytail Girls studied throughout this book. Write them on pretty paper and learn them. Share your favorite with someone else!

Do what is right and good in the Lord's sight.
~ Deuteronomy 6:18

To obey is better than sacrifice.
~ 1 Samuel 15:22

Have you entered the storehouses of the snow?
~ Job 38:22

A kindhearted woman gains respect.
~ Proverbs 11:16

A wise man listens to advice.
~ Proverbs 12:15

Better a meal of vegetables where there is love than a fattened calf with hatred.
~ Proverbs 15:17

Love your enemies and pray for those who persecute you.
~ Matthew 5:44

Do not judge, or you too will be judged.
~ Matthew 7:1

Whatever you did for one of the least of these brothers of mine, you did for me.
~ Matthew 25:40

If the Son sets you free, you will be free indeed.
~ John 8:36

*Jesus answered, "I am the way and
the truth and the life."*
~ John 14:6

I have called you friends.
~ John 15:15

Whatever you do, do it all for the glory of God.
~ 1 Corinthians 10:31

*Everything should be done in
a fitting and orderly way.*
~ 1 Corinthians 14:40

Asking God to fill you with the knowledge of his will.
~ Colossians 1:9

If any of you lacks wisdom, he should ask God.
~ James 1:5

*If we confess our sins, he is faithful and just
and will forgive us our sins.*
~ 1 John 1:9

*And this is his command: to believe in the name of
his Son, Jesus Christ, and to love one
another as he commanded us.*
~ 1 John 3:23

Love one another, for love comes from God.
~ 1 John 4:7

Glossary (glos/ə rē)

Aaron: *air-on*

Abi: *ay-buy*

Acsah: *ak-saw*

Agur: *ah-grr*

Apphia: *ah-fee-uh*

Archippus: *ark-ip-pus*

Asenath: *as-eh-nath*

Assyria: *uh-seer-e-uh*

Caleb: *kay-leb*

Chuzas: *koo-zas*

Colosse: *coh-loss-ee*

Esau: *ee-saw*

Felix: *fee-lix*

Haran: *hair-an*

Hezekiah: *heh-zuh-ky-uh*

Isaiah: *eye-zay-uh*

Jemimah: *jeh-my-muh*

Job: *johb*

Jochebed: *jok-eh-bed*

Josiah: *joe-si-ah*

Jubal: *joo-ball*

Keren-Happuch: *ker-en-hap-uk*

Keziah: *keh-zee-uh*

Laban: *lay-bun*

Lamech: *lay-mek*

Lemuel: *lim-u-el*

Magdalene: *mag-duh-leen*

Naamah: *nay-ah-mah*

Nabal: *nay-ball*

Onesimus: *oh-ness-uh-muss*

Othniel: *oth-nee-el*

Pharisee: *fair-uh-see*

Pharaoh: *fair-oh*

Philemon: *fi-lee-mun*

Phoebe: *fee-bee*

Publican: *pub-lih-kuhn*

Samaria: *sah-mayr-ee-uh*

Si: yes

Sinai: *sigh-nigh*

Answers to Puzzles

Chapter 1

Spot a Bargain, p. 24
1. 39 cents each
2. 3 packs for $1
3. 2 for $10
4. $14 each
5. 55% off

Baby Talk, p. 25
sharing, helping, giving, hugging, teaching, loving

Chapter 6

I've Got Your Number, p. 72
Be 100% for God.

Chapter 7

Right On! Quiz, p. 80
1-E, 2-G, 3-F, 4-H, 5-A, 6-C, 7-B, 8-D

Secret to Success, p. 81
Dare to do right. Put Satan to flight. God helps day and night.

Chapter 8

Bible KP Duty, p. 91
1-E, 2-F, 3-H, 4-G, 5-A, 6-B, 7-D, 8-C

Chapter 11

Searching for Talent, p. 120

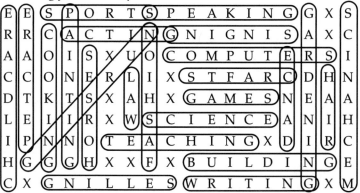

Chapter 12
God's Answers, p. 129
Ask and it will be given to you.

Chapter 13
An A-MAZE-ing Trail, p. 138

Chapter 14
Following Orders, p. 145
1. God's Commands,
2. Him, 3. The Lord Your God; 4. Your Parents; 5. Your Leaders; 6; God's Law; 7. The Words of the Lord; 8. The Gospel

Chapter 15
Stop, in the Name of Love, pp. 152-153
Loving: 2, 4
Not Loving: 1, 3, 5

Chapter 17
Are You a Slave?, p. 173
1. Lying, 2. Shoplifting, 3. Cheating, 4. Oversleeping, 5. Goofing off, 6. Using bad words, 7. Talking back, 8. Snubbing someone, 9. Glued to TV, 10. Not believing God

Chapter 18
Valentine Math Test, pp. 181-182
1. U, 2. O, 3. I, 4. Y, 5. E, 6. V, 7. L, 8. O.
Message: I Love You

Chapter 19
Music, Music, Music, p. 190
1. Harp, 2. Trumpet, 3. Horn, 4. Lyre, 5. Tambourine, 6. Flute, 7. Cymbals, 8. Brass, 9. Bells.

Valentine Heart Puzzle

GET A FREE SCRUNCHIE!

The Ponytail Girls love to give each other gifts. Here is one for you: a free scrunchie! Just fill out the form below and enclose a check or money order for $2.20 to cover shipping and handling. Also, we would love to hear more about you and your thoughts, so please fill out the form on the other side, too.

❑ Send my friend a free catalog, too!

My name _____

My friend's name _____

My address _____

Address _____

City _____ State _____ Zip _____

City _____ State _____ Zip _____

Parent's signature _____

My birth date: _____ / _____ / _____
         month/day/year

❑ Send me a scrunchie and a free catalog!
My $2.20 check or money order is enclosed.

3   Mail this form to: Ponytails • Legacy Press • P.O. Box 261129 • San Diego, CA 92196

Which of The Ponytail Girls books have you read?

- ☐ Meet the Ponytail Girls
- ☐ The Impossible Christmas Present
- ☐ Lost on Monster Mountain
- ☐ A Stormy Spring
- ☐ Escape from Camp Porcupine

My favorite PT is: _____

I am in a Ponytail Girls Club. ☐ yes ☐ no

I am in another club. ☐ yes ☐ no

The name of my club is: _____

My favorite thing to do is: _____

My favorite book is: _____

because: _____

My favorite magazine is: _____

because: _____

The fun devotional that helps girls grow closer to God.

God and Me! is a series of devotionals for girls. Each age-level book is packed with over 100 devotionals, plus memory verses, stories, journal space and fun activities to help you learn more about the Bible.

LP46823
ISBN 1-885358-54-7

LP46822
ISBN 1-885358-60-1

LP46821
ISBN 1-885358-61-X

Attention: Christian babysitters!

This is the only manual you will need to be the best babysitter on the block— and to share about God with others. *The Official Christian Babysitting Guide* is packed with everything you want to know about taking care of kids. Step-by-step instructions will help you learn the best ways to change a diaper, feed a baby or calm a scared child. Plus, get ideas for keeping kids busy with pages and pages of crafts, games, snacks and songs. Most importantly, you will find Scriptures and strategies for serving God as you serve families. Get *The Official Christian Babysitting Guide* and find out how you can be a blessing as you babysit!

LP 48021
ISBN 1-58411-027-9

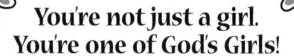

You're not just a girl.
You're one of God's Girls!

Hey, girls, get ready to add some sparkle to your look and a lot of fun to your life. *God's Girls* is packed with tips and ideas to help you make cool crafts. Plus you will read about Bible women and learn how to be a faithful Christian. There is even space included for you to write your deepest thoughts and dreams. So come on and join the party…you are one of *God's Girls!*

LP48011
ISBN 1-58411-020-1

LP48012
ISBN 1-58411-021-X